Reti**ment** Businesses

100 Best Retirement Businesses

Lisa Angowski Rogak

with
David H. Bangs, Jr.

UPSTART PUBLISHING COMPANY, INC.
The Small Business Publishing Company
Dover, New Hampshire

Published by Upstart Publishing Company, Inc.
A Division of Dearborn Publishing Group, Inc.
12 Portland Street
Dover, New Hampshire 03820
(800) 235-8866 or (603) 749-5071

Neither the author nor the publisher of this book is engaged in rendering, by the sale of this book, legal, accounting or other professional services. The reader is encouraged to employ the services of a competent professional in such matters.

Library of Congress Cataloging-in-Publication Data
Rogak, Lisa Angowski
100 best retirement businesses/Lisa Angowski Rogak with David H. Bangs.
    p.   cm.
    ISBN 0-936894-54-7
    1. New business enterprises. 2. Small business—Management.
3. Retirees—Employment. 4. Self-employed. I. Bangs, David H.
II. Title. III. Title: One hundred best retirement businesses.
HD62.5.R63 1994   94-828
658'.041—dc20   CIP

Cover design by Daniel Christmas, Design Alliance, Inc.
Back cover photo of Lisa Angowski Rogak by David Parker.

Printed in the United States of America
10 9 8 7 6 5 4 3 2 1

For a complete catalog of Upstart's small business publications, call (800) 235-8866.

For my mother
—L.A.R.

TABLE OF CONTENTS

INTRODUCTION

What exactly does the expression retirement business mean in the 1990s? For many, the meanings of both *retirement* and *business* have changed radically in recent years, and combining the two has also, by necessity, changed.

Many of the people I spoke with during the writing of this book were quick to tell me, "I'm not retired—go find someone else." For them, their business was a second, third or even fourth stage in their lives, and in virtually every case, they were finally doing what they love to do.

The entrepreneurs profiled in the *100 Best Retirement Businesses* range in age from 43 to 85. Some retired exactly 20 years to the day after they joined the military—thus ensuring that all government benefits and pensions would continue—while others took early retirement, were laid off in their 50s, or just decided it was time to do what they wanted to do for a change. And some followed the old rules: They retired at 65 and then started their businesses.

But everyone's in a different place—you may fall into one of the following categories:

- Like Phyllis Taylor, on p. 163, you may know you want to do *something*, but you may not be sure *what*. Phyllis decided she wanted to work with kids and that she wanted to streamline the business start-up process, so she picked Gymboree, a franchise that allows her to fulfill her dream of working with children.

- Or maybe you find yourself in a similar position as Joan and Lee Yeaton: You may be dissatisfied with the way your life is now and you're thinking about what might be better. Joan and Lee found their ideal solution. (See p. 217.)

- Or you may know that you're going to need an income aside from Social Security and other benefits when you retire, and you're looking for ideas about how to get it. Ed Strom found himself in that situation when he retired from the military. As you'll see on p. 88, he came up with the right answer for him.

- Or perhaps you know exactly what you want to do, but don't know how to do it or if it will work. The assessment exercises and questionnaires starting on p. 14 will be especially helpful to you. The exercises to assess your skills and needs are essential to help you focus on your reasons for starting a retirement business. And browsing through the entire book will provide you with ideas to help you in starting your own business; reading about other people's experiences can add depth to your own ideas.

A few practiced eyes might note that many of the suggested start-up costs for the businesses listed in this book seem low. For the most part, I found that retirees and pseudo-retirees don't need to surround themselves with all the trappings younger entrepreneurs seem to need to acknowledge they are indeed the heads of their enterprise. Instead, the primary concern of most retirees I spoke with is that they're doing what they love. Besides, the majority of retirement businesses are started—and continued—at home.

Though you may already have a good idea of the type of business you'd like to start, leaf through the pages and ponder all 100 businesses. One might have a special twist to it that you could employ in your chosen enterprise, or else a business you never knew existed—like a luxury kennel for cats or a personal moving service—might turn out to be the perfect business for you.

The joy these people have for their businesses shines loud and clear on every page. Use this as a barometer to pick your own business.

After all, in retirement, Rule Number One is to have fun. It's about time.

HOW TO USE THIS BOOK

The *100 Best Retirement Businesses* is more than a book for browsing through to give you ideas about which retirement business to start. In fact, Parts One and Three are designed to help you make sure you'll succeed at whatever business you undertake. These two "before and after" sections will guide you in assessing and planning your venture. In between you will find thought-provoking descriptions of 100 business possibilities.

Part One contains tips for selecting a business as well as several essential self-assessment inventories: a skills checklist, a questionnaire to help you determine if you will be comfortable and successful in retirement business ownership, and two financial data forms—a personal balance sheet and a cost of living budget. Take the time to complete these inventories to lay the proper groundwork **before** you read through the 100 entries and choose a retirement venture. Explore your motives and goals. Think about what the word "success" means to you at this particular stage in your life. Do a little soul-searching to define and put down on paper what your values, interests and abilities are. This self-assessing will pay off later, because the more self-knowledge you can bring to your new retirement business, the more likely you will succeed. Finally, take a good, hard look at your finances. There may be a lot of truth to the old proverb "Where there's a will there's a way," but unless you have a clear notion of your current financial picture, you may find your will to succeed is hopelessly out of sync with your monetary resources.

After you have completed your self-assessment, begin browsing through the entries of the 100 retirement businesses, which appear in alphabetical order. Each entry opens with a handy "at a glance" summary designed to help you make quick comparisons between businesses. These summaries rate each business's **Ease of Startup** as easy, moderate or difficult. They include estimates of the **Initial Investment** you'll need and the **Time Commitment** you'll have to make. Each summary also answers the question, **Can you run the business from your home?**

Finally, the summaries rate the **Success Potential** for each business as easy, moderate or difficult. Since the word "success" can mean very different things to different people, you will need to keep in mind how I've used the term in determining ratings for each business: A business's potential for success depends on *the ease of entering, reaching and staying in the market.* According to this standard, operating a boat tour company (p. 60) has a moderate Success Potential since the business can be seasonal and very competitive, depending on where you live. Similarly, the Success Potential for a land developer is rated as difficult since real estate slumps are hardly uncommon and so much depends on economic trends beyond your control.

Each entry contains helpful facts and tips about starting and running the business and includes references for tracking down more information. The real-life stories of how the owners got started in their businesses should give you many insights that you can successfully apply to your own chosen enterprise.

As you read and zero in on your ideal choice, remember that your real work is just beginning. You'll need to get down to the nitty-gritty of planning your actual business. Part Three of this book guides you through the steps of writing a business plan for your retirement venture. If you think of your business plan as an architect's blueprint, you will realize why it is an essential step in starting any business. Imagine trying to build a house without a carefully prepared blueprint. How long do you think such a building would stand before cracks appear and everything starts to fall apart? If you don't think you are enough of an "architect" to devise a workable business plan on your own, luckily there are many sources you can turn to for free advice and assistance. Part Three describes nine resources that are readily available to help you—starting with your local library.

And so you're on your way. Assess, browse and then plan.

Enjoy, and good luck.

PART ONE

Assessing Your Business

Meeting Your Goals and Fitting Your Resources

What is a retirement business anyway? It might be an extension of a hobby, a part-time affair which requires a minimal investment of time and money such as a small farming operation run out of your backyard. At the other extreme, it could be a country inn, a full-time, all-consuming operation which calls for a very sizable initial investment and total commitment to make it run smoothly and profitably. In between these extremes are hundreds of possibilities, 100 of which are presented in enough detail to help you make an intelligent choice of a retirement business which meets your goals and fits your resources.

These two criteria—meeting your goals and fitting your resources—are the keys to selecting and then running a *successful* retirement business.

Sounds simple enough. But it is more complicated than it appears. You have to know what your goals are, including what you might mean by "a successful retirement business," and you have to know what your resources are. "Resources" includes more than the obvious financial and capital resources. If you have been in business for yourself before, you know you need stamina, family support, pertinent experience or a way to get that experience and an ability to work without supervision. This doesn't mean you have to be some sort of paragon of capitalistic virtue to run a profitable retirement business. You have more experience and capabilities to draw on than you may realize. If you choose your retirement business carefully, running it will be a pleasurable, energizing and fascinating experience.

It is important to run your retirement business as a business. You should know who your customers will be, what they want that you will be able to provide and how to provide those goods or services at a profit that is agreeable to you. Small business is fun—but even a small business can lose startling amounts of money if it isn't taken seriously. The basic managerial chores of organizing, budgeting, monitoring and innovating are just as important to your retirement business as they are to a multibillion dollar, international company. Perhaps they are even more important, as you will be hazarding your own time, energy, emotions and cash on your retirement venture.

This first section and Part Three address the nuts and bolts of starting (or acquiring) and running a small business. Most of the material is covered in greater detail in other books (such as Upstart's *Planning Guide* series).

Starting your retirement business is no different in most ways from starting a business any other time—with two important exceptions. The first is that the goals of most retirement businesses are more modest. A retirement business is seldom intended to do much more than supplement an income or provide an income replacement. Building a retirement business to create capital is unusual. Second, the risks are somewhat different. Most entrepreneurs start businesses while they are relatively young and can therefore recoup losses and recover from severe financial setbacks if that unhappy necessity arises. The failure of a retirement business has more serious consequences, especially if the investment represents a significant percentage of your assets, because there isn't time to recoup the loss.

Otherwise, a retirement business is not essentially different from any other kind of business. The same basic steps must be followed.

Step One: Select the Right Business for You

It is important to select a business consistent with your personal goals, values, interests, skills and abilities. This is easier said than done since it calls for a high degree of self-knowledge. Nothing is more futile than picking a business for the wrong motives (usually "getting rich" or "proving them wrong") and condemning yourself to work hard at a venture you come to loathe.

It may even be more complicated for a retirement business, since questions of level of commitment, location, time involvement and so on will impact your decision.

Don't rush this part of your pre-planning. Ideally this first step takes place over a few years. Realistically it can be compressed to a few intensive weeks. You may have little time to make a decision, especially if you are a victim of down-sizing, right-sizing, RIFing (Reduction In Force), merge & purge or any of the various new ways corporate and institutional America have found to reduce their work force.

Getting Started

You probably have plenty of ideas for some retirement business or businesses percolating in the back of your head. This section will help you sort through some clutter and refine your thinking. Two principal areas of concern are your motivations and capabilities for self-employment. You may find that your purposes would be better served by dedicating your time and energy to charitable work, study, even working part-time for someone else. Small business ownership is a classic tar baby: easy to get stuck to, even when you decide you don't want to be involved any longer. Deciding *not* to go into business may be the best decision for you. There's nothing wrong with that. Most small business experts agree that one of the main reasons for writing a business plan is to avoid going into the wrong kind of business.

For detailed self-examination, the annually updated *What Color Is Your Parachute?* by Richard Bolles (Berkeley, CA: Ten Speed Press) is very hard to beat. *Parachute* has the disadvantage of being a lengthy and lonely process unless you can find other people on the same quest to share notes and ideas with. You can find like-minded people through Small Business Administration programs such as Small Business Development Centers and Service Corps of Retired Executives, through your local Chamber of Commerce, church groups or even in the telephone book. Many cities have programs such as Operation ABLE, 40+ groups, or similar programs for people who still want to work even if they have retired (willingly or not).

If you can avail yourself of outplacement or pre-retirement services, do so. They will provide more than forms, hand-holding and advice. The good ones are designed to help you define your goals and set realistic strategies for achieving them. They are particularly useful in working out the financial information (what can you expect from your pension, social security, investment income and so on), so your retirement planning is realistic.

In almost every instance, a retirement business is a small business with limited costs of entry, small markets and limited growth prospects. You might start a business, buy an existing business or a franchise or buy into a business. These are all options you should investigate. Their virtues and drawbacks differ. A successful startup is usually more difficult to achieve but has the great advantage of being more flexible. You can choose your customers, products or services, location and hours. (Within reason: once you get into it, your customers will dictate most of what you do.) A going business has a client base and a cash flow, as well as established relations with vendors and other businesses. In some cases you can use the business's cash flow to help finance the purchase. A franchise provides a clear structure, detailed operating plans and in most instances a higher degree of safety than a startup.

Preliminary questions to ask:

1. **Why do you want a retirement business?** This is a matter to be exceptionally clear about. Is your motivation income? Filling time? Putting some ideas to work?

2. **What kind of business do you think would be fun?** You don't make these decisions in a vacuum. Your work experiences, hobbies, civic and recreational activities all play a role in what businesses you might consider pursuing. As a general rule, you want your business to be fun—that way you'll stick to it, look forward to the day-to-day effort involved in most businesses, and be able to employ your

---

A note on this and subsequent lists of questions

These lists are short-cuts designed to help you ask and answer some very slithery questions. The lists don't pretend to be comprehensive. If they stimulate your thinking and get you started, they will have served their purpose. The questions are drawn from years of experience with small business owners, and reveal some of their most pressing concerns. The comments are integral parts of the lists. Treat them as background material. They do not substitute for your answers.

Write your answers down as you go along. A three-ring binder is ideal, as your ideas and answers will change. A business which is initially appealing may, on closer examination, not be right for you. Fine; you are one step nearer the initial goal of finding the right business for *you.*

---

favorite aptitudes and skills. Some research and self-assessment before you commit will do more than prevent a disastrous choice. It will open up new possibilities.

This book provides 100 examples. The *Small Business Sourcebook* (published by Gale Research and probably available in your library) will provide several hundred more ideas, though usually for more substantial businesses.

3. **How much capital are you willing to invest—that is, risk?** How much can you afford to risk? This decision demands professional advice, say from your investment counselor or banker, if you are thinking of a business which will require you to invest a major portion of your assets.

4. **What level of risk is acceptable to you?** Risk is subjective. The amount of risk you perceive depends on your experience and your confidence in your own abilities. To counteract excessive optimism, get an outside opinion. The more you understand about a given business the less risky it will be. You certainly don't want to bet the farm

on a retirement business; what happens if it doesn't work?

5. **What do your husband, wife, children or other interested persons feel about this proposed venture?** The support of family and friends is a major success factor. If they begrudge the time and investment you plan to make, you start out with some strong negatives.

6. **Where do you want the business to be located?** Many retirement businesses have a strong geographical bent. You may want to locate in a warm climate, or near family, or in a region where you can pursue some special interests. I've known people who chose to move back into the city to be near cultural events; others who have moved to locations where they can play golf, sail, ski or swim year round.

7. **How much of your time do you want to spend on your business?** Should the business be seasonal? year-round? full- or part-time? Businesses tend to devour time. If you want to make your retirement business part-time or seasonal, choose a business which permits such flexibility. Some businesses—notably hospitality businesses like inns and bed & breakfasts—require constant attendance. Other businesses are more flexible.

Step Two: Prepare for Your Retirement Business

If you have never run a business of your own before, this step may involve taking courses, attending seminars or workshops or simply reading a few books. Most of us have worked for someone else most of our adult lives and as a consequence have become very good at some activities which have limited bearing on running a small business. For example, if you have been an executive for a large business or an institution, you may be expert at financial analysis or outside sales or human resource management. Chances are you haven't had the opportunity to set goals. Even if you have had some input, you may not have experience in setting companywide strategic goals.

"Select a Business" Form

Instructions: Each of the businesses discussed in the following chapters have been evaluated on seven factors: ease of startup, range of initial investment, time commitment, can you run the business from home, pros, cons, and "special considerations," which can be whatever you might think is especially important.

Although you may have a retirement business already chosen, you owe it to yourself to examine alternatives. If your initial choice is a good one, it will still be good after going through this small exercise. If you find there is another business which closely meets your requirements and resources, you have a choice and can make a more considered decision.

Here's a simple way to lay out and compare several alternatives.

Step One: Select three or more businesses which *prima facie* meet your criteria.

Step Two: For each business, make up a T form:

Cons	Pros

Step Three: For each business, fill in the T form, putting positive criteria on the right side, negative on the left. For example:

Country Inn: Cons | Pros

Cons	Pros
hard startup big investment heavy time committment	family involvement build equity fast provides living quarters use our skills great location

Step Four: Then compare the results. If nothing else, this helps you see how the various possible businesses stack up against each other and alerts you to potential problems and opportunities.

In your retirement business you have to be responsible for everything—from product and marketing decisions to financial controls to personnel to dealing with suppliers and bankers and customers. Even if yours is a part-time, one-person business, you have to schedule, organize, monitor and manage yourself. Add employees and it becomes even more complicated.

Seven important questions to answer carefully. Your answers will help you define the right retirement business *for you*. Use your three-ring binder and write down your answers, as none of them can properly be answered off the top of your head. They all call for repeated analysis and re-thinking.

1. **What are you good at? Bad at?** Success in small business comes from being thorough, not brilliant. As marketing expert Ron Michaels puts it, marketing wars are never won. They are always lost. You need to know what you are good at so you can do more of it. You need to know what you are bad at so you make sure that area is covered adequately.

2. **What do you like to do?** As a generality, you will be most successful doing what you like to do. If you enjoy customer contact, that should be the heart of your retirement business. Hospitality or personal services such as massage therapy would be the kind of businesses for you to think of. If you prefer to make things or tinker in the shop, small appliance repair or clock repair would be more appealing to you. A business in which you primarily do what you like is where you will do best investing your efforts.

3. **What skills do you have to acquire or improve?** Work through the "Skills Inventory Checklist" to get a clearer picture of what management skills you have and which ones you need to work on. There are plenty of courses and agencies out there to help you.

Make sure the venture fits your resources—that is, that you have the financial resources or can secure the financial

Skills Inventory Checklist

Following is a summary of the principal functions of small business management. A general familiarity with the basics of each function is essential for successful management of most retirement businesses. Use the functions marked "no" or "uncertain" to map out a study program prior to your acquisition of a business. From *Buy the Right Business—At the Right Price* by Brian Knight and the Associates of Country Business (Dover, NH: Upstart Publishing, 1990).

I have enough knowledge in this area to operate my own business.

I. Sales and Marketing	YES	NO	UNCERTAIN
A. Market Research			
B. Market Planning			
C. Pricing			
D. Advertising/PR			
E. Sales Management			
F. Customer Service			
G. Personal Selling			
H. Competitive Analysis			
Total			

II. Business Operations			
A. Purchasing			
B. Inventory Control			
C. Scheduling			
D. Quality Control			
E. Business Growth			
F. Insurance			
Total			

Skills Inventory Checklist (Continued)

III. Financial Management	YES	NO	UNCERTAIN
A. Bookkeeping/Accounting			
B. Budgeting & Deviation Analysis			
C. Cost Control			
D. Credit and Collections			
E. Bank Relations			
F. Break Even Analysis			
G. Cash Flow/ Cash Management			
H. Ratio Analysis			
I. Taxes			
Total			

IV. Personnel	YES	NO	UNCERTAIN
A. Interviewing and Hiring			
B. Training			
C. Motivating People			
D. Policies			
E. Communicating			
Total			

Skills Inventory Checklist (Continued)

V. Administrative/ Management	YES	NO	UNCERTAIN
A. Problem Solving			
B. Decision Making			
C. Leadership			
D. Using Information			
E. Business Law			
F. Methodology/ Operations Research			
G. Computers and EDP			
Total			

Total "yes" boxes checked: _____ of 35 possible.

Self-Assessment Questions for Retirement Business Ownership

The following questions are designed to help you assess the probability that you will be comfortable and successful in small business ownership. It is not intended as a scientifically valid test, but rather a reflection of certain characteristics which research has shown to be important in a small business career. From *Buy the Right Business—At the Right Price* by Brian Knight and the Associates of Country Business (Dover, NH: Upstart Publishing, 1990).

Answer the questions as honestly and objectively as you can. You will grade yourself, and only you stand to "win" or "lose" as a result of any decisions you make about your career.

	YES	NO	UNCERTAIN
1. Are you willing to work long hours with few vacations and irregular time off in order to achieve your goals?			
2. Are you prepared to place the needs of your business before those of yourself and your family if necessary to preserve the health and continuity of your business?			
3. Does your need to be independent and in control of your work environment make it difficult for you to be satisfied working for others?			
4. Are you willing to take full responsibility for mistakes you make, without looking for others to blame?			

	YES	NO	UNCERTAIN
Can you learn from these mistakes to improve your performance in the future?			
5. Are you able to sustain your energy and motivation in an uncertain or unstable working or economic environment?			
6. Are you willing to take a fair amount of risk in the hope of achieving something you want?			
7. Do you feel you have a high degree of self-discipline? Can you apply yourself to a job that needs to be done even when you don't feel like doing it?			
8. Are you willing to "be on stage" . . . to know that others are watching, evaluating and counting on you?			
9. Do you believe you are able to show "grace under pressure"?			
10. Do you have excellent problem-solving abilities, particularly in crises when others are not thinking clearly?			
11. Are you willing to go against the mainstream—to persist in a course you believe in even when others disapprove?			

	YES	NO	UNCERTAIN
12. When things go wrong, do you pick yourself up promptly and move on to another challenge instead of brooding for a long time and feeling a lot of self pity?			
13. Do you empathize well with others?			
14. Do you have an ability to lead others in a confused or chaotic environment?			
15. Are you willing to spend a great deal of time, as long as you are in business, learning about things that are required or will be helpful in the business?			
16. Do you enjoy most other people?			
17. Do you enjoy working?			
18. Do you have (or are you willing to work hard to acquire) a broad range of business management skills?			
19. Do you possess a high degree of "information consciousness"? That is, do you usually, before starting off on a new course, go to considerable lengths to gather and use extensive information and data to assist you in planning and decision-making?			
20. Do you rely extensively on feedback to test the results of a course of action and make corrections or adjustments as a result?			

21. Check the box that most accurately describes how you feel about each statement:

	AGREE	DISAGREE	NOT IMPORTANT
a. You don't have to "cut ethical corners" to be successful in business.			
b. People need a "sense of mission" in order to be fulfilled in their work.			
c. It is very important for business to provide a service that is worthwhile and useful to others.			
d. I want the credit for my accomplishments and am willing to take full responsibility for my mistakes.			
e. I have a better chance of reaching my goals by working for myself than by working for others.			
f. It is important for a person to have the freedom to be creative in his or her work.			
g. It is more important to accomplish something worthwhile than to earn a great deal of money.			

Scoring the Self-Assessment Questions
Questions:
1-20   ____ (Number of yes or agree responses) x 5 = ____
       ____ (Number of uncertain responses)   x 2 = ____
Question:
 21a-g ____ (Number of yes or agree responses) x 5 = ____
       ____ (Number of other responses)   x 2 = ____

Total
Scores of:
120-140 indicates person likely to thrive in a retirement business.

80-120 indicates tendency toward retirement business ownership with some areas of conflict.

Below 80 indicates person probably not suited for retirement business ownership. Think twice before committing yourself to one if your score is below 80.

Interpretation: The "yes" answers define the profile of a person who will have a high chance of success in most small business ventures. The characteristics reflected by the "yes" or "agree" answers indicate an individual with high independence needs, self-control and self-direction, willingness to face a moderate degree of risk and ability to make a high-level of commitment to the success of a venture. Various studies have identified these characteristics in successful small business owners.

No single person is likely to answer all questions "yes" or "agree." Successful owners of retirement businesses have as much individuality as any other class of person.

resources to make the venture profitable. Lack of capital competes with lack of focus as the top small business killer.

4. **What are your financial resources?** Start with your personal balance sheet. Most small businesses are started with either pillow or house money—e.g., personal savings and family or friends' investment, or by borrowing capital against home equity. Since banks will want to know this kind of information anyway, and since it will affect the kind of business you can realistically become involved with, this is not a step to skimp on.

5. **What income do you want your retirement business to provide?** It may be that you don't want or need any income from your retirement business, but simply want to break even. Or you may need a substantial income. This is a major factor in choosing the right business. Don't guess. The personal budget form below is designed to help you understand what income you need to meet your personal goals; if added income is needed from your retirement business, be as specific as possible. Specific goals with specific timelines make attaining those goals much more likely than vague wishing.

6. **What are your long-term (five-year) goals for your retirement business?** Long-term goals help set direction for your business. In the next chapter, which addressees business planning, tighter business goals will be set. Here, just look ahead. Will you still be in business, or will you want to fold it and move on? Do you hope to build the business into something to pass on to your children or employees? Looking five years ahead doesn't tie your hands, but it will help you focus on what is important in your retirement business.

7. **How will you wind down your retirement business?** All business ventures will end one day. Retirement businesses, almost by definition, have a shorter time horizon than other ventures. How will you "cash out" of your business? Will you sell it? Simply shut the doors? Let it run quietly down?

Personal Balance Sheet

Year ending _____, 199____

Assets
Liquid
    Cash and savings   _____
    Notes, Treasury bills, certificates of deposit   _____
    Life insurance policies—cash value   _____

Illiquid
    Real estate (home, vacation property,
        investment property)*   _____
    Vehicles and equipment*   _____
    Furniture and fixtures*   _____
    Collections (art, coins, stamps, jewelry,
        antiques, etc.)*   _____
    Others   _____
    Total Assets   _____

Liabilities
Current
    Taxes   _____
    Notes—current portion   _____
    Bills (charge cards, professional fees, etc.)   _____
    Current portion of mortgage payable   _____
    Current portion of bank or term loan payable   _____
    Current portion of other long-term liabilities   _____

Long-term
    Mortgage balance   _____
    Notes   _____
    Bank or term loan   _____
    Alimony/child support, maintenance of
        dependent relative   _____
    Other   _____
    Total Liabilities   _____

Net worth = Total assets minus total liabilities
* *Market value*

Cost of Living Budget

(based on average month—does not cover purchase of any new items except emergency replacements)

Regular Monthly Payments
House payments (principal, interest,
    taxes, insurance) or rent   _____
Car payments (including insurance)   _____
Appliance, TV payments   _____
Home improvement loan payments   _____
Personal loan, credit card payments   _____
Health plan payments   _____
Life insurance premiums   _____
Other insurance premiums   _____
Savings/investments   _____
Total   _____

Household Operating Expenses
Telephone   _____
Gas and electricity   _____
Water   _____
Other household expenses, repairs, maintenance   _____
Total   _____

Personal Expenses
Clothing, cleaning, laundry   _____
Prescription medications   _____
Physicians, dentists   _____
Education   _____
Dues   _____
Gifts and contributions   _____
Travel   _____
Newspapers, magazines, books   _____
Auto upkeep and gas   _____
Spending money and allowances   _____
Miscellaneous   _____
Total   _____

Cost of Living Budget (Continued)

Food Expenses

Food—at home _____

Food—away from home _____

Total _____

Tax Expenses

Federal and state income taxes _____

Other taxes not included above _____

Total _____

Budget Summary

A. Gross Income _____

Monthly total A _____

Less Expenses:

Regular monthly payments _____

Household operating expenses _____

Personal expenses _____

Food expenses _____

Tax expenses _____

Monthly total B _____

SAVINGS (A - B) _____

PART TWO

The 100 Best
Retirement Businesses

Listing of 100 Best Retirement Businesses

Acting
Advertising Agency
Antique Mall Kiosk
Antique Shop
Antique Show Exhibitor
Appliance Repair
Auctioneer
Balloon Store
Bed & Breakfast
Bird Raising
Boat Tour Company
Boatbuilder
Book Publisher
Bottled Water Company
Cake Maker/Decorator
Campground
Candlemaker
Cat Kennel
Cleaning Service
Clock Repair
Clown
Coin-Operated Laundry
Community Playhouse/Theater
Consultant
Counselor
Country Club
Country Inn
Crafts Shop
Craftsperson
Dollmaker
Executive Search Firm

Exercise Instructor
Flag Business
Florist
Freelance Writing
Furniture Maker
General Store
Gift Baskets
Gourmet Food Store
Graphic Design Firm
Gymboree
Handwriting Analysis
Hardware Store
Herbalist
Historical Impersonator
Home Jewelry Party Host
House Renovator
House Sitting
Import Business
Information Service
Insurance Agency
Interior Designer
Inventor
Jewelry Designer
Land Developer
Landlord
Llama Raising
Magazine Publisher
Mail Order Food Business
Massage Therapist
Moving Service
Music Hall

25

Musician
Mystery Novelist
Newsletter Publisher
Newspaper Publisher
Nonprofit Organization—
    Environmental Group
Nonprofit Organization—
    Intergenerational
    Communication
Nonprofit Social
    Organization
Nonprofit Organization—
    Urban Booster
Nostalgia Company
Nursery
Orchid Grower
Painter
Personal Financial
    Consultant
Pet Grooming
Photographer
Potter
Professional Golfer
Publicist
Real Estate Agency

Restaurant
Second-Hand Children's
    Clothing Store
Second Hand Clothing Store
Seminar Leader
Small Scale Farming
Special Interest Network
    Group
Specialty Bookstore
Specialty Food Business—
    Large Scale
Specialty Food Business—
    Small Scale
Storyteller
Tax Preparer
Tie Maker
Tour Guide
Travel Matchmaker
Used Bookstore
Video Biographer
Water Filter Distributor
Winery
Yacht Repair Yard

ACTING

Helena Hale, One-Woman Theatre

Helena Hale
Santa Barbara, California

Ease of Startup	Moderate
Range of Initial Investment	$250
Time Commitment	Part- or full-time
Can You Run the Business From Home?	Yes
Success Potential	Difficult

Description of Business: A business in which an individual can perform in productions for other people or produce her own.

Ease of Startup: Moderate. All you need are some 8 x 10 glossy black-and-white photographs, a résumé, a copy of *BackStage* and/or the willingness to stage your own production.

Range of Initial Investment: $250 for the photos.

Time Commitment: Part- or full-time

Can You Run the Business From Home? Yes

Success Potential: Difficult. At any age, the business is cut-throat; if you're not truly talented, you won't make it.

How to Market the Business: Advertising, publicity, word of mouth, referrals, luck.

The Pros: It keeps you active, feeds your ego and you can do what you love.

The Cons: Don't expect to make money. It's difficult to succeed. Quality parts are scarce for older people.

Special Considerations: Acting is for people who are absolutely hooked and are willing to put up with the indignities of the business.

Story of the Business

Once acting gets into your blood, it seems you can never quite shake it. Helena Hale graduated from college as a drama major. She appeared in the first legitimate USO show that was sent overseas during World War II, as well as several Broadway shows. Then she hit tougher times, though she says there was nothing else she wanted to do but act. When it didn't materialize, she turned to the practical career of teaching English and speech to college students.

A few years before she was ready to retire, she started dabbling in acting again. "I'd appeared in a production of famous women artists, portraying Georgia O'Keeffe. One of the arts commissioners in town suggested I perform a one-woman show just on O'Keeffe," she relates. "I did it, and it was quite successful. He then suggested I write my own productions, and I did, one on Louise Nevelson and the other on Mary Cassatt."

Hale started by first previewing her performances, a kind of rehearsal period before the regular shows begin. Then she rented local theaters for $25 a night when it became clear the audiences liked what they saw. "The show kept selling out. I got a reputation, and other people hired me," she recalls.

The performances range from 50-60 minutes each and are complete theater productions with original music, lighting, slides and other special effects. Hale frequently adapts them to special environments, like a classroom or an outdoor gazebo. She also shortens and combines them for certain occasions. In her most popular combination, she transforms herself onstage from O'Keeffe to Nevelson. She began performing full-time in 1987. Though she spends a lot of time on publicity and contacting theaters and groups all over the country, most of her bookings come from word of mouth.

"Someone who sees me in Maine will ask me to come to Nashville or will tell a producer somewhere else to book me," she says. Helena also attends a large, booking-promotion show every year where she performs a showcase. This brings in a few bookings as well.

"It's theater, and it's not commercial," she says. "I get to combine my knowledge of art with theater. There's only a narrow band of people across the country who adore it. Museums and women's groups, for example, love it."

She also does residencies occasionally. She stays for a week in a particular town, leading workshops at schools during the day and giving performances at night. These are usually funded by the state or by local arts councils. The state of New Mexico once funded a special grant so Helena could tour her O'Keeffe production throughout the state. Generally states only fund artists from their own state.

Hale says she spends about 10 weeks on the road each year. She used to take a technical director with her, but at the end of one performance, the technical director told her that most visiting performers use the in-house crew, so she began to travel alone to save money.

It does take time to familiarize the house crew with her performances, however, and she frequently spends up to five hours rehearsing her show with the crew.

Hale makes from three to four figures for each set of performances; the theater always picks up travel expenses. Sometimes she takes a flat fee, and sometimes a percentage of the house. "I try to be fair to everyone and do what they can do," she relates. "I had been charging a little less than other solo performers. They told me I should charge more because I was making them look bad. But I feel I can't price myself out of the market. I enjoy the work so much, I want to be accessible to worthy causes."

Although there are naysayers out there who say Hale's life is essentially over because she is 73, she feels it's just beginning.

"I become more and more of an artist the longer I do this," she remarks. "Each time I perform I discover a whole new way of doing a role. Besides, I've been told I'm a role model for many of the teachers who haven't yet retired."

ADVERTISING AGENCY

Older and Wiser Limited

Ron Phillips, Sandra Inbody-Brick et al.

Los Angeles, California

Ease of Startup	Moderate
Range of Initial Investment	$50,000
Time Commitment	Full-time
Can You Run the Business From Home?	No
Success Potential	Difficult

Description of Business: A business that designs and executes advertising and marketing strategies for clients.

Ease of Startup: Moderate. It can be tough to get that first client.

Range of Initial Investment: $50,000 for office space, equipment and furniture. You can't skimp if you want to win clients.

Time Commitment: Full-time

Can You Run the Business From Home? No

Success Potential: Difficult. The industry suffers in a recession as clients cut advertising budgets. There are already many agencies.

How to Market the Business: Publicity, word of mouth, referrals, sensational presentations.

The Pros: With a background in advertising, it can be satisfying to run a small agency that specializes in one particular market without all the politics of a regular agency.

The Cons: It's an uphill battle. Clients can be fickle.

Special Considerations: Specialty advertising agencies that focus on one market are the way to go for the '90s.

For More Information: *Advertising Age*, 740 Rush Street, Chicago, IL 60611.

Story of the Business

In April 1993 Ron Phillips was sitting at home, not working, and frustrated. As a former creative director at an ad agency, he was able to witness firsthand how the recession had affected the production of commercials. "The field is overcrowded and has shrunk a great deal," he remarks. "In addition, the creative people at the agencies are mostly young today."

When he was a partner at the agency Ogilvy and Mather, one of the oldest and best-respected agencies in the country, he wanted to start a new division to develop advertising for people age 50 and up. The powers that were turned thumbs down on the idea.

Phillips called six of his friends in the business who had all been premier talents in their respective fields and asked if they wanted to start an agency geared toward people past the half-century mark. They all agreed.

The first dilemma was picking a name. Finally Older and Wiser Limited (OWL) was suggested because they agreed it would be a good idea to use an owl logo. The next month, they printed stationery and other promotional materials, hired a publicist and opened for business. Although they've gotten a number of accounts, Phillips says it's been tough.

"We fight an incredible inertia out there," he indicates. "We give them all the facts and figures that show how important the over-50 market is, but people in the business have grown up thinking the 18-49 group is the largest market." He finds that larger corporations are hardest to convince. "The smaller companies go for it right away," he adds.

Among OWLs clients are companies that sell exercise tapes for people over 65, that provide medical care in the home and that make commemorative watches. Unlike many agencies, OWL provides their clients with media consultations and public relations assistance, not just advertising.

Phillips thinks specialty agencies will thrive in the '90s and beyond, as markets begin to fragment even more. "Clients were sold in bulk—the three networks and *Reader's Digest*—for years," indicates Phillips, "but especially now that interactive media is beginning to hit, advertisers will be able to hit their specific markets even more."

Phillips finds working in a small agency much more efficient than working in the big agencies he's familiar with. "When I was working at a traditional agency, I had a staff of 40, and there were a number of people who were deadwood," he says. "Here, we do everything ourselves, and we have much better communication."

To get new accounts, the agency makes a presentation to a new client, showing how they would handle a campaign, using charts, storyboards or ads. Seventy-five percent of the time, OWL wins the account when they're competing against traditional agencies. Though many agencies typically work on a 15 percent commission basis, OWL works with clients on a project basis in some cases.

"Most traditional advertising deals in stereotypes of people over 50," he believes. "They're still patronizing older people portraying them as kindly, demented grandparents and as all aches and pains."

Phillips advises entrepreneurs to find a niche that is really needed. "Find a small market that is large enough that you can sell," he suggests.

ANTIQUE MALL KIOSK

Booth Space/Timber Village Antique Mall

Bruce Magowan
Quechee, Vermont

Ease of Startup	Easy
Range of Initial Investment	$1,500
Time Commitment	Minimal
Can Your Run the Business From Home?	No
Success Potential	Easy

Description of Business: A booth in an antique mall with other vendors.

Ease of Startup: Easy and fun. You need an inventory, which you must restock every month or so.

Range of Initial Investment: $1,500 for stock.

Time Commitment: Minimal; you don't need to staff the booth.

Can Your Run the Business From Home? No

Success Potential: Easy. If you specialize in a particular period or product, your chances are better, especially if no other vendor in the mall carries the same type of thing.

How to Market the Business: Through ads in local papers and by word of mouth.

The Pros: Someone else does the work.

The Cons: You won't make much money, but it gives you an excuse to visit auctions and shop for antiques across the country.

Special Considerations: For people who want to gradually ease their way into a full-time antiques business, this is a great way to test the waters.

For More Information: Antique Dealers' Association of America, Box 335, Greens Farms, CT 06436; *Upstart's Guide to Owning and Managing an Antiques Business* by Lisa Rogak (Dover, NH: Upstart Publishing, 1994).

Story of the Business

In 1987 Bruce Magowan and his wife, Gail, bought a large Victorian house in Bordentown, New Jersey. She started filling it with antiques to such an extent that one day Bruce told her she'd have to start selling some of them. At the time, he owned a men's clothing shop. He offered to turn over some shelf space in the store to Gail for the antiques. She called it—what else?—The Shelf.

A few years later he sold the clothing store and opened an antique shop, which didn't pan out, so he decided to go into a co-op space where all he had to do was stock it.

Then he found Timber Village, a cooperative antique mall on a busy highway in Quechee, Vermont; he started renting a five-foot booth space in 1981. "I stock it, they sell it, and they send me a check every two weeks," he says. "The people are good to work with, over a million customers walk through the mall each year, and it's open 364 days a year. Plus, it gives me a chance to go to Vermont."

The Magowans still buy from their travels, though Bruce admits it's more of a fun thing than a major boost to their income. The rental costs $72 a month; he grosses about $400 every month. He restocks the booth every other month. His specialty is small things, especially matchsafes, of which he has an extensive collection.

Matchsafes are small containers that hung by the wood or coal cookstove in the kitchen at the turn of the century. Some had one cup to hold unused matches, others had two, one of which held the used ones. They were made from tin, brass or leather, and some were give-aways from coal companies. Bruce also has a collection of "what-do-you-call-these-things." His collection attracts the attention of many people who want to puzzle it out; they often end up buying it.

Bruce tags each items with the name and the price. The purchaser brings items to a main counter near the front of the store where the cashier records the sale.

"I put in about five hours a week. Some weeks, I'll spend more time," he reports. "I also travel around looking for antiques, I go to shops, auctions and big antique shows."

He tries to be discriminating in the items he buys. "There's a lot of junk out there; there's stuff from the '50s and '60s that I don't consider to be antiques. I try to go much older." He suggests a person who's interested in starting up a booth in an antique mall seek the advice of someone who knows the business. "A good friend took me out a long time ago and showed me what to look for and what not to look for," he recalls. "I still go back to him and ask for advice on prices. You could be in this business for a lifetime and still not know all the answers."

When they visit Vermont to restock the booth, they stay in a motel room. Bruce's dream is to buy a house in Vermont with an attached garage and a barn where he could open an antique shop. "When my wife retires," he says, "I'll do it."

ANTIQUE SHOP

The Country Loft

Lionel Carbonneau
South Barre, Vermont

Ease of Startup	Moderate
Range of Initial Investment	$20,000
Time Commitment	Part- or full-time
Can You Run the Business From Home?	Yes
Success Potential	Difficult

Description of Business: A store that sells antiques and collectibles.

Ease of Startup: Moderate. It can take a few years to build up a diverse inventory of high-quality antiques.

Range of Initial Investment: $20,000 for inventory.

Time Commitment: Part- or full-time

Can You Run the Business From Home? Yes

Success Potential: Difficult. The business is glutted, unscrupulous dealers and poor-quality inventory have caused people to cut back on their purchases.

How to Market the Business: Advertising, word of mouth, referrals, good location.

The Pros: If you love antiques, buying them for the store feels great. Also, running a shop is an enjoyable way to meet people, both locals and visitors.

The Cons: Good quality antiques are hard to find; competition by dealers drives up prices.

Special Considerations: Running an antique store is a dream retirement business for many people, but like all dream businesses, it's sometimes hard to see the reality.

For More Information: Antique Dealers' Association of America, Box 335, Green Farms, CT 06436; local and statewide associations. *The Upstart Guide to Owning and Managing an Antiques Business*, Lisa Angowski Rogak (Dover, NH: Upstart Publishing, 1994).

Story of the Business

Lionel Carbonneau is a patient man. When he and his wife, Marilyn, were married in 1948, they started to collect antiques, which they both loved. As the years went on, he wanted to get into the business, but with two daughters who Lionel wanted to put through college, his dream was postponed.

In 1972 he was 10 years away from retirement, and he already knew what he wanted to do when he left his job. He started to build his inventory gradually, buying from individuals and knocking on doors. "Since I was in sales, I was used to that," he says.

In 1982 he finally retired, but he had to wait just a little longer. He and Marilyn decided to open the shop in a barn that was attached to an old house they had bought in central Vermont, one town over from the state capitol. Lionel needed to fix up the barn; he put in stairs so customers could get to the loft. Then he filled the barn with all of the antiques he had collected over the years.

In 1983 The Country Loft opened for business. The Country Loft specializes in primitives. Lionel says they sell a lot of rope beds. Local people make up most of his business, and they're familiar with the open "by chance or by appointment" policy of many businesses in northern New England that are located in unheated buildings. "We're not married to the business," indicates Lionel. "If we want to take a day off, we do." The $25,000 to $30,000 gross the shop brings in helps to pay the Carbonneaus' taxes and insurance.

Some of the same people who buy antiques from Lionel also sell items to him. "When we buy, we try to be fair with them on price," he remarks. "If I make a 25 to 30 percent markup on an item, I'm happy."

The most difficult part of the business is finding good merchandise for the shop. "I still go out and look for things," he says. "I also advertise in the paper saying that I'm looking to buy antiques. People call. They think they have an antique, but they don't. For every five items I see, I'll buy maybe one."

Marilyn waits on customers while Lionel is out scouting. "For a good retirement business, the spouse should be interested in the business," he believes. "My wife and I work together, and I think that's what makes a good business. I could see myself doing it on my own, but we do it better together."

Lionel does a little advertising in the local newspapers. He belongs to the statewide organization for antique dealers, but he says most of his customers are people who've dealt with him before.

Both he and his wife like meeting the people who come to the shop. He's amazed at the attitude of the people at some shops he's visited. "I've been places where I've walked in and the owner is grouchy," he reports. "That's not right. You can't expect that every person who comes in is going to buy something."

He suggests that people who are interested in starting an antique shop take their time. "Crawl before you walk," he advises. "You've got to know antiques; otherwise, you'll go out and get stung. You have to love it. I'm happy with what we're doing now; I don't want to get too big."

ANTIQUE SHOW EXHIBITOR

Nan and David Pirnack

Nan and David Pirnack
Boulder, Colorado

Ease of Startup	Difficult
Range of Initial Investment	$10,000+
Time Commitment	Part- to full-time
Can You Run the Business From Home?	Yes
Success Potential	Moderate

Description of Business: An antique dealer who travels to weekend shows to sell antiques from a rented booth.

Ease of Startup: Difficult. You need money to buy inventory along with some background in antiques to know what sells and what's currently popular.

Range of Initial Investment: $10,000 and up.

Time Commitment: Minimal off-season; full-time during the peak show seasons in spring and fall.

Can You Run the Business From Home? Yes, but you need a sturdy truck to cart your merchandise from show to show.

Success Potential: Moderate. It's hard to predict which shows will workl for a particular dealer; trial and error is necessary to determine which shows to repeat.

How to Market the Business: The shows will market the event for you. Once you're there, you market yourself by having quality antiques. You can also ask visitors for their names and addresses to create a mailing list for future shows where you will exhibit in their areas. This can also help you develop a private search business.

The Pros: If you love antiques, you'll love being able to make a living from the business.

The Cons: Living on the road is difficult. Finding quality items that are in demand is harder than you think.

Special Considerations: For antique buffs who love to travel and meet others in the field, they'll have fun and satisfy their wanderlust at the same time.

For More Information: Antique Dealers' Association of America, Box 335, Green Farms, CT 05436. *The Upstart Guide to Owning and Managing an Antiques Business*, Lisa Angowski Rogak (Dover, NH: Upstart Publishing, 1994).

Story of the Business

Though Nan Pirnack had been in the antiques business for almost 20 years with a small shop of her own, it wasn't until her husband, David, retired from IBM that they were able to turn a passion into a thriving business. Neither one had liked working in a shop, so they decided to concentrate on the show circuit.

They took part of Dave's retirement settlement and instead of buying an RV like many retirees, bought a truck to haul the antiques from show to show. It's a Ryder Q Van, which is 15 feet long, seven feet wide and seven feet high.

The Pirnacks buy their antiques from many sources at home and when they're on the road traveling. "We'll buy an item when we think we can sell it for a greater amount of money than the person who has it for sale," he explains. "We've also built up a network of pickers who don't have shops and don't do shows. They like to find pieces and sell them to local dealers or people like us, who are passing through."

In addition, Dave finds items in one part of the country that aren't particularly popular there but are somewhere else. For instance, Western items are reasonably popular all over the country, but they're especially popular in the West. They also tend to be less expensive if bought elsewhere. The Pirnacks buy antiques from people they meet at the shows. They buy very little from garage and yard sales because items from household sales tend to be newer than what they sell. If they find an item they know another dealer would like, they buy it and sell it to the other dealer. There's much less competition among dealers than is thought. "If you specialize in an item, you know more about its value and worth. You build up a base of customers who are looking to buy what you carry," he explains.

When the Pirnacks buy an antique, the first thing they do is polish, repair or refinish it. Then they decide which show would be most appropriate to take it to. Nan and Dave travel to about 18 to 20 shows all over the country each year. Some shows they go to every year; others they try out for the first time.

"We'll decide to do a show by talking with other dealers to see how they've done there. We also ask whether they think our type of merchandise would sell well at the show," indicates Dave. "Sometimes our own customers tell us we should do a particular show as well." Of five new shows they exhibited at in 1993, they'll go back to only two of them next year.

The size of the booth used at a show and whether there is another show nearby are also factors in their decisions. "We generally will not go to a show unless we can get a booth that's eight by 20 feet," says Dave. Eight by 16 is the minimum; they have displayed their antiques in a space as large as 30 by eight feet. Some shows have full walls with quality wallpaper on the walls; if they don't, the Pirnacks bring their own.

"We try to bunch our shows so we don't have to do so much travel," he indicates. "We just got back from two shows, one in Birmingham and the other in Atlanta. We only made one trip, doing the shows on successive weekends."

Exhibiting at a show requires much more than just showing up and being nice to the people who stop by your booth. Depending upon how elaborate you want your booth to be, it can take up to three days just to set up. The shows last from two to four days, and then you have to break everything down and travel to the next show.

Booth fees range from $150 to $2,200, and the Pirnacks budget $100 a day for expenses on the road. Some shows charge admission, while others don't. All are open to the public, and the number of exhibitors can range from 30 to 1,200.

"Our style has changed over the years," remarks Dave. "For a while, we sold a lot of pure American country antiques; then we went to Western items, then sporting items. You have to keep up with the trends, but a lot of it is determined by what you can find."

The Pirnacks have been selling antiques on the show circuit since 1989, but they say they paid their dues for the 15 years Nan had her shop. "You have to know something about antiques before you go into it as a business," warns Dave. They keep a library of 500 reference guides and a variety of trade publications handy to research different styles.

"The biggest challenge is finding the best items," he remarks. "You don't find the really special items very often."

APPLIANCE REPAIR

Mel Applebee
Westport Island, Maine

Ease of Startup	Difficult
Range of Initial Investment	$5,000
Time Commitment	Full-time
Can You Run the Business From Home?	Yes
Success Potential	Easy

Description of Business: A one-person business in which a skilled person travels to local homes and repairs household appliances.

Ease of Startup: Difficult. You need several years of experience or schooling before you can begin.

Range of Initial Investment: $5,000, not including a vehicle.

Time Commitment: Full-time

Can You Run the Business From Home? Yes

Success Potential: Easy. If you have the technical ability, you'll always be in demand.

How to Market the Business: Newspaper ads, word of mouth and repeat business.

The Pros: It's a lucrative business for one person to run.

The Cons: Gaining the experience takes a long time.

Special Considerations: If you've always dabbled in appliances around the house or have worked in the field, this is a great business.

For More Information: Local vocational/technical schools.

Story of the Business

Mel Applebee spent 20 years in the Air Force as an Aircraft Environmental Technician, which meant he spent a lot of time in the guts of planes. Once you've done that for awhile, troubleshooting a faulty washer seems like a piece of cake.

Before Applebee left the service, he signed on with Project Transition, a program offered by the military to help retiring personnel decide what they want to do when they get out. He worked at a Sears store in Champaign, Illinois, for awhile learning how to repair household appliances because it was something he always wanted to do.

Today Mel runs his own business repairing dryers, refrigerators, stoves and dishwashers. He works Tuesday through Saturday from eight in the morning until six at night. He has more than enough business to keep him busy. Sometimes his waiting list is two weeks long.

He does all repair work at his customers' homes and charges according to the distance he has to travel, within a 30-mile radius. In the Westport area, it's $24 for a service call; for Bath, which is 18 miles away, he charges $28. Parts are extra.

He's able to work six or seven jobs in one day, depending upon the distance. Each job averages about an hour. He usually plans his jobs a week or two ahead, calling his customers in the evening. "The biggest problem I face is that people are not always there when I am," he relates. "In that case, they'll tell me to just go into the house, but sometimes I need to talk over a problem with them and they're not home."

In addition to a small newspaper ad in the local paper, Applebee often gets referrals through an appliance store in

Bath when people call to have an appliance serviced the store calls him. The store doesn't get a percentage, but if Applebee declares an appliance to be DOA, there's a good chance the customer will buy a new appliance from the store. "I always tell a customer when it would be more economical if they bought a new appliance instead of having me fix the old one. They listen to my advice most of the time," he reports.

When he started his business in 1983, Applebee invested in a vehicle, some hand and power tools and spare parts like belts, water pumps, timers and valves. He uses a pickup truck, though some other repairmen prefer a van.

Applebee says that anyone who's thinking about getting into this business must be able and willing to go to special classes run by the appliance manufacturers as often as possible. "Appliances are changing all the time, they're getting more technical and electronic; you need to stay current," he explains. Three times a year he attends one-day classes run by companies like General Electric and White Westinghouse, though he works on all brands of appliances.

Applebee also does some warranty work for General Electric. He contacted the company and told them he wanted to get on their list for warranty work in your area. Warranty work, however, accounts for only one percent of his business.

Though it's good to have a general proficiency for electrical appliances, Applebee says a person can attend a technical school for six months and learn the necessary skills, especially if he's been tinkering around at home and is mechanically inclined to start with.

"It's a good trade," he says. "After all, everybody has at least five major appliances in their home, and they're changing all the time."

AUCTIONEER

Francis O'Loughlin
St. Augustine, Florida

Ease of Startup	Moderate
Range of Initial Investment	$5,000
Time Commitment	Part- or full-time
Can You Run the Business From Home?	Yes
Success Potential	Easy

Description of Business: A business that organizes, promotes and then conducts an auction of merchandise or real estate.

Ease of Startup: Moderate. You should attend workshops and classes to become licensed by the state.

Range of Initial Investment: $5,000 for instruction, licensure and initial promotion.

Time Commitment: Part- or full-time

Can You Run the Business From Home? Yes

Success Potential: Easy. There's a dearth of skilled auctioneers in some parts of the country.

How to Market the Business: Advertising, word of mouth.

The Pros: Being an auctioneer is exciting, and you'll gain first-hand knowledge of many different types of merchandise.

The Cons: It's hard work; it takes time to develop your own business after interning for other auctioneers.

Special Considerations: If you're outgoing, have a fast tongue and reflexes and have an impeccable background, you could be a superb auctioneer.

Story of the Business

What do you do after you spend 30 years as a cop, all the while working on your cattle ranch in your spare time? You become an auctioneer, of course. Francis O'Loughlin spent many years living on cattle ranches and all of his working career in law enforcement. When he gave that up, he got into real estate. He began to see how auctioneering could help his business. In 1990 he went to an auction school that offers a two-week immersion course in the fundamentals of becoming an auctioneer.

"The first thing they teach you is how to speak clearly and let people know you're trying to sell them something," he relates. "I didn't know how tongue-tied I was. It took me two months before I could loosen up enough to lead an auction."

Everything was hands-on, with students attending auction barns and sales every day of the course. "There was constant movement from one instructor to another. Each one has a technique designed to teach you how to handle a crowd," he recalls.

After several years in the business, he's convinced that a good ring man is the most important part of running a successful auction business. "He's the guy gathering the bid," O'Loughlin explains. "The auctioneer is calling the bid, but the ring man is doing the work."

After he left school, O'Loughlin contacted some auctioneers in his area to arrange to intern for them; he wanted to call bids or play ring man. "Interning at other auctions—especially benefit auctions—is the best free advertising you can get," he says.

Many states have very strict rules on licensing auctioneers; Florida is one of the strictest. After the aspiring auctioneer passes a test, the state does a background check and conducts a hearing to make sure they're not bringing in a person of questionable character. After all, an auctioneer handles a lot of money and is entrusted with people's goods.

Besides interning in the beginning, auctioneers can get experience by going to other auctions and letting the auctioneers know you're a licensed auctioneer. They'll give you something to do. "It gives a little pizzazz to an auction. It also provides the auctioneers with a break, especially if they're alone," explains O'Loughlin. "Even established auction houses will put you to work."

O'Loughlin opened his auction business in collaboration with his partner, Terry Pacetti, who runs a real estate agency. They average two to eight auctions each month. They conduct several different kinds of auctions. Cattle auctions require the auctioneer to deliver in rapid-fire because he's moving a lot of animals. Antique auctions are slow by necessity.

"The first rule of auctioneering is that you should have some knowledge of what you're auctioning off," indicates O'Loughlin. He occasionally does an auction of exotic birds, which is his specialty.

In recent years, real estate auctions have become popular, but O'Loughlin says they're the hardest kind of auction to conduct. The auctioneer must get everything in order in advance because he's essentially closing on a house. Whenever they're planning an auction of merchandise, they try to include a piece of property. Some of the properties they auction off are foreclosures and owned by the bank; they haven't moved for months or even years. "The property might not sell that day, but I guarantee we'll sell it within two weeks," he remarks. "Auctions bring people out who normally wouldn't have looked at the property. An auction is one of the best marketing tools I've ever seen."

BALLOON STORE

Ann's Balloons

Ann White

Birmingham, Alabama

Ease of Startup	Easy
Range of Initial Investment	$2,000-$5,000
Time Commitment	Part- or full-time
Can You Run the Business From Home?	Yes
Success Potential	Easy

Description of Business: A business that sells, delivers and decorates with balloons.

Ease of Startup: Easy. The various wholesalers in the field will help you get started.

Range of Initial Investment: $2,000-$5,000 to rent helium tanks and buy other necessary equipment and merchandise to augment the balloons.

Time Commitment: Part- or full-time

Can You Run the Business From Home? Yes

Success Potential: Easy. Many florists offer balloon services. If you're talented and specialize in just balloons, it's relatively simple to succeed.

How to Market the Business: Advertising, publicity, word of mouth, referrals.

The Pros: Customers are very appreciative; it's a fun business.

The Cons: Expect to work around the clock during holidays.

Special Considerations: Creative people who like to deal with the public should do well with a balloon store.

For More Information: National Association of Balloon Artists and *Balloons and Parties Today Magazine*, Festivities Publications, 1205 W. Forsyth Street, Jacksonville, FL 32204.

Story of the Business

Ann White stumbled into the balloon business. In 1982, when her husband was laid off, they decided a good way to make a living would be to buy discontinued or returned toys and sell them at discount prices.

The Whites added a few balloons to the merchandise they offered. They figured that when people came in to buy birthday presents they would buy balloons as well. They didn't display the balloons, but kept them in a box. They soon noticed the balloons were outselling the toys.

That's when Ann decided to get serious about balloons. She signed up for a balloon seminar. When she got back she told her husband she couldn't believe the things people were doing with balloons. He scoffed a little, but then they both attended a balloon convention. By that point they had fallen in love with the idea of working with balloons. They put all of their toys on sale for half price and changed the name of their business from Ann's Toys to Ann's Balloons.

Ann loves working with balloons because they're beautiful and they send a loving message to the person who receives them. "You can buy a balloon for less than you can buy a greeting card, and it's much more visible," she explains. The business also provides decorations for a lot of weddings. "I tell the bride if she wants people to come in, relax and have a good time, she should try balloons because they just change people's attitudes."

Just selling balloons on a string won't bring customers in because they can buy that at the grocery store. "You have to be creative and able to put different things together," relates Ann. In one day, for instance, three of the balloons she made were a Pilgrim, a baby boy and a money balloon filled with bills. She learned how to design with balloons by attending seminars and reading *Balloons Today*, the industry magazine. A lot of her ideas come from her customers. "They ask if I can do something. I say, 'Of course.' After I hang up, I wonder, 'How am I going to do this?'"

But it always works out. Today, Ann's Balloons has five full-time employees—including herself and her husband. They hire part-timers for special occasions, like the time they had an order for 8,000 balloons on New Year's Eve.

When they first started to concentrate on balloons, they didn't have a lot of money, so they worked out barter arrangements with local businesses for promotional work. They continue the arrangements today. She works with one of the local radio stations for their remote broadcasts. If the station wants balloons to hand out to the children, she provides them. They both keep a tab. When it's built up, she schedules some radio advertising.

One time, she persuaded the director of a Birmingham mall to let her arrange a balloon display in the middle of the mall to promote her business for a weekend. She also sent out invitations to potential clients, like hotels, for a special breakfast before the mall opened one morning. She often trades with bridal shows by decorating their main entrance in exchange for a booth.

Ann says a balloon business is good for someone who is creative and doesn't have much money. You can rent helium tanks, but you must buy regulators, air compressors and various merchandise that accompany the balloons like stuffed animals, coffee mugs and candy.

"You have to like people, since you're going to be dealing with the public," she adds, "but it's very seldom that we don't get a phone call from a bride or other customer who says they're happy we were there."

BED & BREAKFAST

Paisley and Parsley B & B

Bea Stone
Jackson, New Hampshire

Ease of Startup	Moderate
Range of Initial Investment	$10,000-$400,000
Time Commitment	Full-time in season
Can You Run the Business From Home?	Yes
Success Potential	Difficult

Description of Business: A private house with a number of guest rooms to rent out overnight or longer to guests. Breakfast is served each morning.

Ease of Startup: Moderate. It's necessary to be licensed by the state. Make sure your home and guest rooms are welcoming to guests.

Range of Initial Investment: $10,000-$400,000.

Time Commitment: Full-time in season.

Can You Run the Business From Home? Yes

Success Potential: Difficult. If you're in a tourist area, you'll do well, but don't expect to make your sole living from a B & B.

How to Market the Business: Guidebooks, advertising, national and local publicity, the Chamber of Commerce and the local bed-and-breakfast association.

The Pros: You'll meet interesting people who will envy your lifestyle.

The Cons: You won't have a lot of free time; it's more work than just making beds and cooking breakfast.

Special Considerations: For people who have a few extra rooms and who truly enjoy meeting all types of people, running a B & B will be a satisfying business.

For More Information: American Bed & Breakfast Association, 1407 Hugenot Road, Midlothian, VA 23113; *Upstart's Guide to Owning and Managing a Bed and Breakfast* by Lisa Rogak (Dover, NH: Upstart Publishing, 1994).

Story of the Business

"Everybody who comes to stay at our bed & breakfast tells us they want to live like we do," remarks Bea Stone. She opened Paisley & Parsley, a three-room B & B in prime White Mountain tourist country in 1989. "It's their dream. What they don't realize is they need a lot of energy and a background in cooking and entertaining. They also need to like living in a state of near-crisis and operating on a shoestring all the time. If all those things are true, then I'd say this is the perfect business for them."

Stone and her husband are in an enviable position. When they retired, they sold their home in Mountain Lakes, New Jersey and used the proceeds to buy the house in Jackson. "For four years, we traveled every weekend looking for a house that would make a good B & B," she recalls. "We traveled from New Hampshire to North Carolina looking for an old house. Instead we ended up buying a new house with an incredible view of Mount Washington."

They decided on the new house because the rooms were spacious, and they didn't have to take down walls or redo plumbing fixtures, even though the house hadn't been used previously as a B & B. "Since we used money from the sale of our other house to finance it, there was no risk because we were going to live there anyway," explains Bea. "As a result, we feel we can take time off for ourselves. Someone with an incredible mortgage might feel they wouldn't be able to do that."

Once they bought the house, they made sure the house met state safety codes; they had to install a hardwired smoke and fire alarm system. Then they were licensed to operate as a B & B by the state. "We read some innkeeping books, found a good lawyer, an accountant and a bank. We joined the Chamber of Commerce and the local association of resort owners," she says. She also investigated places to advertise, the AAA, and the various inn and B & B guidebooks.

They've spent about $375,000 on the house, including the purchase and $25,000 for a new well. "When we bought the house, we didn't know a new well was necessary, but fortunately we had the money for it," she says. "These are the kinds of things people need to roll with if they want to get into the business."

Bea also upgraded everything in the house. She bought brand-new beds, down comforters and beautiful linens. Her biggest expense has been the landscaping and developing herb and perennial gardens. "We're up to about $30,000 on the gardens alone," she remarks. She admits it's not necessary, but that it enhances the B & B. "It would have been pretty plain without it," she points out.

The Stones live in the house. This has its good and bad points, but they've managed to create their own private spaces. The busiest seasons are summer, fall foliage and February's peak skiing. Rooms range between $65 and $95 a night for a couple. The breakfast is gourmet quality. Bea uses a lot of the produce from her gardens to prepare it. A typical summertime breakfast consists of mushroom crepes, fresh kiwi and strawberries and zucchini muffins. The occupancy rate ranges between 50 and 75 percent. They get a lot of referrals from guests who have stayed there before. "Many people walk by when they're on vacation. They'll come in and book a weekend later in the season when they're up here again," she reports.

Bea hires a maid to work an average of 10 to 12 hours a week. She pays her $10 an hour, which is high for the area. She justifies it because that's what she paid a cleaning woman back in New Jersey.

The B & B grosses between $20,000 and $25,000 a year, and all profits are plowed back into the business.

"You have to really like people to do this," indicates Bea, "because you don't have a lot of free time. Having a good sense of humor also helps. When guests tell me they like what I've done, it's really good for my ego."

BIRD RAISING

White Flight

Susan Severson
Sioux Falls, South Dakota

Ease of Startup	Moderate
Range of Initial Investment	$1,000+
Time Commitment	Part- or full-time
Can You Run the Business From Home?	Yes
Success Potential	Moderate

Description of Business: A business that sells birds wholesale to retail shops after raising them from eggs.

Ease of Startup: Moderate. You need to set up cages and incubators; then you can order breeders through the mail.

Range of Initial Investment: $1,000 and up for cages and birds.

Time Commitment: Part- or full-time

Can You Run the Business From Home? Yes

Success Potential: Moderate. It's important to focus on a number of species and raise sufficient volume in order to make it. Not everyone has the knack for raising birds.

How to Market the Business: Word of mouth, referrals.

The Pros: You're helping to perpetuate a species.

The Cons: You're tied to the house. It's also hard to arrange for backup help when you want to go on vacation.

Special Considerations: Nurturing people who love birds and can tolerate the constant sounds of birds will do well.

For More Information: Society of Parrot Breeders and Exhibitors, POB 369, Groton, MA 01450.

Story of the Business

On Mother's Day in 1990, Susan Severson's husband bought her a two-week-old lovebird. Little did he know the monster he had created. "I raised him until he was full-grown and had a great time doing it," she recalls. "I then decided to start raising birds. I got a couple pairs of lovebirds and was able to get them to breed."

Today, she has 250 birds in the house at any time. She raises cockatiels, cockatoos, parrots, parakeets and lovebirds. She keeps the breeders in the basement. She had to put a 25 x 30 foot addition onto the house to serve as a showroom for the birds. She prefers to sell her birds to pet stores in town. Occasionally, people come to the house to buy birds.

Severson says several factors can influence breeding success. "First, you need the right size breeder cages," she indicates. "Then, a lot of it is in the seed, fruits and vegetables you give them." It's also necessary to manipulate the amount of light the birds receive, since they require a set amount of light each day to bring them into the breeding season.

In the beginning she contacted the stores in town to sell her birds. "Handfed birds are really the only way to go for a pet," she believes. "I pull them from the parents so young that they have a good success rate. They're really human imprinted, tame and almost talking by the time they leave," she indicates. She currently supplies birds to four stores in town.

"I started on a wing and a prayer," Severson recalls. She raised four pairs of lovebirds; three of them were given to her by a man who wasn't having any luck breeding them. Her husband built cages for them. She invested about $500 in the business and was off. Today she estimates she has about $10,000 invested in equipment and $40,000 in birds.

Since news of her talent in breeding birds has gotten around, a few people from town call Susan to have her incubate their babies and handfeed them. Eggs take anywhere from 18 to 25 days in the incubator before they hatch. She sells birds to stores at ages that range from 10 weeks to five months. The price she charges the pet stores is determined partly by the rarity of the birds and partly by how difficult they are to breed. She sells cockatoos for $400 to stores, lovebirds for $35 and parakeets for $75.

Severson works at the business full-time, spending six hours a day cleaning cages and several more hand-feeding babies. Sometimes she's not able to leave the house for more than an hour because the babies need to be fed frequently. "You're tied to the house, and you're not going to be able to go on vacation," she relates. "If you're interested in the business, you should really examine what kind of a lifestyle you want to have. My daughter-in-law occasionally covers for me, but I have a lot of money tied up in those birds. If I plan a vacation and I've got a sick bird, I decide to stay at home with the bird."

Severson's eventual goal is to open her own store in town, so she concentrates now on building her stock and putting as much back into the business as she can. "It's easy money, I'm a homebody anyway, and I really love the birds," she admits. "It's not just a hobby or a passing thing, it's very demanding. I'm helping to propagate the species, since some people aren't able to raise them and I am. That gives me a good feeling."

BOAT TOUR COMPANY

Balmy Days Cruises

Diane and Bob Campbell
Boothbay Harbor, Maine

Ease of Startup	Difficult
Range of Initial Investment	$50,000
Time Commitment	Full-time in season
Can You Run the Business From Home?	No
Success Potential	Moderate

Description of Business: A company that offers excursions and transportation for tourists and residents via boat.

Ease of Startup: Difficult. You have to buy and equip a boat, get licensed and attract customers.

Range of Initial Investment: $50,000 and up.

Time Commitment: Full-time in season

Can You Run the Business From Home? No

Success Potential: Moderate. Depending upon where you live, the business can be seasonal and very competitive.

How to Market the Business: Advertising, word of mouth, local tourist attractions, publicity.

The Pros: You're literally the captain of your own ship. You get paid to run a boat.

The Cons: The weather can determine your success.

Special Considerations: Running a boat tour operation will seem like heaven for people who love boats.

For More Information: National Association of Charterboat Operators, 655 15th Street NW, Suite 310, Washington, DC 20005.

Story of the Business

Diane and Bob Campbell were living in Massachusetts when a rare opportunity came their way. They had the chance to buy a couple of excursion boats on the coast of Maine. The Campbells had spent vacations sailing in Maine, and Bob had worked on a boat as a child. He had been friendly with a tour boat operator during the summers he spent in Maine. When he found out the boats were for sale, he approached the owner and bought them. As Diane put it, "It didn't take long to make up our minds."

The *Balmy Days II* serves as one of the ferries to Monhegan Island; the *Maranbo II* is the sole form of transportation to Squirrel Island, where many summer residents have their homes. The *Balmy Days II* can carry 150 passengers; it makes one trip a day to the island in season. It drops off and picks people up, and then returns to shore for a dinner cruise each night. The trip to Squirrel Island takes about an hour on the *Maranbo II*, which holds 69 passengers and makes from seven to eight trips a day.

When they bought the boats, Diane became the business manager in charge of sales and marketing. Bob took on the responsibility of running the boats and captaining them. Diane didn't know a thing about marketing and promotion when she started. She began by writing and designing a brochure that described the trips. She attended seminars and workshops sponsored by the Maine Publicity Bureau. Her membership in that group allowed her to place brochures in five tourist information booths throughout the state. "We advertised in several magazines and joined the local Chamber of Commerce," she relates. Diane also hangs signs on the booth for the boat and places brochures in local motels and hotels.

Their efforts worked well enough that they were able to add a sailboat called the *Bay Lady*, with a capacity of 15, to their fleet. Diane also runs a bed & breakfast called the Anchor Watch Inn year-round, though winters are pretty slow.

The total staff for all the boats comes to 14 for the full season. One of the benefits of running your own business is you can hire whomever you want. In the Campbells' case, that means family. "My father and my daughter work for us; my son is captain and operations manager in charge of the crew; his wife does the bookkeeping," says Diane. "The whole family is involved. It's a real pleasure to see the kids all the time in the summer and work together."

The biggest challenge the Campbells face is the weather. "It's the critical factor for success in any given year," indicates Diane. "If we have a good year weatherwise, it doesn't matter what's happening in the rest of the world, we'll have a good year. But if the weather's bad, it doesn't matter how great the economy is or how many Europeans are traveling in this country, we'll have a bad year."

The *Balmy Days II* runs every day from early June through September; it runs on weekends through Columbus Day. The *Maranbo II* runs year-round; in winter it runs three days a week for the two people who stay on the island as caretakers. The Campbells estimate they carry up to 7,000 passengers a year on their three boats.

"When people ask us if we like our retirement, I say we gave up our nine-to-five jobs for five-to-nine jobs," jokes Diane. "But there's no problem with that because we love what we do. We enjoy meeting so many interesting people. It's a short season, though, so the rest of the year we lead a more normal life."

BOATBUILDER

Small Craft Builder

Dick Harrington
Hancock, New Hampshire

Ease of Startup	Easy
Range of Initial Investment	$3,000
Time Commitment	Part- or full-time
Can You Run the Business From Home?	Yes
Success Potential	Difficult

Description of Business: An individual who designs and builds boats, working on speculation, on custom orders and for retail outlets.

Ease of Startup: Easy. Most people who start a boatbuilding business already have the equipment since they've been dabbling for years.

Range of Initial Investment: $3,000 for tools and supplies.

Time Commitment: Part- or full-time

Can You Run the Business From Home? Yes

Success Potential: Difficult. The business is directly affected by economic downturns. There's lots of competition.

How to Market the Business: Advertising, word of mouth, referrals, retail, signs and products on front lawns.

The Pros: This is a dream business for some people.

The Cons: There's no guarantee your boats will sell.

Special Considerations: For many people who built boats—full-size or model-size—as a hobby, the money from a boat-building retirement business is of secondary concern.

For More Information: American Boat Builders & Repairers Association, POB 1236, Stamford, CT 06904.

Story of the Business

Dick Harrington spent the majority of his working life in the electronics and computer industries, but he always wanted to build boats. He even worked a couple of times for sailboat manufacturers, which whetted his appetite even more. When he retired in 1990, he finally started building boats and airplanes, ostensibly to supplement his Social Security income, but you know it's much more than that.

He sells his boats by placing them on his front lawn with a "For Sale" sign. "I usually just have one boat on the lawn at a time," he says. By the time the boat sells a few weeks later, his next boat is ready to replace it. He sells his planes not on the front lawn, but through advertising in various specialty publications.

Building a boat from scratch takes about four to six weeks. He builds boats eight to 16 feet in length, selling them for $100 a foot. Until late 1993, Dick was editing a magazine that took three weeks of his time out of every month. He was only able to build three boats a year, and one plane every other year. He builds planes and boats because the same aerodynamic principles are involved in both. He plans to increase his production from 1994 on.

Harrington's shop is 18 feet in length: this has limited the size of his boats to 16 feet. He built a temporary structure next to his shop where he is working on a 23-foot light schooner. This will diversify his business.

Harrington says that his biggest problem is finding wood. "I have to constantly shop around," he remarks. He gets plywood from a Massachusetts firm that imports its materials from Finland, where they use waterproof glue in the production of the wood. He visits local and regional lumberyards for additional sources.

He also does boat restorations. People advertise that they're looking for someone to restore an old wooden boat to its original condition. "I also ask around to see if anyone knows anybody who wants a boat restored, and generally keep my ears and eyes open," says Harrington. He only charges ten dollars an hour for restoration, which he admits is not much, but it reimburses him for the time, effort and materials he puts into it.

He's thought about selling his boats through a dealer on consignment, but he's turned down that idea. "A dealer doesn't really put much emphasis on selling the boat, though it does get more exposure," he remarks. Harrington hopes to build two 23-foot schooners over the course of eight months. He plans to sail one at Lake Sunapee in New Hampshire, a lake that's big with recreational sailors. If anyone inquires about the boat he's sailing, Harrington will let them know it's for sale.

"I've had a shop for as long as I can remember," he says. "My father was very handy. He taught me a lot of what I know. I was never this busy while I was working, but I'll take this any day."

BOOK PUBLISHER

Thornapple Publishing Company

Robert Redd
Ada, Michigan

Ease of Startup	Difficult
Range of Initial Investment	$10,000+
Time Commitment	Part- to full-time
Can You Run the Business From Home?	Yes
Success Potential	Moderate

Description of Business: A company that publishes a small number of books—sometimes fewer than one each year—usually on related subjects, which become a niche within a niche.

Ease of Startup: Difficult. You need equipment to process words and typeset, a trustworthy printing company, a good topic and lively writing.

Range of Initial Investment: $10,000 and up.

Time Commitment: Part-time to write and produce the books; full-time to market.

Can You Run the Business From Home? Yes

Success Potential: Moderate. The more people you know, the better. If you can be persuasive, you can do quite well.

How to Market the Business: Through publicity, bookstores, specialty shops, even at flea markets and groups that have a special interest in your books' topics.

The Pros: There's a book in everyone; publishing it yourself will ensure it gets out.

The Cons: It's expensive to publish a book. More than 50,000 books are published every year; you have to be loud and/or different in order to be heard.

Special Considerations: Contrary to what you may think, bookstores may constitute a very small percentage of your sales.

For More Information: *Publishers Weekly*; *The Self-Publishing Handbook* (Para Press) by Dan Poynter.

Story of the Business

Many small publishers get started because a big publisher shunned their book idea. Publisher Robert Redd is no exception. He also found a very specific niche that no publisher was currently serving—which stemmed from a personal interest—and he created a product to serve that niche.

"I retired in 1986 and felt quite terrified by the idea of not having something to do every day," he remembers. "I researched the information that was out there about retirement planning. Most of it centered around finances and where to live. I sensed there was a need to broach the idea of emotional adjustment, particularly among executives. You see, everyone in this country identifies with their jobs. When you go to a cocktail party and say you're retired, people just walk away from you."

Redd felt he had lost his identity. He also had a strong desire not to let his life stagnate. He began to write a book advising retired executives how they could cope with their new status. During the writing process, Redd also analyzed himself; he even participated in counseling to work through the transition to retirement, which he believes is the most important change in a person's life.

As he worked on the book, he addressed these issues in a narrative style. "I wrote about what people are doing," he relates, "from teaching school to running a business."

He called the book *Achievers Never Quit* and submitted it to a few publishers. He quickly learned his book fell into a particular social niche and that he would be able to better reach his audience by publishing it himself.

He makes it sound easy: "I got a listing in *Books in Print*, received an ISBN number, did my own typesetting, took it to a printer and started circulating material about it," he recalls. "Dupont bought some copies for their retiring executives, and so did Weyerhauser and a few others."

Whew. Back up. *Books in Print* is a multivolume set listing all books that are still in print by American publishers. An ISBN number identifies you as a publisher and makes it easy for customers and bookstores to order from you. With the myriad of desktop publishing systems available, virtually all small publishers design their books and page layout themselves. Book printers are found in all parts of the country; their prices and quality vary widely, so shop around and ask for samples.

What Redd calls "circulating material" is the most important part of the publishing process. If you don't get the word out about your books, no one will know they exist. Marketing techniques include book reviews and feature stories that mention the book as a resource.

Back to niches. "I was a member of the International Society of Retirement Planners. I saw my market as the retiree who needs something to take home," says Redd. "I also work with financial advisors who like to give a gift to people who come in to talk about retirement." He sells *Achievers Never Quit* in bulk to businesses for about $3 a book; the cover price is $6.95. Redd considers the book, in its third printing, a success. Selling in bulk he makes about the same amount of money he would by selling single copies through bookstores, which usually buy through distributors.

But Redd says the problem with distributors is that they take about 50 percent and usually don't want to touch small publishers. "If they do, they put the book in and take it out in three months if it doesn't sell," remarks Redd. The best way to sell books is through direct sales: The publisher keeps the entire cover price. But Redd is quick to add this requires a significant amount of time devoted to marketing.

Achievers Never Quit is a 140-page paperback book that measures 6 inches by 9, with a two-color glossy cover. It cost Redd $1.50 to print each book; his printings average 3,000. He uses a Macintosh computer with a laser printer, a scanner for photographs and other artwork, and PageMaker software for layout and design. He can go from design to finished copies on a book in three months once the book is written.

His second book is called *Whimsey, Wit and Wisdom*, which is a book he wrote with his wife. It's a compilation of columns Redd wrote for a regional senior magazine with cartoon illustrations. He's planning his third book now on how to cope with losses.

Redd pulls in about $10,000 a year; he is content to add another book every year or two. For him, money isn't the issue.

"You can publish books anywhere, and you can get into it for less than ten grand," he points out. "It's better to do it yourself, because with the big publishers—unless you're George Bush's dog—you don't have a chance."

BOTTLED WATER COMPANY

Vermont Pure Natural Spring Water

Jack Maguire

Randolph, Vermont

Ease of Startup	Difficult
Range of Initial Investment	$1 - 20 million
Time Commitment	Full-time
Can You Run the Business From Home?	No
Success Potential	Easy

Description of Business: A company that sells bottled spring water.

Ease of Startup: Difficult. You need to buy a spring, meet agricultural requirements, conduct testing to determine the mineral content and purity and then market it.

Range of Initial Investment: $1 - 20 million

Time Commitment: Full-time

Can You Run the Business From Home? No

Success Potential: Easy. Water safety is a big issue for the '90s. As bottled water sales increase, so will every company's market share.

How to Market the Business: Print and radio advertising, promotional event tie-ins, publicity, coupons, billboards, free samples.

The Pros: The business is booming and will only get bigger.

The Cons: It's very expensive and takes time to achieve market share.

Special Considerations: Starting a water company that caters to home and office use—offering five- and 10-gallon jugs—is an option that is much less expensive and easier to start.

For More Information: International Bottled Water Association, 113 North Henry Street, Alexandria, VA 22314.

Story of the Business

What do you do for an encore when you've spent nine years as president and CEO of Evian Water? You buy your own small bottled water company—preferably in Vermont, regarded as the lower 48's most pristine state—and proceed to build it up like you did with Evian.

Jack Maguire bought his spring from an existing company called Vermont Hidden Spring that focused on the home and office market. He had spent a year tromping through fields looking at springs throughout northern New England, but he always came back to Vermont because he had vacationed in the state and had a house in Woodstock. When he found the spring in Randolph, he was attracted by the mineral content and the flow, which he felt matched what the Europeans have.

"All the things I learned working for Evian gave me the confidence that it could be done with an American label," he says. "My aim was to develop a premium American water using a Vermont spring. I always thought America could compete with a European water if the quality was there."

He had certain criteria he was looking for in a spring. He sought a glacial area because he had a feel for where natural springs occur from the topography and the history of the glaciers. The spring he was looking for always flowed, the temperature never varied, the mineral content never changed and the water contained no sodium. Other springs he looked at met some of these conditions, but not all. The spring in Randolph met all of them, and it was certified. This means the owners had agreed to keep the area free of contaminants. The spring itself is on a 25-acre plot; Maguire bought an adjacent 100-acre plot of land to further protect the purity of the water.

"The deterioration of municipal tap water systems is fueling the bottled water industry," he explains. "As a result, water has to be marketed as something that's healthy and pure. In addition, Vermont has the image of being healthy and pristine."

After he positioned the product, Maguire decided to take the company public to raise the funds necessary to market it. The first market the company went after was the Albany, New York area, then he proceeded to the metropolitan New York area and to Burlington, Vermont. He uses a variety of marketing vehicles, including radio and print advertising, coupons in Sunday supplements and outdoor advertising—except in Vermont where billboards are illegal. Future plans include Washington, D.C., the South and Florida, where the per capita intake of bottled water is three times that of the Northeast.

Vermont Pure Natural Spring Water relies on sales reps to sell the product to stores and supermarkets in the target areas. The company has not had the problem some new products face like being discontinued and pulled off the shelf. "We just keep increasing our market share," he relates. "As long as I've been in this business, the industry has grown 10 to 15 percent every year, except in 1990 when Perrier was taken off the shelf." The industry as a whole increased 13 percent in 1992 alone; a premium market like Maguire's has increased 26 percent. When Maguire bought the company he started with seven employees; in 1993 he had 45.

Maguire advises business people to stay within their expertise when looking for a retirement business to start and then look for certain niches within that framework. "You may be small, but the big guys don't care about small," he points out. "Then position it and come up with something the big guys aren't doing, because it's all salesmanship at this point."

Indeed, although all natural waters are different, each with a different thumbprint, the tangible difference comes through marketing. The bigger you get the more money you need.

"Our first year, we sold a quarter of a million cases," says Maguire. The second year they were up to 750,000 cases, followed by 1.5 million the third year.

In the beverage industry, it's said you need $20 million to get into it and succeed, but with home and office, one million would be adequate. In fact, home and office water delivery are growing quickly. "I think most people could succeed in a growth industry, not a flat one," advises Maguire.

CAKE MAKER/CAKE DECORATOR

Barbara Stinson
Hanover, New Hampshire

Ease of Startup	Easy
Range of Initial Investment	$250-500
Time Commitment	Part-time
Can You Run the Business From Home?	Yes
Success Potential	Easy

Description of Business: An individual who makes custom decorated cakes for special occasions that are sold through stores or by word of mouth.

Ease of Startup: Moderately easy. You should get some training. You will have to buy the equipment and ingredients, then publicize your business.

Range of Initial Investment: $250-500 for pans and ingredients.

Time Commitment: Part-time

Can You Run the Business From Home? Yes

Success Potential: Easy. Skilled cake decorators are in demand, especially in areas without a bakery.

How to Market the Business: Advertising, publicity, word of mouth, referrals.

The Pros: It's a happy business, and it's creative.

The Cons: There might not be enough demand in your area for you to rely solely on the income.

Special Considerations: A person who likes to stay at home and doesn't mind receiving orders on short notice will do well.

For More Information: Cake decorating course at community schools or through the Wilton Cake Decorating Company, Wilton, Connecticut.

Story of the Business

Barbara Stinson got into the cake business by default. She and her husband, Jack, had recently opened a general store. About a year into the business, they bought a freezer so they could sell ice cream.

The ice cream didn't budge. Barbara was still teaching psychiatry at the nearby Dartmouth-Hitchcock Medical Center when her secretary brought in a couple of cakes she had made. They were beautiful and delicious. Barbara decided to hire her secretary to make cakes on the side to encourage people to buy the ice cream.

After awhile, the secretary's prices increased and she wanted to make just two a week. The business was demanding two a day. "I decided I had to do the cakes, or get someone else to do them," remembers Barbara. Since she couldn't find anyone to make them, she decided to do it herself. She spent a day with a known cake decorator in a nearby town, and then started making the cakes for the store.

"After I learned how to make flowers and do the edging, we put a couple of them in the window. The business increased to the point where I left my job," she says.

The Stinsons make all their cakes from scratch. "I convinced Jack to be the baker because he's an engineer and much more precise than I am. I do the decorating," she remarks. "Our success is due to the fact that we make the cakes from scratch; they're not fluff cakes."

They make the cakes at home because there wasn't room in the store and because their office is in their home. "It was natural for Jack to work in the office, so when the buzzer went off, he'd take them out of the oven. When I got home, I'd decorate them," she says.

They make the most cakes—mainly white and yellow cakes—in summer because people don't want to be bothered with a hot oven. In the wintertime, chocolate cakes are popular. Sixty percent of their cakes are for birthdays, wedding cakes make up 30 percent of demand, and all-occasion cakes account for about 10 percent of their business.

The Stinsons charge $13 for an 8-inch one-layer cake, and $15 for a 10-inch cake. She concentrates on single-layer cakes because she's a perfectionist. With two layers, there's a distinct line that separates the two layers. With sheet cakes, she puts the cake on plywood boards covered with aluminum foil to prevent the cake from cracking, as it tends to do on cardboard. An 11 x 15 inch sheet cake is $25, and a 12 x 18 cake is $35; a carrot cake with cream cheese frosting costs $7 more.

Barbara suggests that a person who wants to get into the cake business start by offering to serve as backup help. "I've tried to find someone to make them for me, when I'm busy or tired," she indicates. "Cake decorating is somewhat demanding. If I look at the cake book and see I have to make five cakes on Friday, I know I'm not going out that day."

She can decorate a cake in seven minutes. Her record is 27 cakes in one day. The occasion? Valentine's Day. "After that, I had tennis elbow for a week," she laughs.

CAMPGROUND

Aunt's Creek RV Park

Neil Hartwell
Branson, Missouri

Ease of Startup	Difficult
Range of Initial Investment	$200,000+
Time Commitment	Full-time in season
Can You Run the Business From Home?	No
Success Potential	Easy

Description of Business: A campground that offers RV hookup, repair service and a convenience store for patrons and outsiders.

Ease of Startup: Difficult to start from scratch due to zoning, construction permits and landscaping.

Range of Initial Investment: $200,000 and up.

Time Commitment: Full-time in season

Can You Run the Business From Home? No

Success Potential: Easy. RV travel is increasing. While customers are at the campground, you have a captive audience, so the more services you can offer them, the better.

How to Market the Business: Through guidebook descriptions, ads in RV magazines, word of mouth and repeat business.

The Pros: If you're located in a popular tourist area, you'll be booked solid.

The Cons: It's hard work and the hours are long.

Special Considerations: If you can do most of the maintenance and repair on the buildings and facilities and enjoy dealing with people from early morning until late at night, you'll do well in this business.

For More Information: National Campground Owners Association, 11307 Sunset Hills Rd, Suite B7, Reston, VA 22090.

Story of the Business

Neil Hartwell sounds like a million other corporate executives who always dreamed of doing something else. The difference is that he actually did it. For many years, Hartwell managed what he calls "losing divisions of major companies" in several big cities, but he was losing his taste for it. "I was fed up with big American business, spending a lot of my time sitting in meetings and on airplanes," he recalls. "I decided I wanted to work with my hands."

He left corporate America and bought an 11-1/2-acre piece of property near the town of Branson, Missouri, intending to build a campground. "I felt if we bought a piece of property and developed it, we'd get the capital appreciation," he explains. He bought the land for just under $50,000 in 1984, put in about $180,000 worth of improvements over the years, and has turned down an offer to sell the park for $310,000.

Aunt's Creek RV Park is the smallest four-star campground in America; it has only 16 pads, though Neil is adding seven more. One-and-a-half of the acres of the original plot of land are across the street from the main campground. A convenience store is located there, along with facilities for boat storage and a repair building for boats and RVs.

The RV pads are unique in that each bay is separated; this is a welcome contrast to the sardine cans patrons find at many other parks. Hartwell's campground features manicured gardens, TV, sewer, water and electrical hookups. There is also a table with an umbrella at each site. Each bay has an extra-large tent pad because many people come with their kids. The parents stay in the RV, and the kids pitch a tent outside.

The season in Branson is longer than in other areas. Hartwell opens the park on March 15th for fishermen and stays open through the end of October. He picked the area because there were no mosquitoes, and land and taxes were cheap. "Land is expensive now, it's gone up 10 times since I bought it," he says.

In recent years, Branson has eclipsed Nashville as the country music capital of the nation with 37 country and western theaters operating in 1993. The theaters are owned by Loretta Lynn, Johnny Cash and Andy Williams—among others. When Hartwell bought the land, no one knew that Branson would become such a hot spot. "Part of life is luck," he says.

He spends a typical day at the park picking up sites, collecting garbage, mowing lawns, fixing roads and RVs and pumping gas, which he admits makes for long hours. "I enjoy dealing with the people," he says. "They come from all over the country and Canada, too." The park is perched on a lake, which is an added enticement to travelers.

Though 80 percent of Hartwell's business comes from referrals and repeat business, he still advertises in all the major RV publications and the local Chamber of Commerce book. He also sends out general mailings to his own mailing list.

Hartwell built all the buildings on the land himself, serving as carpenter, electrician and plumber. "I was lucky enough to have a father who made me do all that when I was young," he reflects. He still does all the on-site work himself, without hiring help. He believes running a campground is a good business for someone who retires early and is in good health. Later on, the owner would have to hire help, which would mean fewer financial rewards.

Back when Hartwell bought the land, Branson was one of the few areas of the country that didn't require building permits or zoning, though today it does. "I work full-time in season, but the rest of the time I goof around," he says.

CANDLEMAKER

Clem Block
Grand Rapids, Michigan

Ease of Startup	Easy
Range of Initial Investment	$100
Time Commitment	Part- or full-time
Can You Run the Business From Home?	Yes
Success Potential	Easy

Description of Business: A business in which a craftsperson makes themed candles for sale, selling them through retail outlets and to individuals.

Ease of Startup: Easy. You need to buy a variety of molds and waxes.

Range of Initial Investment: $100 for supplies.

Time Commitment: Part- or full-time

Can You Run the Business From Home? Yes

Success Potential: Easy. Personalized candles for special occasions sell well.

How to Market the Business: Advertising, word of mouth, referrals, retail outlets.

The Pros: It's an easy business to operate. You can make several candles at one time.

The Cons: There's not a lot of money in selling customized candles.

Special Considerations: Making candles is a good business for creative people who like to keep busy, but not too busy.

For More Information: *Homemade Money*, by Barbara Brabec, POB 2137, Naperville, IL 60567.

Story of the Business

Sometimes a seemingly innocuous comment or image will plant a seed that launches an entirely new venture. At least, that's what happened one day to Clem Block.

Clem is a published poet who is frequently invited to read his poetry at functions and special occasions. He read his poem "Divided Highway Ends" at a wedding back in 1970. At the wedding, he noticed that one of the candles at the service had a copy of the wedding invitation embedded in it. Clem sought out the man who had put the invitation on the candle and had him make a candle with a copy of his poem on it. Clem sold the candle to the new bride for $15. She liked it so much she showed it to all her friends. From this, Clem had several inquiries about candles. He went back to the candlemaker and offered to refer business to him if he would make the candles.

"I asked him what he would pay for my poem. He replied 25 cents," says Clem. "I didn't think that was nearly enough for a $15 candle, so I went to a high school girl I knew who made candles and started to work with her." After they worked together for a while, she started college. The work started to be too much for her, so Clem taught himself to make candles.

Block displays his candles in florist shops and at printers because prospective brides and grooms frequent them. They can order a candle through the printer, who forwards the order and a copy of the invitation. Clem makes a candle for them, with the invitation on one side and his poem "Divided

Highway Ends" on the other. Usually the couple only orders a candle for themselves. Occasionally Clem has made more; one family ordered nine, providing candles for all the aunts and uncles in the family.

Clem starts out by making core candles that measures 3 x 9 inches. He makes 25 of the cores at a time in commercial molds. Next he staples the invitation and the poem to the candle. He then frosts the candle with wax at a different temperature, so it looks like the icing on a cake. He puts a small sticker on the bottom of each candle with his name, address and phone number. When other people admire the candle, a seed is planted.

A number of years ago, the winner of the Miss Teenage America Contest was a resident of Grand Rapids. She was supposed to take something from her state to a national convention. She contacted Clem and asked him to make 50 candles for the convention. Another winner did the same a few years later. Clem even sent President Ford a candle for the Bicentennial; it's now kept in the President's museum in Grand Rapids.

Clem makes candles for Christmas, Halloween, Thanksgiving and Mother's Day. His Grandparents' candle is very popular. He charges $2.50 for the smallest candle he makes and still charges $15 for the wedding candle.

Block spends an average of five to 10 hours a week making candles. During the Christmas season, he increases his hours to 15 a week. He offers 48-hour service on orders. Generally he waits until he gets orders for six candles because he can make six just as easily as he can make one. People pick up their orders at his house. If he mails candles out, Clem charges for postage and handling. He makes about 1,000 candles in the course of a year.

CAT KENNEL

The Cat's Pajamas

Toni Miele
Lincolnville, Maine

Ease of Startup	Difficult
Range of Initial Investment	$20,000
Time Commitment	Full-time
Can You Run the Business From Home?	Yes
Success Potential	Easy

Description of Business: A luxury boarding facility geared toward cats and kittens who stay overnight or longer.

Ease of Startup: Difficult. You need to build a separate, heated facility that has the cats' best interests at heart.

Range of Initial Investment: At least $20,000 to build the facility.

Time Commitment: Full-time

Can You Run the Business From Home? Yes

Success Potential: Easy. Yet another niche that combines quality with caring, important factors when it comes to people and their pets.

How to Market the Business: Newspaper advertising, publicity, word of mouth and repeat business.

The Pros: It's perfect for cat lovers.

The Cons: You can't leave spontaneously; when you do leave you must arrange for backup care.

Special Considerations: Many kennels are utilitarian, barracks-like facilities. Without conventional cages and with a focus on cats, this business will receive a lot of attention, and therefore, business.

For More Information: American Boarding Kennels Association, 4575 Galley Rd. #400A, Colorado Springs, CO 80915.

Story of the Business

As with many entrepreneurs, Toni Miele started her business when she couldn't find a particular service she needed. "In 1987, my husband Michael and I went overseas for six months," she recalls. "The only problem we had was finding a quality boarding facility for our three cats. When we got back, I decided to open my own. When we designed and built our own house, we planned the cat kennel as part of the house. The cats are on the ground floor, and we're on the top floor."

Toni worked as a respiratory therapist for many years. In opening the kennel, she started working at what she always wanted to do as a child: taking care of animals.

There are no cages. The cats' space is L-shaped with commercial grade linoleum. There are upper and lower sleeping lofts in each of the cats' "rooms." Every cat gets a sheepskin to lie on, and there's a floor-to-ceiling climbing pole made of sisal rope. The rooms are eight feet tall and designed for two cats, with 72 cubic feet per cat. Michael, who's a builder, helped with the construction, which kept the costs down.

"They can get a lot of exercise in the room, but I allow each cat out into the room, one at a time, all day long," says Toni. "They play in an exercise area with a cat tree and a carpeted window ledge that faces the woods where they can watch the birds and squirrels at the feeders. They can also sit on my desk, my lap or on top of the aquarium."

Miele spends about 20 minutes with each cat every day, depending upon how needy the cat is. She says that when both of the cat's owners work, the cat isn't used to being around people all the time and tends to stay by itself. She pays special attention to homesick cats, petting them and holding them a lot and giving them special treats.

When The Cat's Pajamas—which Toni calls "a bed & breakfast for cats"—opened in May of 1989 the media pounced on the story. Local and statewide newspapers ran articles on the business; they also had spots on the nightly TV news. "Now that we're established, our clients and local vets refer new people to us," she reports.

Her routine remains the same every day. In the morning, she prepares the food—special foods supplied by Toni or the owner if necessary—cleans out the rooms, administers medications and then starts to groom the cats. At that point, the phone begins to ring and she takes booking reservations; the average stay is 10 days to two weeks. Many people come from two hours away to board their cats with Toni. Out-of-state vacationers also bring their cats because they often stay at inns or motels where cats aren't welcome.

The busiest time of year is from October to April, and she has to turn many people away during the holidays. Even so, her year-round occupancy rate is 90 percent. Toni expanded the business from a capacity of 12 to 18 cats after her first year. She is expanding again, this time to 24 rooms. "And then that's it, because it's all I can handle by myself," she says. She sometimes hires workers on a contract labor basis so she and Michael can take a break and leave town, but she prefers not to hire regular employees.

Miele suggests that people who are thinking about starting a B & B for cats research local building ordinances, licensing requirements and zoning. Also check out local cat ownership numbers; Maine has lots of cats and dogs. "Check out your competition by visiting all the boarding kennels and vets in the area," she adds.

"You want to be very different from what the competition is doing so people can make an intelligent selection. I'm different because of the amount of space for each cat, the excellence of service and the degree of care," she continues. The Cat's Pajamas is one of the few kennels in the area that can accommodate multi-cat families and long-term boarding.

Miele's business grosses about $50,000 each year, and her operating expenses are low. "Food and litter go up," she points out, "but you get smarter about ordering and usage."

Miele says this is the best business she could ever be in. "I'm doing something I would be doing anyway. I have lots of free time, and I don't have to commute or dress up. During my lunch break, I can go out and bicycle or kayak on the bay."

The only members of the Miele household who might not be enthusiastic are her three cats, who never venture into the kennel.

CLEANING SERVICE

Workenders Cleaning Franchise

Ed Strom
El Dorado Hills, California

Ease of Startup	Easy
Range of Initial Investment	$100-$20,000
Time Commitment	Full-time
Can You Run the Business From Home?	Yes
Success Potential	Easy

Description of Business: A small business that cleans houses and apartments on an ongoing or one-time basis.

Ease of Startup: Easy, whether you start with a franchise or on your own.

Range of Initial Investment: $100-$20,000, depending upon whether you go with a franchise and/or invest in a vehicle.

Time Commitment: Full-time

Can You Run the Business From Home? Yes

Success Potential: Easy. More working couples means less time. There's a desire for cleaning, even when the economy is bad.

How to Market the Business: Advertising, local direct mail, brochure distribution and word of mouth.

The Pros: You'll be in demand from the beginning.

The Cons: It's hard to find good help to keep up with the work.

Special Considerations: For people who don't mind the stigma and hard work of cleaning, it's easy to make a good living.

For More Information: *Everything You Need to Know to Start A House Cleaning Service* (Cleaning Consultant Services), by Mary Johnson, 206-682-9748; Workenders, POB 810455, Boca Raton, FL 33481, 800-634-1717.

Story of the Business

When Ed Strom decided he had to do something after 20 years of military service, he looked around for a business to run that would be a success from the beginning. "I had a very nice income, but it was cut down to about a third of what it was," he recalls. "The problem was that my lifestyle stayed at the old level. I couldn't go out and beat the streets for six months to a year looking for a job that would probably pay me less than the difference between what I made before and what I have now. I decided I either had to make it as an entrepreneur or downscale my lifestyle, and I didn't want to do that."

Ed began to investigate franchises as a way to have some support while he got the business off the ground. "I picked cleaning because it seems to be the expanding service industry of this decade," he explains. "I live in a very affluent area, and I saw a great need for it here." He picked Workenders because the franchise fee was low at about $3,000. Other cleaning franchises Ed investigated charged up to $20,000.

The franchise fee includes support via an 800 number with experts at the main office to answer a franchisee's questions. Workenders also supplies Strom with products cheaper than he can get them elsewhere.

Workenders stresses the team approach to cleaning; this makes more money for the franchisee because they are able to take on more jobs. Instead of one person spending the whole day in one house, three people can clean two or three houses in one day.

"I wear a lot of hats. For me that is the most stressful part of being an entrepreneur," Ed admits. "I market the business, advertise for employees, research their backgrounds, train them, set up a daily schedule, stock the van with supplies and wash the cleaning towels. I also call my clients periodically to get their reaction to the job we did."

Another hat Ed reluctantly wears is that of employee; he often can't find and retain enough good employees. Even though he has three full-time employees, he's looking for more to increase the number of cleaning teams and, thus, his income. "My biggest challenge is finding good employees and keeping them motivated," he remarks. "I've learned to target people who already have an income and are looking for a sideline." In addition to working alongside his team, he also likes to go out with a new team to be assured they're doing a quality job.

Ed focuses on cleaning an entire house rather than on spot jobs. When a cleaning team arrives at a house, one person is assigned to clean bathrooms; a second works in the kitchen. The third team member dusts and vacuums, which is the biggest job. "Each house has to be carefully thought out before you attack it," he advises. "There's a lot of trial and error in the beginning."

Strom markets the business primarily through direct mail. He sends a brochure to people above a certain income level; he also delivers them in bulk to a local coupon pack mailing company. He has an ad in the phone book and is a member of the Chamber of Commerce in two of the communities he serves. Lately he has had to stop advertising temporarily because of the lack of good help. "I still get two or three calls a day," he reports.

After five months in business, Ed was expecting to have two full-time cleaning teams and another starting up shortly. He still hasn't gotten to his second team. If he were to stop growing right now, his income would be $450 a week, and the business would gross $67,000 a year from just one cleaning team.

"Because this is a rural area, I don't have a lot of clients close together," he indicates. "If they were closer, it would minimize the downtime between houses." He pays each employee six or seven dollars an hour. For every $100 in payroll, he pays $31.50 for worker's compensation, Social Security, unemployment taxes and other payroll expenses. His company is bonded for $25,000 per employee; if one of his workers stole something, the bonding company would pay off.

Per house, Ed charges $75 for a four-hour job. He pays a four percent royalty to Workenders; another two percent goes into a separate marketing fund at the company, which is used for national campaigns. He's happy with his cleaning business and with the franchise. "The business has really taken off," he says.

CLOCK REPAIR

Ray and Linda's Clock Repair

Ray Pinson
Tustin, California

Ease of Startup	Moderate
Range of Initial Investment	$1,000
Time Commitment	Full-time
Can You Run the Business From Home?	Yes
Success Potential	Easy

Description of Business: A service that repairs and restores new and old clocks.

Ease of Startup: Moderate. You need to have some mechanical skill and to invest in a necessary set of tools.

Range of Initial Investment: $1000 for tools.

Time Commitment: Full-time

Can You Run the Business From Home? Yes

Success Potential: Easy. Not a lot of people specialize in clock repair; there is a ready demand in most markets.

How to Market the Business: Advertising, word of mouth, referrals.

The Pros: You'll be dealing with people who are entrusting treasured possessions to you, so they're usually pleasant to deal with.

The Cons: You'll need to do house calls.

Special Considerations: Tinkerers who appreciate antiques and enjoy working with people have a good chance of running a successful clock repair business.

Story of the Business

Ray Pinson says he and his wife Linda couldn't have picked a better business to start back in 1979 when he retired from the Marine Corps. "It started as Linda's hobby, and then we talked about doing it as a business," recalls Ray. They worked together in the shop for a number of years before Linda began her own business helping people start their own businesses.

They started the business by phoning an ad in their local pennysaver and by printing up fliers to distribute in their neighborhood. Within a year, they had an ad in the Yellow Pages, which was all it took. "At times it seems like more business than is comfortable," he indicates, "but I've managed." Ray has actually reduced the size of his ad in the Yellow Pages to thin the volume of business.

At any time, Ray will be working on six different clocks in his home office. They might include cuckoo clocks, an antique wall clock or the movement of a grandfather clock. "Sometimes I'll just adjust the swing of the pendulum, which takes five minutes; other times the clock will need a complete overhaul," he says.

An important part of his business is making house calls: He often visits a customer's house to service a grandfather clock. Ray estimates he spends about three half-days each week at clients' homes. He might bring the movement back to the shop if it needs work, or he spends a few hours to clean the movement, oil it and test it there.

Ray works primarily on clock movements that are weight-driven or have windup mechanisms. Clock repairers don't require specialized tools, like watch repairers do. "I use all kinds of pliers and screwdrivers, tweezers and clamps," he says. Possibly the only power tool necessary is a jeweler's lathe with many accessories.

He charges by the job. Determining prices was the toughest ordeal they had when they first started the business. "We didn't have the technical expertise in the beginning, but learned as we went along," he says. "We hung in there and saw we could get more and more. Now, we've been in there long enough that we know what we can get away with without ripping people off." His fees vary: he often adjusts a pendulum swing for free; he charges $600 to overhaul a large grandfather clock. He grosses about $60,000 a year.

"It's strictly a mom-and-pop or one-man operation," remarks Ray. "If you work by yourself, there's never enough time. If a person wants a supplemental income, this is pleasant, clean work; it's not grueling or unhappy."

Dealing with customers is not tough. "It's more personalized than TV or auto repair," he says. "Your customer is bringing in a clock given to her grandmother on her wedding day.

"There's a certain mystique and charm about clocks and people," he adds. "People sometimes think I'm a magician."

CLOWN

Samuel Clinton VanDusen Kilbourn
South Portland, Maine

Ease of Startup	Easy
Range of Initial Investment	$0
Time Commitment	Part- or full-time
Can You Run the Business From Home?	Yes
Success Potential	Moderate

Description of Business: A business in which a clown is paid to perform at schools, fairs, businesses and other events.

Ease of Startup: Easy. Just get dressed up and you're in business. It's recommended you invest in classes or workshops to hone your skills.

Range of Initial Investment: $0

Time Commitment: Part- or full-time

Can You Run the Business From Home? Yes

Success Potential: Moderate. If you're good at it and keep your name out there, you'll do well.

How to Market the Business: Publicity, word of mouth, referrals.

The Pros: If you've always been good at clowning, you'll love being able to make a living from it.

The Cons: Clowning requires constantly changing your act so it doesn't become stale.

Special Considerations: Clowning isn't necessarily wearing a fright wig, big shoes and lots of makeup. You should be able to adapt to different situations, performing in street clothes or even a business suit.

For More Information: Clowns of America, POB 570, Lake Jackson, TX 77566-0570.

Story of the Business

Sam Kilbourn was a lawyer who changed his profession to become a clown. He's heard all the jokes already: he didn't really change jobs at all, etc. The truth is Kilbourn saw the effect he could have on people the first day he went to the law office dressed in a clown suit. That got him thinking that maybe he could do this for a living after all.

It all began in 1977 when he took an evening clown workshop for adults. "It was a revelation because I was asked to be totally physical and just let go. That was the complete opposite of what I was doing at the time," he remembers. "I became a whole different person."

Kilbourn and the other participants liked the workshop so much they talked the instructors into giving more classes. Shortly after, a local school put on a Clown Day and invited Kilbourn to participate. "I went to the office in the morning and worked for a few hours, then I went to the school and got dressed as a clown. It was so much fun and I was so high off of it that after it was over I went back to the office in full dress," he recalls. "I saw clients, and I walked into a closing. People loved it."

At that point, though, it remained a hobby. He regularly performed at local fairs and festivals. "I never thought about turning it into a job," he remarks.

Until, that is, he attended a three-week clown workshop. "When I got back, I wanted to do more of clowning, so I handwrote my resignation and put it on all the partners' desks," recalls Sam. He was in business.

Kilbourn has never advertised; he gets all his business through word of mouth. "People find out about me when they see me do a show," he says. "They'll see me perform, and they—or someone they mentioned me to—end up in a situation where they need a clown for a fair or festival." Kilbourn is also listed in the state directory of artists; some events he performs at are subsidized by the state.

His work is very diverse: Kilbourn works at schools, theaters, fairs and festivals, vaudeville shows, corporations and as roving entertainment at theme shows. Sometimes he works in traditional clown clothes; but frequently, especially at corporations, he performs in a suit and tie.

"The most exciting thing about my job is that I never know what to expect," he mentions. "My challenge is to keep adapting to the situation at hand since it's always different. If I can't do my high balancing act on a stack of chairs because the ceiling is too low, then I do something else."

When he's not clowning, he's working on the business end, arranging bookings, making phone calls or sending out contracts and press releases. He sometimes works seven days a week—though he averages three or four—and is generally busier in the summer.

He sets his fees according to certain variables, including the size of the audience, the nature of the sponsor, the work involved and the amount of setup and technical work. "Can I just show up, or do I need a lot of props?" he asks. "I shoot from the hip and work it out. Generally, I try not to do something for less than a hundred dollars." His performances range from 30 to 45 minutes.

Sam suggests that prospective clowns study as much as possible. "Go to as many shows as you can that involve theater and mime," he remarks. "Study and practice—from juggling and acrobatics to acting—as much as you can. There are just so many different realms to this."

Since clowning is a fairly physical job, he recommends that prospective clowns start working out if they don't already. "You have to get your body so it can move any way you want it to," he explains.

"Clowning is an attitude, and you don't necessarily need silly clothes," he adds. "The spontaneous ways in which we goof around are our biggest source of material. You can use your own voice and face instead of makeup."

Though he still does some legal work on the side, Kilbourn spends most of his time being a clown. "I'm being trusted to take care of people at an event," he says. "Clowning is counteracting all the things in society that tell us we need to be serious."

COIN-OPERATED LAUNDRY

The Village Laundry/The Quick Wash

Ben Russell

Elmwood Park, IL/Schiller Park, IL

Ease of Startup	Easy/Moderate
Range of Initial Investment	$40,000 - $400,000
Time Commitment	Part-time
Can You Run the Business From Home?	No
Success Potential	Moderate

Description of Business: A business that offers self-serve laundry facilities—either staffed or unattended.

Ease of Startup: Easy/Moderate. Easy if you buy an existing facility, moderate if you start from scratch.

Range of Initial Investment: $40,000 - $400,000, depending upon the area.

Time Commitment: Part-time

Can You Run the Business From Home? No

Success Potential: Moderate. Competition has intensified in this business in the last decade. Also, utility costs are always increasing.

How to Market the Business: Being responsive to customers, offering freebies, encouraging repeat business.

The Pros: In most cases, a laundromat runs itself with little input or time required from you.

The Cons: You're tied to the business to collect the money; an extended vacation is sometimes difficult to manage. As utility costs rise, it's hard to raise your prices and still stay competitive.

Special Considerations: Mechanical skills help, but aren't necessary. This business doesn't require education or particular skill. You can leave the business for a day or two.

For More Information: *American Coin-Op Magazine*, 500 N. Dearborn Street, Chicago, IL 60610.

Story of the Business

When Ben Russell was considering what his retirement business would be, he had several requirements. He needed a business that would provide him with a good retirement income, since the companies he had worked for had no pension or retirement plan. He didn't want something that would take up all his time, and he didn't want to hire employees.

He was also the editor of *American Coin-Op* magazine for 14 years, which ultimately influenced his decision. Several years before he retired, he established the foundation of his retirement business. He bought his first laundry in January 1986. He bought his second laundry in 1988. When he retired in 1992, his businesses were up and running.

Russell's laundries are small—1,000 square feet—and unattended. Each has 22 top-loading washers, four front-loading washers and thirteen driers. He is able to run them without attendants because the doors to the building operate on a timer, locking and unlocking at certain times of day.

"When I bought the first laundry, I initially spent very little time there," he explains. "I was working full-time, so I visited the laundry three times a week to collect the money and see if anything needed repair." He ordered supplies, paid the bills, replenished the change machine and collected the money in 10 to 12 hours a week.

Looking back, Russell says it wasn't the best way to run a laundry, though it did work for him because he was familiar with the business through editing the magazine. "I don't want to give the impression that all you have to do is go out and collect a few times a week because a laundry can quickly deteriorate if you don't pay attention to it."

Since retiring, he's had more time for the business. He's paid more attention to the laundries, and it's paid off. "I've found that since I spend more time at the laundry, business is up," he indicates. "I go at different times of day and meet and talk with the customers." He took a survey in which he asked customers what improvements they would like, and he responded to several of the suggestions. "The customers began to see I was a serious owner and that I treated them well," he adds. He believes this accounts for the increase in business.

A laundromat can be located almost anywhere, but certain characteristics predict success. Russell says the ideal location is a densely populated area with a number of apartment buildings. The average income level for each family should range from $25,000 to $30,000, and each family should have a number of children. Even when landlords place washers and driers in the basements of their buildings, many tenants choose to go elsewhere, because the machines are often broken and the laundry rooms are dark and uninviting.

Russell bought existing laundries—which can be purchased for $50,000 to $400,000, depending upon the location. The average startup cost for a new laundry is $150,000 for 35 washers and 18 driers. He's thought about buying a third laundry, but he's decided he is content to spend 30 hours a week working on the two. They gross $50,000 and $70,000 a year.

Russell chooses to do other promotions during a Customer Appreciation Month, where he gives away groceries and gift certificates. He warns that prospective laundry owners should research the business before they get into it. These days there are more laundries competing for a fixed number of customers. Price wars have resulted in some parts of the country with some laundries giving away services, like free drying.

"A good lease is extremely important to a coin-op laundry," he says. "Some cities require machine taxes and hookup fees. In many cases, the previous owner won't tell you about them.

"The profit margin is not what it used to be in the business," he adds. "Utilities were once much lower, and people didn't expect that much from laundries. That's not the case today."

COMMUNITY PLAYHOUSE/THEATER

Hackmatack Theater

Carl Guptill

Berwick, Maine, and Dover, New Hampshire

Ease of Startup	Difficult
Range of Initial Investment	$50,000+
Time Commitment	Full-time
Can You Run the Business From Home?	Yes
Success Potential	Difficult

Description of Business: A seasonal or year-round theater company that produces plays, musicals and community workshops.

Ease of Startup: Difficult. If you start from scratch, you need to build a theater, develop a repertory company and do endless promotions.

Range of Initial Investment: $50,000 and up.

Time Commitment: Full-time

Can You Run the Business From Home? Yes, if you have a barn that's gathering dust.

Success Potential: Difficult. It's expensive, risky and requires a good location, preferably in a tourist area.

How to Market the Business: Newspaper ads, fliers, radio ads, publicity, tie-ins with local businesses.

The Pros: It's very satisfying.

The Cons: It's very difficult to start. Actors and other artistic people you deal with can be temperamental.

Special Considerations: If you've always had the theater bug, here's a way to make a living from it.

For More Information: American Association of Community Theater, c/o L. Ross Rowland, 8209 N. Costa Mesa Drive, Muncie, IN 47303.

Story of the Business

Carl Guptill is fond of saying he started his first Hackmatack Theater because he had the chance to get his hands on some seats very cheaply. "I've always been involved in community theater in the area, and the opportunity was there. We thought it would be fun to have a theater in the barn," he recalls.

So back in 1970, that's just what he did. He turned an old cow barn on his farm in Berwick, Maine, into a theater. Performances are held three nights a week in the summer. All of the actors, stagehands, ushers and musicians that first year were volunteers. A few years later, he began to pay the techs, then the actors. Tickets were three bucks.

Today, Guptill runs three musicals and two plays during the summer season. He hires a pianist, bass player and drummer for musical accompaniment and pays everyone something. Each play runs for two weeks with six performances a week, including a matinee on Thursday. A ticket for one of the theater's 217 seats costs $15.

Berwick is in an area that's loaded with tourists in the summer. To pull them in, his number one draw is his location on a major highway. "Where the theater is located is the most important thing," he says. "If we weren't on a regular route, we'd be in trouble. But if we were on a busier road, I'd need 200 more seats."

With the success of the summer theater, Guptill decided to start a theater in nearby Dover, New Hampshire, in 1987. It runs from September through May. The summer theater runs in the black most of the time, but Guptill is lucky if the 183-seat Hackmatack Repertory Theater in Dover breaks even. "It's much tougher in the winter because the percentage of people who go to the theater around here is very small," he explains. The Dover playhouse features a play every month, children's theater presentations, a touring program in the school and children's theater classes.

Guptill built the Dover theater inside an existing building. It cost $35,000—a figure he says is very low—to buy the seats, build the bathrooms and do all the inside work. He already had the lights and costumes from the summer theater, which helped keep expenses down.

Carl's biggest expense, surprisingly, is royalties for the right to produce the plays and musicals. In the summer of 1993, Guptill produced *Annie Get Your Gun* for three weeks; it cost him $4,000 in royalties. Building and designing the sets runs about $5,000 for the summer. He also pays local residents a fee to provide room and board for several interns whom he doesn't pay. Actors come from both the community and New York; some have been working with Guptill for more than 17 years.

To promote the performances, Guptill advertises in local papers; he barters for radio time in the winter. In the summer, he hires a person to walk the beaches distributing cards and fliers, hanging posters and visiting motels.

Guptill serves as producer on every show and director on some of them. He also selects the plays and musicals; in the summer, they have to be pretty commercial. In winter, they can be less so. "There has to be a musical. We need to draw people in order to survive," he explains. "I'm always torn between the things we ought to be doing and the things we have to do to survive."

Both of the theaters are nonprofit organizations. This encouraged a local bank to give the group money in the past, but Guptill says that doesn't happen too often.

Though both theaters each gross about $110,000 per year Guptill points out that it's a labor of love, and he's not operating the theaters for his economic survival.

"There aren't too many small theaters around here that have gone on for 20 years," he reports. "We never expected it to continue and grow for this long."

CONSULTANT

Optics Consultant

Richard Weeks
Wiscasset, Maine

Ease of Startup	Easy
Range of Initial Investment	$1,000 - $10,000
Time Commitment	Part- or full-time
Can You Run the Business From Home?	Yes
Success Potential	Moderate

Description of Business: A person with a particular expertise who consults on a project basis with outside companies.

Ease of Startup: Easy. You have to put the word out at your old haunts that you're in business.

Range of Initial Investment: $1,000 - $10,000 if you need a computer.

Time Commitment: Part- or full-time

Can You Run the Business From Home? Yes

Success Potential: Moderate. There's good potential if you've built up the contacts and have the ability to back it up.

How to Market the Business: Word of mouth and referrals.

The Pros: You'll make much more money working as a consultant than as a staff member. Also, you can probably live where you want.

The Cons: Income can be unpredictable.

Special Considerations: Professionals who have a particular specialty and lots of contacts in that field will do well.

For More Information: Consultants' Network, 57 W. 89 Street, New York, NY 10024; *Successful Management Consulting: Building a Practice with Smaller Company Clients* by W.M. Greenfield (New York: Prentice-Hall).

Story of the Business

"In the optics business," says Richard Weeks, "everyone knows everyone else."

That is the basis of becoming successful in a consulting business. Years of experience also helps. Weeks started his consulting business when he was still working as a division manager at Polaroid, where he had previously worked as director of optical engineering. He started his own business because he was unhappy working there.

"Four times a year I gave a dog-and-pony show, and the rest of the time I watched everyone bicker. So I went to my boss on January 4th, 1980, and told him I wanted to resign," recalls Weeks. "He said that I couldn't do that, and I said, 'Watch me.' We ended up negotiating so that I could work half-time for Polaroid on a consultant basis." Weeks also arranged the deal so he would be released from his obligation not to work for any other company because there were other firms that wanted to hire him.

As it turned out, he didn't do much work for Polaroid and spent most of his time working for the other companies. He set up an office at home and hired lawyers to set up his business.

His workload varies widely. "If I have clients, I work 30 or 40 hours a week, and on a real hot case I can get up to 50 or 60. But if I don't have clients," he says, "I don't work."

He has never advertised for work, and gets all his assignments through word of mouth. He'll occasionally contact

Teltec, a clearinghouse for technical consultants in Minneapolis, and tell them he's looking for work. When things get slow he also calls up his consultant friends to see if they have any overflow from their work to pass along.

"I pass jobs along to them when I'm overloaded, so they do the same for me," relates Weeks. "And I generally won't take a job if I know there's someone who can do it better than I can." He also travels to conventions and technical meetings where he gets updates in the field, keeps in touch with other consultants and touches base with the companies that do the hiring.

Besides the office politics, Weeks says he became a consultant because he can live in Maine; before, he lived in Lexington, Massachusetts, and in Connecticut. "I can accept or refuse jobs, and choose who I want to work for. I don't have to put up with the hassles you get working for a big company."

The income from consulting, especially in such a specialized field, can vary. "There's no average income," he says. "Some years I make less than $5,000; since I also subcontract work, I earn some money from that."

To deal with the uncertain income, Weeks says a consultant needs to have a lifestyle that can contract when times are tight, which is nothing more than simple Yankee economics: "When I don't have the income," he says, "I don't spend the money."

COUNSELOR

Center for Interim Programs

Neil Bull

Cambridge, Massachusetts

Ease of Startup	Easy
Range of Initial Investment	$500
Time Commitment	Full- or part-time
Can You Run the Business From Home?	Yes
Success Potential	Moderate

Description of Business: An individual who offers consultations and advice to people and corporations, based on his past experience.

Ease of Startup: Easy. Develop the business basics—stationery and an office—and then network, network, network.

Range of Initial Investment: $500

Time Commitment: Full- or part-time

Can You Run the Business From Home? Yes

Success Potential: Moderate. If you're charismatic and can convince people and businesses you can help them, you should be able to succeed.

How to Market the Business: Publicity, advertising, word of mouth, referrals.

The Pros: The money can be good; you'll be helping people live their lives better.

The Cons: It can take awhile to get started; you're selling an intangible service that might be difficult for some people to grasp.

Special Considerations: A person with a solid background in a particular field who enjoys advising people about their options will do quite well.

Story of the Business

"My mother's side of the family was very entrepreneurial," remarks Neil Bull. "My father was a writer and dreamer. He made no bones about the fact that he'd always hated work."

Today, Neil runs the Center for Interim Programs, a business that advises both students and adults on how to take a breather from their busy lives. He seems to consist of equal parts of both parents. He's had wide experience; he taught in private schools before becoming a headmaster, an admissions director and holding various other positions. The family spent a number of years living in Vienna, where he was headmaster at the American School. "I was always giving myself sabbaticals," he explains, "because I wanted to give my children different experiences and myself different challenges."

Bull noticed other people were less adventurous than he. He thought they might like to know how to lead happier lives. He advises about 200 people a year. Most of them are students who are about to start college or are a year or two into it. They need to take some time off to figure out what will make them happy.

"This business has grown organically out of everything I've ever done," explains Bull. "Parents came to me and asked, 'What am I going to do, my son is allergic to school?'"

When Bull first started the Center, he called on all his contacts to see if they would like to have an intern who's disillusioned with a fast-track academic lifestyle. He doesn't suggest students take a year off from school and do nothing. Rather, he talks with the student at length to help him decide whether he would like to work on a ranch in Wyoming for a few months or go to Micronesia to work on an anthropology project. Then they draw up several options.

Bull arranges these trips by contacting people he's met in his travels. He lived abroad for 12 years and has taught for 10. "I use my old students all the time," he explains.

He speaks frequently at private schools and colleges. Most of the people who use his services have heard him speak. "When I work with a kid from a school I haven't been to before, I write to the school and tell them I'm working with their student. I inquire if they would like me to come and talk with their kids. Ninety percent of the time, they say absolutely," says Neil. As a result, many schools are now including the concept Bull espouses in their regular college advising program.

Bull does a lot of his work at home on the phone at night when people are at home. He doesn't want employees, preferring to do most of the counseling himself. He runs the business with his daughter and a few other people. He is looking forward to becoming involved with the business in a different way in the future. "I'd like to be a roving ambassador for Interim, traveling to Bali or Italy to find new programs," he explains. "I don't ever want to stop doing this. Like most people, I'm driven by John Calvin in that I want to be needed. I think that when people stop being needed, they die."

He's never spent a cent on advertising. He has received a lot of publicity because of the unusual position he takes. "My biggest challenge is convincing people to believe they can do this," he explains. "I'm nonjudgmental; that's vitally important in what I do. I have no *shoulds* and no *oughts* for anybody. I'm really subversive; I want people to rethink their lives. In essence, I'm giving people permission to do some of the things I've done and what I've wanted to do. "No one has ever come back and said their time off was a waste of time."

COUNTRY CLUB

Woodlake Golf and Country Club

Valery Platzer
Lakewood, New Jersey

Ease of Startup	Moderate
Range of Initial Investment	$10 million+
Time Commitment	Part- to full-time
Can You Run the Business From Home?	No
Success Potential	Easy

Description of Business: A country club with golf course, restaurant and banquet facility that offers private memberships and is open to the public.

Ease of Startup: Moderate. Most country clubs are bought outright, not begun from scratch.

Range of Initial Investment: $10 million and up.

Time Commitment: Part- to full-time

Can You Run the Business From Home? No

Success Potential: Easy. A country club in an affluent area will typically succeed, as many members belong to more than one.

How to Market the Business: Through newspaper advertisements and word of mouth.

The Pros: It can be lucrative, and you get to play golf for free.

The Cons: If your staff and management aren't on the ball, a club can go downhill fast.

Special Considerations: For people with experience in the hospitality business and lots of money or investors, this is considered a dream business.

For More Information: Public Golf Management Association, 8030 Cedar, Suite 215, Minneapolis, MN 55425.

Story of the Business

For their primary careers, Valery Platzer was a teacher with a master's in school administration. Her husband Fred was in the hotel and restaurant business, which Valery joined after she left teaching because she thought the restaurant business was more exciting.

"In 1983, my husband said, 'Why don't we retire and travel around the world?'" recalls Valery. "So we did, for a year. We came home so we could appreciate the next trip." Then a great opportunity fell into their laps.

"When we got back, our accountant told us there was a country club in dire need of professional direction and management. He thought we'd be interested," she continues. Two of the Platzers' restaurants had been on golf courses, so they were familiar with the format. They decided to take the plunge. "We saw great potential," remembers Valery.

Woodlake Golf and Country Club, in central New Jersey, has an 18-hole golf course, a 500-seat banquet room and a dining room that seats 150. But it needed some TLC and an overall facelift, which the Platzers provided after they bought the club. They spent the next 10 years building up the membership and the banquet facilities at the club.

To raise the funds necessary to buy the club, the Platzers put together a limited partnership. They got 18 investors to put up $150,000 each; a bank supplied a loan for the balance. The Platzers paid $3.5 million for the club in 1983.

Woodlake is run as a semiprivate club that's open year-round with two different membership levels. Full membership gives first priority on weekends for golf; associate membership gives members a 24-hour advance over the general public for weekend tee times. Members have a locker room that's separate from the public locker room. There are 280 golf members in all. A major part of Woodlake's income is from catering and banquets for weddings, bar mitzvahs and civic affairs.

"Golf is not something you have to really market, since TV and sporting goods company do a lot of the work," says Valery. She advertises in local papers in the spring, announcing the opening of the new season, but beyond that there's not a lot to do.

Running a country club means interacting with a large percentage of retired people. "It's an expensive sport, so you're dealing with an elite clientele," she remarks. It also doesn't involve much effort. "You put people out on a golf course, it takes them about four hours to play. You really don't have to worry about them," she says.

In February 1993 Fred Platzer died, and Valery took over his responsibilities. Previously she was in charge of the decorating and additions to the buildings. "It was a massive change," she recalls, adding that the business runs itself with the right staff.

Today she is the owner and operator of the club. She leaves the day-to-day details to a manager, but Valery is responsible for the monthly profit-and-loss statement. She signs all the checks and approves changes in the menu, rates or staff. "In the summer, I'm usually there a few hours each day, but when it's running smoothly, I really don't have to be around," she admits.

Regardless, for people who are dreaming about running a country club, Valery wants to bring them down to earth. "I don't think the business is anything you can just walk into. You really have to know what you're doing," she warns. The business is best suited to someone with a background in the hospitality field or to someone who has owned or managed a restaurant. Unless you have a great greenskeeper, you need some knowledge of the greens and fairways, and shouldn't go into it totally blind. If you owned a restaurant before, and bought one with a golf course attached, it might seem easier since you're not constantly trying to bring in new people for dinner because you have a built-in membership. She adds, "You should play a lot of golf and spend a lot of time at country clubs."

COUNTRY INN

West Mountain Inn

Wes Carlson
Arlington, Vermont

Ease of Startup	Difficult
Range of Initial Investment	$300,000 to $1.5M
Time Commitment	More than full-time
Can You Run the Business From Home?	Yes
Success Potential	Moderate

Description of Business: A multi-room inn open year-round with a restaurant open to guests and the public.

Ease of Startup: Difficult, if you're starting from scratch. Moderate, if you're buying an existing inn.

Range of Initial Investment: $300,000 to $1.5 million and up.

Time Commitment: More than full-time

Can You Run the Business From Home? Most innkeepers live on the premises.

Success Potential: Moderate. Location, ambiance and your dedication and hard work will determine whether you make it or not.

How to Market the Business: Through inn and travel guidebooks, hosting travel writers, publicity and regular mailings to repeat guests.

The Pros: The people.

The Cons: The hard work—it's not as easy as it looks. Also, innkeeping is a money-hungry business, whether it's for repairs, mailings or labor.

Special Considerations: For people who've always dreamed of being innkeepers *and* recognize the endless work it involves, the business can do quite well. If you can buy the inn outright, you'll live with a lot less stress.

For More Information: Independent Innkeepers Association, POB 150, Marshall, MI 49068, 800-344-5244.

Story of the Business

According to Wes Carlson, who's owned the 15-room West Mountain Inn for 16 years, the best part of being an innkeeper is that the world comes to see you.

That's the most important part of having a country inn: the people. You've probably visited country inns on vacation and thought it looked easy. That's the first bubble you should break. The second is that because your guests are on vacation, they'll be on their best behavior and it will be easy to please them.

Truth is, if you don't absolutely love people, don't get into the business. The aura of hosting a country inn will wear off within the first week, and there, revealed in all its splendor, will be the 80-hour workweeks and, yes, the occasional ornery guest.

Wes Carlson was an elementary school principal in Hastings-on-Hudson in New York state when he retired to move to Vermont. "We had a friend who was trying to run the inn, and we came up to help him," Wes recalls. "My wife, Mary Ann, who was a teacher, could get a job up here and we were going to take life easy." As with most fantasies, the reality turned out to be quite different.

When they arrived, the inn was referred to locally as a bunch of "hippies on the hill" and Wes' friend was ready to bail out due to lack of business. After Carlson spent one summer at the inn, his friend did pull out—he was leasing the inn—and Carlson took over. He started by paying off the debts, cultivating repeat business and by working very closely with the town. "It worked out," he says. "We're pretty gregarious people."

He has innkeepers who take care of the day-to-day concerns, from taking reservations to ordering supplies and supervising housekeeping staff. Wes takes care of general management, but he takes it easy and lets his staff take care of things. "Basically, it runs itself," he says. "There are always nitty-gritty problems with the inn, but never anything that's totally insurmountable. Every one of our staff thinks it's their inn."

Why, in a field where burnout is almost inevitable after seven years of innkeeping, are the Carlsons still going strong? From the beginning, they decided what they wanted to do themselves and what they wanted to delegate to others. In an inn this size, with a number of staff, this is possible.

"Neither one of us were cooks, and we didn't like to clean," says Wes. "The main thing that helped is that we were out there with our guests. Many people who open inns today become so involved with cooking and cleaning and running the inn that they don't have time for their guests."

To look at the handsome, yet casual inn, it seems like it's had several large common rooms downstairs, and 13 rooms upstairs—all with private baths—since it was built back in the mid-19th century. Nothing could be further from the truth, and it's another reason why the Carlsons have longevity at the inn. They do a little expansion or improvement to the inn each year.

"When we came, there were only three shared baths for nine guest rooms," says Wes. Today, each of the 13 rooms in the inn and two more rooms in a house down the road has a private bath. "The expansion has been gradual, but we've maintained the ambiance." One year, the inn added a garden, another year, they added some llamas.

The Carlsons market the inn today through writeups in a few guidebooks, but say that their primary sales technique is word of mouth. "Caring for people is the main thing," says Wes. "The best person to come back is the customer you have right now. Treat them right, and they become regular customers." Each guest takes home an African violet and a chocolate llama, and a bowl of apples is found in each guest room.

The town hasn't used the phrase "hippies on the hill" in years. "We support the community," says Wes. The inn offers a high school scholarship to a local student who "works locally and thinks globally," as Wes put it. He also offers free meeting space to local nonprofit groups, which builds good will and helps the business.

Perhaps the main reason why Wes can kick back and combine a leisurely retirement with a bustling country inn is because the mortgage is paid off and the inn has a 70 percent occupancy rate year-round, which is high for the industry, even in Vermont. The inn is valued at $1.5 million, and grosses about $700,000 a year. The inn's busiest months are August and October, and least crowded in April and May. From May 1st through mid-June of that first year, Wes says there might have been six couples who stayed at the inn. "Right now, we're considered to be one of the better inns in Vermont," he says. "Next time around, I want to retire at 21."

CRAFT SHOP

Patches

Pat Nottle
Emmaus, Pennsylvania

Ease of Startup	Easy
Range of Initial Investment	$2,000+
Time Commitment	Full-time
Can You Run the Business From Home?	No
Success Potential	Moderate

Description of Business: A store that sells crafts, decorations, antiques and other hand-crafted items.

Ease of Startup: Easy. You can start accepting things on consignment, or you can buy stock from suppliers or local craftspeople.

Range of Initial Investment: $2,000 and up, depending upon your goods.

Time Commitment: Full-time

Can You Run the Business From Home? No

Success Potential: Moderate. If you set yourself apart from the other craft shops that abound, you'll succeed.

How to Market the Business: Advertising, word of mouth, publicity, and promotions.

The Pros: It's fun and will keep you involved with people.

The Cons: The work never stops. You must be discriminating and buy merchandise that appeals to your customers.

Special Considerations: People think running a craft shop is easy. Think again.

Story of the Business

"People come into the shop and think I've made everything," reports Pat Nottle of her country decor shop, Patches. "Of course, I haven't, but that's the impression the shop gives them."

Nottle sells candles, pottery, dolls, cards and reproduction furniture in her 2,600 square-foot store located in an old Victorian house. This is the third location she's had since starting the business in 1988. "Anyone can have a store," she remarks, "but you have to take the time to run it. You can't just open a store and have somebody else run it for you."

When she started in the first location—a tiny 500 square feet was all she could afford—she spent six weeks fixing up the shop. "I had always wanted to do this, but I never had the nerve. We had next to nothing in cash," she remembers. Nottle took on a lot of consignment items in the beginning, and many people helped with the shop.

"This is a unique store," she says. "I always tell people I buy dirty. It has to look primitive and old. I won't buy it unless I see it, so we spend lots of time antiquing and decorating the store for different seasons.

"We have a very friendly atmosphere," says Pat. "People come in to tell me everything from 'I hate my mother-in-law' to 'I left my husband.'"

The business is Nottle's child. She admits she wishes she could be there 24 hours a day, even though she does have a couple of part-time employees who help her out on occasion. "We've talked about opening a second store, but I don't think so because I'd lose that personal contact," she remarks.

"Some customers come in when I'm not here, and they immediately leave. That bothers me," she adds, though there's not much she can do about it.

She no longer takes consignments. That involves too much paperwork, and she wasn't getting what she was looking for. To find stock, she attends several major gift trade shows each year. "It's hard to decide what to buy because what I like isn't necessarily what's going to sell," she says. "You can't always tell what will be a hot item, and when something really sells, you can't get stock on it anymore, especially during the Christmas season."

Today, the shop grosses $250,000 a year, largely due to Pat's personality and love for her business. Though she advertises in the local, weekly paper, most of her business comes by word of mouth. She also sends mailings to her list of 2,500 names several times a year.

But what undoubtedly draws the most people to the shop are her monthly special events like the Two-Day Broom Sale she held at Patches one spring. "It was a clean sweep sale: 20 percent off everything in the store with an extra 10 percent off if you brought a broom," she remembers. "We had valet broom parking; my husband was on the porch handing out tickets as customers checked their brooms."

One woman brought a whisk broom and hid it in her purse because she was embarrassed. Another woman went to the hardware store in town and bought a broom just for the sale.

"Shopping can be boring," says Pat. "Stores should hold more special events. We try to schedule something at least once a month. People call up to ask when the next event is."

CRAFTSPERSON

Marilyn Herman
Pomfret, Vermont

Ease of Startup	Easy
Range of Initial Investment	$100
Time Commitment	Part- or full-time
Can You Run the Business From Home?	Yes
Success Potential	Moderate

Description of Business: An individual who makes a particular line of crafts and sells them retail, wholesale, on consignment and at craft shows.

Ease of Startup: Easy, especially if you concentrate on craft shows.

Range of Initial Investment: $100 for supplies.

Time Commitment: Part- or full-time

Can You Run the Business From Home? Yes

Success Potential: Moderate. The field is crowded; your products must stand out from the crowd.

How to Market the Business: By visiting shopkeepers, going to shows, having your own shop and using some word of mouth.

The Pros: It's fun and easy. Most craftspeople run their business from home.

The Cons: It's highly competitive, shopkeepers can be condescending and there's not a lot of money in it.

Special Considerations: For people who always made crafts anyway and can be satisfied with the small amount of money it brings, give it a shot.

For More Information: *Homemade Money*, by Barbara Brabec, POB 2137, Naperville, IL 60567.

Story of the Business

Marilyn Herman has always been responsive to market trends when it comes to crafts. She spent a number of years making quilts for an artists' cooperative shop in Bar Harbor, Maine, when quilts were popular and reasonably priced. When there was a downturn in the demand for quilts, she switched to making crafts from birch bark and never looked back.

Even within her second crafts career, Marilyn has kept aware of the changes from year to year. She opened a shop next to her home. It was successful for the first two years, but she saw that her wholesale business was bringing in more money. Now she's thinking seriously about discontinuing the shop to concentrate fully on the wholesale end of the business.

That's the secret to being successful in the crafts business: anticipating what the market needs and then filling it. There are already too many people out there making knitted dolls, potholders and the like. When Marilyn started making birch baskets in 1990, she saw the burgeoning interest in anything remotely related to Native Americans would be popular. At the time there were only a handful of craftspeople who were making birch bark crafts.

"I did some experimenting with birch from trees on my farm. I learned about its malleability and the best time to harvest it," she recalls. She also collected sweetgrass and grapevine to use in the baskets. She sold them in her own shop and a few others in the area, including a shop in

Woodstock, which has heavy tourist traffic. The manager at the Vermont State Crafts Center saw the baskets and placed an order. She's been busy ever since.

Marilyn makes a variety of crafts from the bark, including shelves, mirrors, baskets and canoes. The miniature canoes are her best-selling item. She collects the bark in June and July when the sap is running and the bark is most pliable. Then she weights it down to keep it flat; she stores the bark so she can use it year-round.

She ships her crafts to stores or delivers them herself. Stores take different commissions. In her area, if she sells on consignment, the store gets 30-35 percent; if they buy outright, they take 50 percent. Herman's baskets sell from $35 to $85 retail. Some shops prefer to buy the baskets wholesale, but Marilyn says you have to be careful. "They say they'll pay in 30 days, but lots of times it ends up being closer to 120," she remarks. When working with a new customer, Marilyn prefers to get paid when she delivers the order, and after she's developed a history with a particular store, she'll give more flexible terms.

Herman still sells quilted crafts like potholders and pillows to some of the local shops, but they specify what they want and she fills the order. She has a freer rein with her birch bark crafts.

Though she says she doesn't make a lot of money, she mentions a friend in Maine who supports her family on the $27,000 a year she makes from birch bark crafts. "Even she's found the market to be quite narrow, so she's expanded into jewelry and other products," Herman indicates.

Perhaps more than with other businesses, craftspeople must be versatile and willing to change in order to make a living. "It's a fun way to make a living," says Marilyn. "I'm compelled to make my crafts, I have to be creative. I'd rather do this than anything else."

DOLLS—REPRODUCTIONS AND REPAIR

The Different Drummer

Lillian deGiacomo
Barnard, Vermont

Ease of Startup	Difficult
Range of Initial Investment	$5,000
Time Commitment	Part- or full-time
Can You Run the Business From Home?	Yes
Success Potential	Difficult

Description of Business: Making reproduction dolls and restoring and repairing old dolls.

Ease of Startup: Difficult. You need a kiln, molds, special paints and clay and reliable suppliers for the clothing and hair.

Range of Initial Investment: $5,000 for equipment and supplies.

Time Commitment: Part- or full-time

Can You Run the Business From Home? Yes

Success Potential: Difficult. It's a very limited market. You must have skill and creativity.

How to Market the Business: Retail, wholesale, mail order, word of mouth.

The Pros: You can exercise your creativity in many different ways. You'll make a lot of people happy.

The Cons: Demand is small. The work is expensive, and it can be physically demanding.

Special Considerations: For people who loved the dolls from their childhood, the business fulfills a childhood dream to have all the dolls you ever wanted.

Story of the Business

Lillian deGiacomo is in her second childhood. She spends her days making dolls. Some have porcelain heads and cloth bodies, while others are entirely porcelain with several jointed sections.

She starts with plaster molds of the original dolls and pours porcelain slip—the finest ceramic clay available—into the mold, to form a head, part of a leg or an arm. Lillian allows it to form a shell before pouring the excess out; she lets it sit before opening the mold and letting it dry. She then fires it in the kiln and sands it down to soften the rough seams. She paints it, then fires it again.

Her husband Wally strings the doll parts together, and Lillian makes the clothes that the doll will wear. She buys wigs for the dolls from a supplier. After everything is assembled, the doll is ready for sale.

The styles of Lillian's dolls date from the late 1800s and range from a five-inch Bye-lo reproduction to a 30-inch Art Deco classic. She has 75 doll-part molds of arms, legs and heads with different expressions. Even though she might make several dolls from the same head mold, every doll is different. "You might pour it out of the same mold, but by the time you get it painted and dressed, it's an entirely different doll," she points out.

She spends 30 to 40 hours a week making the dolls. She can pour three head molds in one day but keeps a careful eye on the weather. If it's humid or damp out, she doesn't get good pouring. She makes 100 dolls each year and signs, dates and numbers each one. She also puts Barnard, Vermont

,on each. Every doll comes with a certificate attesting to the fact that it's a reproduction, not an original.

"People have been known to make reproductions and pass them off as originals," she reports. "We make it very clear that our dolls are reproductions. Our trademark is a necklace or a hand-painted pin they wear."

She sells the dolls in local shops and in the Vermont State Crafts Center in nearby Windsor. The dolls range in price from $35 to $295; the shops take a 40 percent consignment fee. The dolls priced from $85 to $100 are the most popular. She and her husband also have a shop in their barn called The Different Drummer. They sell lamps, nativity sets and jewelry, which they also make. There are also a few antiques for sale in the shop.

Lillian and Wally also repair both antique and modern dolls. Local newspaper columnists Anne & Nan—the Heloises of the north country—frequently refer readers with doll questions to Lillian. She gets most of her restoration business from the column. Articles about her business that appear occasionally in local papers also bring in work.

As with many retirement businesses, Lillian's work started as a hobby and grew into an industry. She suggests aspiring dollmakers start slowly. "Take lessons to see if you enjoy it," she says. "Start slowly because it's expensive. The prices of the molds and porcelain keep going up, and the electric rates during a Vermont winter are very high. I try to get as much firing done before December as I can."

Lillian says there is a large market for reproduction dolls, but at their stage of life, she and Wally don't want to get that big. "Every time I say we're going to cut back, something else comes up," she remarks. "We don't want to get much bigger than we are now, but the business seems to grow a little more each year."

EXECUTIVE SEARCH FIRM

Ability Resources, Inc.

Noel Ruppert
Alexandria, Virginia

Ease of Startup	Moderate
Range of Initial Investment	$30,000+
Time Commitment	Full-time
Can You Run the Business From Home?	No
Success Potential	Difficult

Description of Business: A company that specializes in seeking high-level executives to fill jobs. The fee is paid by the employer.

Ease of Startup: Moderate. You need contacts in many corporations; prospects will find you.

Range of Initial Investment: $30,000 and up, for first year's overhead.

Time Commitment: Full-time

Can You Run the Business From Home? No; it's important to appear as corporate as possible.

Success Potential: Difficult. Though a lot of money can be made from one placement, they sometimes can be few and far between; the competition is cutthroat.

How to Market the Business: For clients: schmoozing, cold calls and current contacts. For prospective employees: help wanted ads and word of mouth.

The Pros: It can be very lucrative.

The Cons: Recession can easily put a search firm out of business, and you'll get rejected frequently by prospective clients.

Special Considerations: This business is good for people who have a lot of contacts at companies in a particular field.

For More Information: Association of Executive Search Consultants, 230 Park Avenue, Suite 1549, New York, NY 10169.

Story of the Business

People who retire from the military after 20 years of service usually have enough energy to plunge right into a business that will provide them with the same challenges Uncle Sam once did.

This pretty much describes Noel Ruppert, who retired from the Navy as an aviator and assignment officer in February 1990. When he first left the service, he thought he was job hunting; he didn't know he would end up running a high-powered executive search firm that specializes in high-end placements.

"When I first retired, I probably made most of the mistakes I'm now teaching people to avoid by writing a poor resume, marketing myself insufficiently and not developing a network," he recalls.

Despite his beginnings, a small recruiting company asked Ruppert to work with them as a consultant because a client was looking for someone with prior military experience. Five months later, the company came to Ruppert to ask if he wanted to buy the firm. A few months later, it was his.

"My goal from the beginning was to work exclusively with retiring military officers from all the services," he remarks. Ruppert helps with their transition, critiques their resumes and places them in jobs suitable for their experience.

One such placement was for an army officer with an artillery background, whom Ruppert matched with a company with a few army contracts. Lots of companies in the

Alexandria area specialize in professional services; they will hire a senior military person because of who he knows and what doors he can open. "But," warns Ruppert, "frequently, once the company has picked his brains, it will pitch him out if they don't have room for him." Then they come back to Ability Resources for help.

Noel belongs to the Retired Officers Association. He sometimes learns of companies that are asking the association for candidates or advertising in the group's paper. "I wait a couple of weeks, then I call and tell them I have someone who would fit the job," he says.

But he doesn't like to do cold calls; he says they're not effective. "Instead, through networking and the various associations, I find out which companies have landed a major contract, what it involves and if, for example, they need Air Force people with space systems background. Then I call and tell them I have someone for them," he explains.

Getting candidates for the job has not been a problem. "I speak at some of the career transition seminars and panels for the military. The only way I work is face to face with people. I never take somebody's resume, make 20 copies and send it out. That's a good way to make money, but not a fun way to run a business."

Ruppert has two principals and three consultants who work for the firm. "I spend about 25 percent of my time being presidential and 75 percent on administrative support," he remarks. He enjoys the administrative support because it provides diversity to his job.

An executive search firm is not an employment agency. "If I make five placements a year, I will be doing very well," he points out. The fees Ruppert's firm earns will vary with the economy and the city. They range from 15 percent to 35 percent of the candidate's annual salary. Ability Resources grosses an average of $250,000 to $300,000 a year; this includes placements done by other members of the staff.

Ruppert is currently developing a sideline to his business. He is working with a major corporation to develop a course in career management for retired military officers and for those who are about to leave. "We'll start with three-day transition seminars here; then we'll take them all over the country," he reports. "The difference is that I'm pursuing individuals, not corporations as I do with my search business." The advantage of going with a major corporation is that they underwrite the marketing budget.

Ruppert plans to develop his mailing list for the seminars by getting the names of officers who are leaving the military in the next year through the Freedom of Information Act. He charges $450 for the three-day workshop, keeping each seminar under 50 participants.

EXERCISE INSTRUCTOR

The Dancin' Grannies

Beverly Gemigniani
Sun Lake, Arizona

Ease of Startup	Easy
Range of Initial Investment	$10,000
Time Commitment	Full-time
Can You Run the Business From Home?	No
Success Potential	Easy

Description of Business: A business that offers exercise instruction through classes, videos and other products. Demonstrations provide another source of income.

Ease of Startup: Moderately easy. It's a good idea to become certified and to work through another studio before you start your own business.

Range of Initial Investment: $10,000.

Time Commitment: Full-time

Can You Run the Business From Home? No

Success Potential: Easy. Good instructors are in demand, especially if they cater to a particular group.

How to Market the Business: Advertising, publicity, word of mouth, referrals.

The Pros: You're helping people become healthy and fit. It's a fun business.

The Cons: Even if you're in great shape, teaching up to six classes a day is exhausting.

Special Considerations: A physically fit, outgoing person with charisma and a dance background will do well in this business.

For More Information: *Fitness Management Magazine*, POB 1198, Solana Beach, CA 92075.

Story of the Business

Beverly Gemigniani likes big challenges; in fact, she wants nothing less than to change the public's image of older age. "I want to show it as something that is likable and adventuresome," she says. "No one's done this before, and I've always felt I'm on unproven ground."

You've probably seen The Dancin' Grannies at the video store or at the White House. Beverly Gemigniani is the force behind The Dancin' Grannies, an aerobic dance troupe of grandmothers over 60 that performs all over the country. She started her own business because she was looking for someone to teach her how to exercise as an older person, and that person did not exist.

Before she began working out in the early 80s, Beverly was a size 16. After two years of aerobics and one of weightlifting, she'd transformed her body to a size 4.

She'd always worked as a machinist for her husband, who owned several machine shops over the years. Then they moved to a retirement community in Arizona so her husband could build a new shop. She looked around for something to do and discovered the gym. "I love to share, and pretty soon I was helping other women work out," she remembers. Beverly had to sneak around the gym because one of the employees resented her teaching the members.

Her husband's plant opened up, and she went back to work. The women at the gym still called her asking for instruction.

She decided she wanted to teach after all, but she needed certification. She joined IDEA, an organization of aerobic dance teachers, and The Dancin' Grannies was born.

"I keep pushing out the boundaries of what we can do," she says, which has included holding health seminars, performing at senior expos and lecturing, but the group gets most of their visibility through their four exercise videos.

After the Dancin' Grannies appeared on The Phil Donahue Show, Beverly was approached by four video companies. She ended up with an independent producer who specialized in marketing businesses to mature people. In fact, the producer was so thrilled with the concept that she financed the project herself when a bank loan fell through. The first video—their best-seller—has sold almost 800,000 copies.

Beverly believes many people who go into this business eventually fail because they focus on too small of a market. "With physical fitness, they'll join one organization," she says. "What we do is also show business, which reaches another audience." As a result, the Dancin' Grannies have performed in the Macy's Thanksgiving Day Parade. Beverly has also been involved with the National Council on Aging.

"You have to constantly come out with new products," she remarks. The Dancin' Grannies are planning a walking tape, a relaxation tape, a poster and a calendar. All will be sold through a distributor.

The Grannies perform at fairs and expos, earning $2,000 for two performances. Beverly gets $1,500 for a lecture. She grosses $200,000 a year, but calls the business a labor of love, due to the high expenses of travel, costumes and training.

But not everyone has such lofty aspirations. You could build a local reputation and succeed as a part-time business by forming your own specialized dance and/or exercise troupe and appear at local benefits and functions.

FLAG BUSINESS

All American Flag Company

John Sorenson
Grand Rapids, Michigan

Ease of Startup	Easy
Range of Initial Investment	$400
Time Commitment	Part- or full-time
Can You Run the Business From Home?	Yes
Success Potential	Easy

Description of Business: A business that sells a large variety of flags to retail stores, wholesale accounts and by direct mail to consumers.

Ease of Startup: Easy. You need a small inventory.

Range of Initial Investment: $400 for merchandise.

Time Commitment: Part- or full-time

Can You Run the Business From Home? Yes

Success Potential: Easy. There's not much competition in this business.

How to Market the Business: Through sales reps, mail-order catalogs and to groups.

The Pros: One person can handle it and make a good living.

The Cons: Travel is involved; also a mail-order business takes some time to develop.

Special Considerations: Someone who wants to run a small, manageable business independently and likes to juggle tasks will do well.

For More Information: John Sorenson, All American Flag Company, 1004 Hall Street SE, Grand Rapids, MI 49507.

Story of the Business

John Sorenson was in the office-supply business in 1978 when myasthenia gravis forced him to retire and sell the business. By July 1979 he had recovered enough to think about going back to work and wanted to do something that would get him out of the house. He started a flag business because he was amazed at how few stores were selling American flags back then. He also wanted to start a business he could handle by himself.

He spent the first two years traveling around Michigan, Ohio and northern Indiana, visiting retail stores he thought would be able to sell a steady number of flags. He narrowed his market by visiting towns with a population of about 8-10,000. He called on the local hardware store or tent and awning shop to sign them up to sell flags. Most would buy a couple dozen at a time.

He stayed away from big cities like Minneapolis and Omaha because they already had large stores that sold nothing but flags and banners. Shops in the smaller towns were more receptive to selling Sorenson's flags.

The All American Flag Company sells foreign, state and college flags, though the American flag is Sorenson's biggest seller. Four people work full-time filling orders, which are shipped by UPS the same day the order is received. Today, Sorenson's two sons run the business while John handles the finances.

The company primarily sells in an eight-state region around Michigan. Sorenson's best customers are VFWs and

American Legion halls; he sends a promotional letter to these groups each year. He also sends a flier and a price list to selected mailing lists annually. If they request more information, he sends a full-color catalog; most new business comes through these direct-mail promotional efforts.

Sorenson has developed a sideline, setting up people who want to start a flag business in their own area. "We've started up lots of smaller businesses across the country," he reports.

Sorenson is gradually phasing out of the business and leaving it to his sons. He still welcomes inquiries from people who are thinking about getting into flag selling. Be forewarned, though. "It started out as a hobby," he says, "but it totally ran away from me."

FLORIST

Martin Downs Florist

William Uber
Palm City, Florida

Ease of Startup	Moderate
Range of Initial Investment	$50,000
Time Commitment	Full-time
Can You Run the Business From Home?	No
Success Potential	Difficult

Description of Business: Selling fresh flowers, plants, and gift items to retail customers and through wholesale channels.

Ease of Startup: Moderate. You need some background through classes or experience; you'll also need equipment and lots of patience.

Range of Initial Investment: $50,000 for equipment and inventory.

Time Commitment: Full-time

Can You Run the Business From Home? No

Success Potential: Difficult. The business can be cutthroat. If you don't order properly, you'll end up eating your profits.

How to Market the Business: Advertising, word of mouth, referrals, corporate functions.

The Pros: It's an enjoyable business, and frequently you'll be making people happy.

The Cons: It can be extremely fast-paced part of the year and very slow at other times.

Special Considerations: Creative people who love to work with flowers and who possess stamina will make good florists.

For More Information: *Florist Magazine*, 29200 Northwestern Highway, Box 2227, Southfield, MI 48037.

Story of the Business

When William Uber started his retail flower shop in 1988, he thought his 20 years of experience as vice-president of operations for Armellini Express Lines—the largest cut-flower hauler in the continental U.S.—would be sufficient to run the shop. Little did he know.

"I thought I could open a retail florist shop and run it from my kitchen," he relates. "The biggest surprise was the amount of effort and time it involved. I was also surprised by the intensity of being self-employed in this type of business."

He knew his shop was going to be a family business: his son, his daughter-in-law, his wife and his daughter work in the shop. His wife and daughter went to a flower design school for a month before the shop opened. A year later, Uber left Armellini and began to work full-time at the shop.

"We lived in Palm City, which already had one florist," he says. "We offered to buy the shop, but it wasn't for sale. We knew a lot of people since it was our hometown, so we decided to open anyway." He leased a 1,400-square-foot storefront and named the shop after a local residential community. Four years later, he bought a 2,400-square-foot building and moved the business. The next year he opened his second shop, Harbor Bay Florist, in nearby Sewall's Point where the market is larger and more prestigious.

"When I left my job, I was making good money," he says. "In running your own business, if you're doing all your numbers correctly, your pay can be 10 percent of the gross, and the return on your investment should also be 10 percent of the gross," he indicates. "I can't live on the income from one shop. My goal from the beginning was to have two or three shops. You can usually figure in another $50,000 in salary if you're doing everything right."

The Martin Downs shop grossed $250,000 in 1992, which Uber hopes to increase. But he has also learned patience in the course of reaching that goal.

"I think you have to have one full year under your belt before a business starts to grab hold," he remarks. He has concentrated on generating corporate accounts, because then business can be steady. "We give presentations to businesses. They nod their heads and say they're glad we're here, and then frequently play hard to get. It takes awhile to make any kind of inroads. I get commercial accounts by having a good product, excellent service and knowing some people. I do a lot of my marketing through the local Chamber of Commerce," he says.

Running a flower shop is a tough business because the product is not a necessity. Furthermore, flowers are highly perishable. The bulk of the business comes all at once at holidays. "If I could spread my business out over 12 months, then I could handle it," says Uber. "Valentine's Day is worse than any of them because it's just one day. All my customers want everything ordered, wrapped and delivered in one day."

He loves the business, though, especially since his family is involved. "My wife and I have been married 34 years. When we opened the business, we got even closer," he says. "It was difficult in the beginning because the business I came from was very heavy-handed. It took me awhile to settle down. But we've found our niche, and everyone works very well together."

FREELANCE WRITING

Barbara Bell Matuszewski
Sewall's Point, Florida

Ease of Startup	Easy
Range of Initial Investment	$1,000-$2,500
Time Commitment	Part- or full-time
Can You Run the Business From Home?	Yes
Success Potential	Difficult

Description of Business: A one-person operation in which a writer sells articles to magazines and newspapers, and/or writes books.

Ease of Startup: Easy. You need a computer, some market guides and stationery: no quills or inkwells, please.

Range of Initial Investment: $1,000-$2,500 for computer equipment.

Time Commitment: Part- or full-time

Can You Run the Business From Home? Yes

Success Potential Difficult. *Write what you know* isn't as easy as it sounds. You have to match your topic and style to a particular publication, get the timing right and hope you catch the editor in a good mood.

How to Market the Business: Read a year's worth of the magazine you want to write for; then design query letters that show you've done your homework. Despite repeated rejections, you must submit and resubmit manuscripts.

The Pros: Recognition, satisfaction and the potential to break into other fields.

The Cons: Poor pay, no guaranteed income, *lots* of competition and rejection.

Special Considerations: If you're not self-motivated, forget it. If you are, become an expert on a topic and create a niche.

For More Information: *Writer's Market*; *Writer's Digest*; *The Writer; How To Get Happily Published*, by Judith Appelbaum (Bantam).

Story of the Business

In 1974, at the age of 45, Barbara Bell Matuszewski and her husband retired and moved from Wilmington, Delaware, to Sewall's Point, a tiny town in southeast Florida. She had been employed for 26 years at a small advertising agency and worked her way up from the mail room to just outside the boardroom. One month after she arrived in Florida, Barbara joined a writers' club. She had taken courses in journalism and feature writing in the past, but now she wanted to write for publication.

Barbara sold a few features that first year about her experiences as a semifinalist in cooking competitions. She also took a few courses in nonfiction, fiction and poetry. In 1981 she wrote to a local daily newspaper suggesting a weekly column called "Questions of Cuisine." She enclosed a sample column, and the editor gave her the go-ahead.

By 1983 the newspaper was publishing in a second city. Barbara wrote food and travel features for both papers. She added restaurant reviews to her repertoire in 1987, and today her "Dining Out" column appears weekly.

Based on her renown, Matuszewski was invited to attend competitions among professional chefs; she served widely as a judge—at local, regional and national cookoffs. In 1988 she went to the quadrennial international Culinary Olympics in

Frankfurt, Germany, where she observed 2,500 chefs representing 30 countries competing for medals in various events. By 1990 she was also teaching gourmet cooking at her county's continuing education department.

In 1987 Matuszewski was researching a travel feature about the Brandywine Valley of northern Delaware and southeastern Pennsylvania when she got the idea for a book. She had spent the first 45 years of her life in that area. She used her knowledge to outline *Bounty on the Brandywine*, a book about the area's heritage of natural beauty, history, art and fine food. She submitted the outline and three chapters to a publisher who specialized in books about the region. He bought her proposal, and the 341-page book was published in May 1988.

Barbara became a consulting editor to *The National Culinary Review*, the publication for the American Culinary Federation (ACF), which is a professional organization of chefs in the United States. The *Review* sent her to the 1992 Culinary Olympics. The next year she won the magazine's annual Henry Award given to the best editorial feature for her article about the event. She also won an award for runner-up for best technique feature for her article about experimental cuisine. Her work has also been recognized by the National League of American Pen Women.

Barbara is happiest at her computer, but she and her husband, Mat—who takes photographs for her food and travel articles—spend many weeks on the road each year. Freelancing isn't making her wealthy, but she says she's doing what she loves to do. While some freelancers earn a healthy income, the average freelancer earns less than $5,000 in a year. Barbara made about $500 the first year.

Even though she loves writing despite the erratic and low income, Barbara has one regret about her career. "The law of averages predicts I will not live long enough to write all I want to write," she says. "I wish I had started freelancing 15 years earlier."

FURNITURE MAKER

John Alden
Gorham, Maine

Ease of Startup	Moderate
Range of Initial Investment	$3,000-5,000
Time Commitment	Part- or full-time
Can You Run the Business From Home?	Yes
Success Potential	Moderate

Description of Business: Making chairs, tables and other items for individuals and retail stores.

Ease of Startup: Moderate. Many woodworkers have had shops set up for years.

Range of Initial Investment: $3,000-5,000 for equipment and supplies.

Time Commitment: Part- or full-time

Can You Run the Business From Home? Yes

Success Potential: Moderate. There's a lot of competition out there. If you specialize in one area and are skilled, your chances are good.

How to Market the Business: Advertising, word of mouth, referrals, through retail furniture shops.

The Pros: If you've always worked with wood as a hobby, doing it for money will be a joy.

The Cons: It takes time to build up a clientele. You might have to charge a lot to make money or cut your prices to sell your work.

Special Considerations: Custom and hand-built furniture is in demand, though it can be affected by the economy and a limited market.

For More Information: *Fine Woodworking Magazine*, POB 5506, Newtown, CT 06470.

Story of the Business

With traditional Yankee foresight and caution, John Alden, who builds furniture with an emphasis on Early American styles, planned his retirement business according to a blueprint that would work for many aspiring entrepreneurs. He began planning his business a few years before he retired, developing it while still working at his job as engineer.He retired at age 62 to work full-time building furniture, taking time for a little sailing, now and then.

Alden has always built furniture. During the Depression he and his family made most of their own furniture. When he had children of his own, he made a lot of his family's furniture. "I enjoyed it and thought I would start doing it for other people," he explains. "While I was working at my job, I began to get things ready so when I retired I could start right in."

In the beginning Alden advertised in local papers and distributed a brochure to attract customers. After he developed a reputation in the area, he discontinued the brochure and ads. He says that if he continued the marketing, he'd get more business than he could handle by himself. He has no desire to add to his business by having employees. "I keep busy just by word of mouth," he indicates.

John made chairs and other items for a furniture shop in Connecticut, but he says there were problems. "When you build furniture by hand, it's difficult to make it inexpensively enough so a shop can double the price and still have it be affordable," he explains. "I prefer to sell direct. That way I can price pieces so they're reasonable enough that people can afford them."

To determine the price of a chair, Alden accounts for his overhead, estimates the cost of the materials he uses and adds in the labor he puts into a piece. He's built clocks, chests of drawers and tables. Windsor chairs are the most labor-intensive piece he builds, taking 20 hours for each chair. He prices a side chair at $350 and an armchair at $450.

Alden gets most of his wood from his 50 acres of woodland. "I try to use the same species of wood that would have been used in the original," he points out. "I cut and dry the timber here in my own building and use it as air-dried lumber."

He works 50 hours a week, which is more than he spent at his engineer position, but says he thoroughly enjoys it. "I work a full day nearly every day, but I don't feel pressured to do it," he says.

"My goals are quite different from someone who's starting a new business because I have no desire to build it up and have employees," he remarks. "Consequently I end up doing many of the menial tasks that would normally get passed on to an employee, like cleaning and getting rid of the sawdust."

Though he specializes in chairs, he does do custom work, building whatever a customer wants. "My expertise is the ability to copy Early American pieces," he says.

"I'm going to stick with it as long as I'm physically able. This kind of work gives me the opportunity so that when the weather is right for sailing, I sail. The other days I work in the shop. And people understand."

GENERAL STORE

Westport General Store

Bob and Lorraine Caristi
Westport Island, Maine

Ease of Startup	Difficult
Range of Initial Investment	$200,000-$400,000
Time Commitment	Full-time
Can You Run the Business From Home?	Yes
Success Potential	Moderate

Description of Business: A convenience store geared toward a rural community serving both locals and tourists.

Ease of Startup: Difficult. If you're starting from scratch, you'll need to renovate a storefront and set up accounts with suppliers. It is easier to buy an existing business.

Range of Initial Investment: $200,000-$400,000 for inventory and building, which usually includes owner's quarters.

Time Commitment: Full-time

Can You Run the Business From Home? You should live upstairs or nearby.

Success Potential: Moderate. The larger variety of products you carry and the more centrally located the store, the higher the success rate.

How to Market the Business: Carry a large selection of products at reasonable prices and provide good service. Advertising and other promotion won't bring in new people if they have to drive any distance.

The Pros: When you're the only store in town, you're important to the community.

The Cons: The hours are long and the work is physically hard.

Special Considerations: Owning a general store is one of the top three businesses people dream of, mostly to escape the city. In each of these businesses—innkeeping and gift shops are the other two—the dream does not even begin to match the hard work of the reality.

For More Information: National Grocers Association, 1825 Samuel Morse Drive, Reston, VA 22090.

Story of the Business

Listen to how Bob Caristi describes the difference between his corporate job—which he left to move up to Maine with his wife, Lorraine—and their general store, which opened for business in June 1992:

"At my corporate job, I seldom put in 40 hours," he relates. "Here, we work untold hours for relatively little money, but the compensation is in a different form; we're no longer being paid in dollars. Anyone thinking about doing what we did better realize you have to do everything yourself. Most people tend not to know what that's like. It also takes a tremendous range of talents to do this: you have to be bookkeeper and businessperson, personable, physically strong and willing and able to work long hours."

Undoubtedly, many of the people who come to the Westport General Store in the summertime are in the very position that Bob hated enough to leave and envy his new career. It may look easy, but running a general store after the age of 50 is a daunting experience, especially if you choose not to hire help, like Bob and Lorraine. They sat down one day back in Massachusetts and realized they both wanted to leave their jobs. They asked themselves the question, "How do you do what you're good at, get away from what you don't like, live where you want and yet somehow make a living?" They decided their skills were complementary—Lorraine is more people-oriented, while Bob likes to deal with tangible objects and manufacturers. They put it all together and decided to open a mom-and-pop store on the coast of Maine. "I handle the business and mechanics, and she primarily deals with people," explains Bob. "This type of business is such that unless you're an idiot, you're going to make money from the beginning."

They started saving for the purchase in 1986 and bought the store in 1991 while they were still working in Massachusetts. They saved enough to buy the store outright to avoid the pressure of a mortgage. They finally moved to Maine in April 1992. They spent two months fixing up the store and opened for business at the end of June.

The store is 1,500 square feet. They carry beer and wine, canned goods, bread and dairy products. The Caristis also have an extensive grocery line, which most general stores don't do. When they first opened, they guessed at what they should sell. In the year and a half they've been open, they have chosen new products according to the demand that comes from two distinct communities: locals and the summer residents.

"There are two Westports," explains Bob, "and there are fundamental differences in the nature of the two." For instance, the summer residents want bottled water and antifreeze for their toilets and sinks at the end of the season. The year-round people want other things.

"Your customers are your boss, which can be trying at times, but the minute you forget that, you're out of business," he warns. "It's nice to be a central point in the town and to have people rely on us to provide services and products."

Unlike other nearby general stores, the Caristis have deliberately chosen to limit their product line. "There's a lot of call for the lottery, but even though it has a significant impact on gross, we don't want to do it because it's a pain in the butt," he remarks. "We also don't want to sell prepared food and sandwiches because of the potential for waste of perishable items."

They also refuse to have employees; this makes for some very long days and nights. Besides not having to pay high rates for worker's compensation in addition to payroll taxes, Bob says he does it himself because no employee cares like he does. "Especially with a new business and with this kind of business, I want to make sure that customers are being appropriately served. There's also no pilferage and no errors."

His marketing campaign consists of being pleasant to people, carrying the merchandise that people want and being impeccably honest and service-oriented. "You're only going to attract people within a convenient driving distance, so if you do things right, you're going to maximize the draw within the geographic area," he explains.

They didn't know anything about running a general store when they started, but they thought they could translate what they knew into a viable business, and they have. "We did it with intelligence and guts."

GIFT BASKETS

A Basket Case

Janet Booth
San Jose, California

Ease of Startup	Easy
Range of Initial Investment	$300
Time Commitment	Part- or full-time
Can You Run the Business From Home?	Yes
Success Potential	Moderate

Description of Business: Packaging merchandise in baskets for people to give as gifts. Baskets can be organized around a theme like a new home or a baby shower.

Ease of Startup: Easy. You can obtain supplies retail as you start out; contact wholesale suppliers later on.

Range of Initial Investment: $300 for initial inventory.

Time Commitment: Part- or full-time

Can You Run the Business From Home? Yes

Success Potential: Moderate. The wider the variety of baskets you offer, the larger your market will be.

How to Market the Business: Advertising, word of mouth, referrals, retail stores.

The Pros: The gift basket business is fun: you can be creative in designing the contents of each basket.

The Cons: Buying items wholesale from suppliers who require high minimum orders can tie up your money.

Special Considerations: For people who have physical and health problems but lots of ideas, this is a good business.

For More Information: *How to Find Your Treasure in a Gift Basket*, by Ron Perkins, Home Income Publishing, 2796 Harbor Blvd., Suite 107, Costa Mesa, CA 92626.

Story of the Business

Janet Booth's sister, Nancy Ingham, was sitting at her home in Natick, Massachusetts, one day in 1990, watching television with her daughter. They were viewing a tape on how to start a business. Right then and there, mother and daughter decided to start a gift basket business. They called it Baskets for Babies, specializing in baby baskets aimed at new mothers.

"My sister called me and told me what she was going to do. I got the bug, too," remembers Janet, who started her basket business in California the next year. They began by showing their baskets at craft fairs on both coasts. Nancy has expanded into retail stores, a step that Janet will soon follow.

Janet retired from the field of x-ray technology before she started her business, while Nancy still works full-time as a medical coder and is planning to retire in a few years. They both run their businesses part-time. The months preceding Christmas are the busiest time of year.

Janet designs a variety of themed baskets, but says her best seller is a small tin with a few cosmetics in it that she sells at the craft shows for $5.50. "They bought them faster than I could make them," she reveals. The usual markup for baskets is to charge twice the cost of materials.

They pick their fairs on the recommendations of other craftspeople and by trial and error. Janet did an outdoor show in the summer in California once, which she says was a disaster. "The products started to melt. I had to take everything home and rewrap them," she recalls. "Plus, I think summer is the wrong season for craft shows: the shows are poorly attended."

Janet can't work full-time due to medical problems. This business enables her to stay at home and make baskets.

The advantage of running a gift basket business is that, except for food baskets, she can make them up in advance and tote them to the fairs and stores. When she attends a show as an exhibitor, her kids help her get there and set up.

To expand a gift-basket business, it's almost necessary to get into different markets because the industry is so seasonal. Nancy has placed baskets in a craft store and a beauty salon; Janet hopes to follow suit. She's thinking of marketing a golf basket to pro shops at golf courses and golf retail stores. She's also thinking of a basket geared toward new homeowners that realtors could buy as gifts. "I thought I'd just walk in with one of them and ask 'Do you like these?'" she says.

Janet indicates that the biggest challenge to a gift basket business is finding adequate supplies, since some suppliers require high minimum orders of $250 and up. She buys some items at retail. Sometimes basket purchasers buy items for her to put in the basket. "We only sell sparkling cider or de-alcoholized grape juice. If someone wants to give a bottle of wine, they buy it and we put it in the basket." In all, she keeps about $3,000 worth of inventory on hand for the different types of baskets.

It's a creative business that frequently requires a bit of brainstorming. "Right now we're trying to find a basket and products for triplets," she says.

GOURMET FOOD STORE

Treats

Paul Mrosinski
Wiscasset, Maine

Ease of Startup	Moderate
Range of Initial Investment	$50,000
Time Commitment	Full-time
Can You Run the Business From Home?	No
Success Potential	Moderate

Description of Business: A specialty shop that focuses on high-end products that aren't available in supermarkets.

Ease of Startup: Moderate. You need some expertise in specialty foods. It's important to create a shop that shows them off to their best advantage.

Range of Initial Investment: $50,000.

Time Commitment: Full-time

Can You Run the Business From Home? No

Success Potential: Moderate. This is fairly easy in an area where there's no competition and there are people who appreciate specialty foods.

How to Market the Business: Advertising, publicity, tastings, quality products.

The Pros: It's a great business if you love good food.

The Cons: There are thousands of specialty food producers out there; you'll be inundated with their products.

Special Considerations: For people who love high-quality food and are located in a high-traffic or exclusive area, a gourmet food shop will do well.

For More Information: National Association for the Specialty Food Trade, 8 W. 40 Street, New York, NY 10018.

Story of the Business

Paul Mrosinski had been working as an architect for many years. He loved his profession, but he had been commuting 45 miles each way to his job in Portland since he and his wife, Sharon, moved to Maine from California in 1987. In 1993 he was looking for something else to do when a gourmet store right across the street from their house went out of business and the space became available.

Sharon was already running an antique business from their home. When Paul saw the vacant store staring out at him, he thought it would be a way they could bring their two lives to one spot.

Paul opened Treats in the spring of 1993. Even after he acquired the space, there was still a lot of work to do.

"We changed the physical appearance of the store a lot," he says. "We're right on the main road through town, with a lot of traffic. When we opened a lot of local people told us they had never noticed the shop." The first thing he did was to increase the visibility of the store from the road. He put in awnings, placed clear signs outside and changed the interior walls from dark green to white.

Mrosinski also removed the dirty carpet and arranged the store in a much more efficient way "so customers can get excited about buying," as he puts it.

Mrosinski focuses on four niches. Fresh-baked bread—something which was unavailable in that part of central Maine—is delivered daily to the store. He also carries a selection of fine cheeses, good coffee and domestic and imported wines at both ends of the price scale. Wine is his biggest seller.

He doesn't need to market the store; he feels a good product will find its clientele on its own. Of course the increased visibility of the store brings people to the door.

Treats is open seven days a week at least 10 hours a day, year-round. "Reducing the number of hours in winter doesn't make sense to me," he remarks. "Locals need to realize this is a serious business. If they want some cheese, bread and wine on a Sunday afternoon in winter, they know where they can find it."

He hires high school students to help out at the store in the summer. Even so, his hours amount to full-time plus. He doesn't have a background in gourmet foods, though he's always been a consumer of them.

There are thousands of large and small specialty food companies selling everything from salsa to banana bread mix vying for a spot on his shelf. How does he decide what products to carry?

"I pick the products by tasting them," he reports. "I know what I want and what I don't want. You have to know what you're selling so customers gain confidence in your ability to steer them in the right direction," he explains. "Therefore, I'm not going to listen to a salesman who tells me a particular product will sell well in the store. I trust my own judgment."

The projected annual gross for a comparable store can be more than $150,000. Though he still does a limited amount of architecture work, Mrosinski devotes most of his time to the store.

"The biggest thing I've learned is that whatever happens in that store, I only have myself to blame," he says. "You'd better like the products you sell, or you're not going to be able to sell them."

GRAPHIC DESIGN FIRM

Eagle Graphics

Don Carter

Alexandria, Virginia

Ease of Startup	Moderate
Range of Initial Investment	$5,000
Time Commitment	Part- or full-time
Can You Run the Business From Home?	Yes
Success Potential	Moderate

Description of Business: A company that designs printed matter, sets type and coordinates printing for businesses.

Ease of Startup: Moderate. You need to buy typesetting and/or a desktop publishing system.

Range of Initial Investment: $5,000 for a system.

Time Commitment: Part- or full-time

Can You Run the Business From Home? Yes

Success Potential: Moderate. More companies are doing their own desktop publishing, so the business is more competitive than it was.

How to Market the Business: Through brochures, word of mouth, ads, direct mail, barter.

The Pros: You can exercise your creativity.

The Cons: It's highly competitive, and people are more concerned about price than quality.

Special Considerations: For people who have an eye for
design and layout—and who can convince a business it's better to use a professional than doing it in-house—graphic
design is a good business.

For More Information: Association of Professional Design
Firms, 1 Story Street, Cambridge, MA 02138.

Story of the Business

Desktop publishing is all the rage in businesses today—the
prevalent feeling is if you don't have your own system,
you're a step behind everyone else—but there are advantages
to going to a professional firm.

Unfortunately Don Carter—who started Eagle Graphics in
1982—must spend a good amount of time explaining the difference between what he does and what a secretary who's
assigned to do the company newsletter using a layout program manual can do.

When he retired from the Army as an officer in 1974,
Carter found a job working with a local trade association,
where he was responsible for publishing the membership
directory. "When you work for a trade association," he
warns, "new board members each year mean new ideas and
more work with no accompanying increase in staff."

He put up with the frustrations of the job. When his children graduated from college, he decided to start his own
graphics business. While he was at the association, he frequently met with staff members from other trade associations that represented many different kinds of businesses.
He made a lot of contacts. Many of the other associations
also had an overworked graphics department, so when he
opened his business, they were happy to steer the extra
work his way.

Though he began with professional typesetting equipment, Carter says these machines—Linotronic 300s and

Compugraphic 8400s—are almost obsolete because the quality of desktop publishing improves every day. The advantage of typesetting machines is that they set type through a photographic process at 2,600 DPI, or dots per inch. This results in the clear resolution of each letter. Many laser printers today, on the other hand, produce characters at 300 DPI: Many of the characters have ragged edges and look shoddy when reproduced.

New technology is producing laser printers that approach 2600 DPI, are faster than the typesetting machines and allow for more flexibility in letter size and line length. Most businesses are still working with 300 DPI printers. Frequently their employees—who don't have a graphics background—design documents. Fixing their mistakes has become a big part of Carter's business.

"I've had to get into desktop publishing in order to accept floppy disks from people who think they've got their work camera-ready and don't," he reports. "Then they come to me, and think they're going to get it redone for peanuts." Computer service bureaus that prepare the data for the printer in his area work with businesses and accept work over a modem; the bureaus then send it back for almost nothing with the job half-done. "The businesses then have to send it back to get all the parameters plugged in. The bureaus really make their money off the second effort."

But sometimes they go to Eagle Graphics for the second round. Carter says when he takes in work, he usually needs to do a lot of extra keyboarding whether a client hands it in on disk or not. "Half my business comes from military-oriented clients, and some don't even want to look at a computer," he says. "Sometimes it's typed, sometimes it's just handwritten, and I take it and work with that."

Carter also works as a printer broker for several local and out-of-town printers. The printers give Carter a discount when clients want him to do everything including the printing of the final document. He keeps the discounted amount, increasing the amount of money he receives for doing the work.

From the beginning, Carter didn't want to deal with walk-in business; he wanted to qualify his customers over the phone first. He has an ad in the Yellow Pages, but gets most of his business through his old contacts and word of mouth. "I used to do work for a guy who was the publicity director of a local community college 12 years ago. Now he's at the Salvation Army, and I do work for him there," he relates. As for the community college, they do most of their design and printing in-house now.

Carter suggests that people who are interested in starting a graphic design firm have experience in printing or publishing and are proficient working with computers.

"Computers change so rapidly," he reports, "that if it works, it's out of date."

GYMBOREE

Gymboree Franchisee

Phyllis Taylor
East Lansing, Michigan

Ease of Startup	Easy
Range of Initial Investment	$35,000
Time Commitment	Part- or full-time
Can You Run the Business From Home?	No
Success Potential	Easy

Description of Business: A franchise that offers group exercise classes for children with parents in attendance.

Ease of Startup: Easy. The franchise provides the foundation. It's up to you to get the word out.

Range of Initial Investment: $35,000 for equipment and franchise fee.

Time Commitment: Part- or full-time

Can You Run the Business From Home? No

Success Potential: Easy. The franchise determines location and interviews franchisees. If you make it in, you'll probably do well.

How to Market the Business: Advertising, word of mouth, referrals.

The Pros: If you like kids and like to be active, Gymboree is a perfect business.

The Cons: You might have to start by offering just a couple of classes to build up your reputation.

Special Considerations: For energetic retirees who will never have enough grandchildren, this is a good business.

For More Information: Gymboree, 700 Airport Blvd., #200, Burlingame, CA 94010.

Story of the Business

Phyllis Taylor had jumped in and out of jobs and businesses for most of her working life. She worked for other people; she ran a 7-11. She never found a career she really enjoyed; consequently, she never stayed with anything for very long.

In 1994 she had her tenth anniversary as a Gymboree franchise operator and signed a contract for her next 10 years with the company. She's even thinking about developing another site in the area. This would mean paying another franchise fee, but Taylor doesn't care. She's found her niche in life.

"I love what I do," she says of her Gymboree franchise. Back in 1984 she read an article about the then-new company. It looked interesting, so she called the California headquarters to request information. She and her daughter were looking around for a business they could run together that involved children. They didn't want to run a day-care center. Phyllis is very athletic, so Gymboree was particularly appealing.

Taylor filled out the necessary forms and sent them back; she attained financing from a local bank. She and her daughter left for California to be interviewed. They were accepted as franchisees and entered the next training session.

Franchise training sessions can vary in depth and quality. For Taylor the 10-day Gymboree training was very informative. "We were introduced to the program, learned how to advertise and how to run a class," she says.

Phyllis came back, rented a church for classes and opened for business. Her timing was good, since Gymboree was a relatively new concept then. Taylor opened her franchise six months after the first two in Detroit were started. "There was lots of visibility for the program," she remembers. The local paper and television stations interviewed her, giving her valuable publicity. The phones rang off the hook.

Today Taylor runs 16 classes a week within a three-day period. She still teaches half of them. She has hired two teachers to handle the morning classes. Each 45-minute class can have up to 20 children plus their parents. Each class costs $7, and participants have the option of taking another class in the same week for half price.

Taylor's workload varies. With each new session she advertises the new classes, takes enrollments and answers the phone at her home office; she spends about 10 to 12 hours a day at the business. Once the session is underway, she spends eight to 10 hours a week in the office and eight hours teaching classes.

As with any franchise, a certain percentage the gross goes to the parent company. Taylor pays a six percent royalty to Gymboree and one and a half percent into a general advertising fund to pay for national advertising and marketing campaigns.

Taylor's daughter has since pulled out of the business. Today Taylor does all the paperwork and planning. She says it never seems like work to her, even when she has to deal with some of the parents.

"I deal with all kinds of people," she remarks. "Everyone thinks her child is special. I have to let them know I think so too without favoring one child over another. I love both the children and their parents, and I love doing classes."

HANDWRITING ANALYSIS

Lillika Weinberger
Montclair, New Jersey

Ease of Startup	Moderate
Range of Initial Investment	$1,600
Time Commitment	Part- or full-time
Can You Run the Business From Home?	Yes
Success Potential	Easy

Description of Business: A one-person business that includes lectures to social groups, employee screening for businesses, personality assessment, cruise ship entertainment, compatibility studies, document examination and vocational guidance.

Ease of Startup: Moderate. You need to complete a formal course of home study to become certified, which can take up to 18 months.

Range of Initial Investment: $1,600 for the correspondence course.

Time Commitment: Part- or full-time

Can You Run the Business From Home? Yes

Success Potential: Easy. Graphologists are in demand in many areas; the demand exceeds the supply of skilled analysts.

How to Market the Business: Local social organizations and businesses, attorneys and advertising for individual evaluations.

The Pros: It can be lucrative, you can do it anywhere, and you'll be in the public eye.

The Cons: The initial training period takes time.

Special Considerations: Graphology is a good business for people who are curious about people and for those who like to juggle a variety of tasks.

For More Information: Contact Lillika Weinberger, POB 1212, Montclair, NJ 07042-1212; International Graphoanalysis Society, 111 N. Canal Street, Chicago, IL 60606.

Story of the Business

Lillika Weinberger was a successful professional artist. Her sculptures and wall murals were found all over the New York metropolitan area, from the windows at Tiffany's to private homes. Over the years, however, she found she wanted to spend more time with people, as her work was very solitary. Her father had been a graphologist. She decided to continue the family tradition, since it would get her out into the world and involved with people.

She took a home-study course through the International Graphoanalysis Society in Chicago and became certified as a graphologist in 1981. From the beginning, she hasn't had to solicit work; everyone has come to her. She began with one hour a week at a local club.

"I wanted to join a local club because I like to swim. The social director said that in exchange for a membership, I could talk about the art of handwriting analysis one hour a week," she recalls. "That's how I got started. I met people, and some who belonged to other clubs asked me to speak at their clubs. Still others wanted me to analyze their own handwriting. People continue to find me."

Lillika also served as a guest speaker at a luncheon for employers and their secretaries during Secretary's Week that first year. She did some sample analyses for a few members of the audience, then a couple of employers called her to do analyses of prospective employees. It hasn't stopped since. She also occasionally spends a week on a cruise ship, giving lectures and doing individual analyses.

"I'm an entertainer, too," she admits. "There are so many facets to this field and so many ways to practice it. Handwriting is a graphic form of body language; it tells a lot about someone's personality. It's not fortune telling, but a psychological tool."

When she works with businesses who are screening employees, they might be considering two or three people for one job. "They want more of a profile," reports Lillika. "Some employers pay for psychological testing, but it usually takes time to get the results. I deal only with a piece of paper, and usually don't see the person. In a matter of hours, I can arrive at a personality profile that is uncannily accurate." She says more and more businesses are using graphology to screen employees.

Another part of graphology is document examination. A graphologist works with attorneys to examine the accuracy or validity of handwriting or of a signature. Weinberger says document examination is the most lucrative part of handwriting analysis. "If you are required to go to court—you have to sit and wait until you're called—your day is worth $500," she indicates. "Writing a report is paid on an hourly basis, from $100 and up per hour. One woman I know, who's around 80 years old, told me she made $80,000 last year from handwriting analysis and document work." A new part of legal graphology is jury screening. An analyst will work with a lawyer to help select the right jury for a particular case. "I think you're only limited by the extent of your imagination," suggests Lillika.

A private analysis, which can take from four to five hours, costs a minimum of $100. Her fee for lectures varies, depending on her travel time, the type of group hiring her and whether it's a nonprofit or a corporation. The range is from $150 to $2,000. The sponsoring group pays for air fare and other travel expenses; she charges per mile if the travel is local.

Weinberger teaches an introductory course in handwriting analysis at Florida Atlantic University; formal certification must come from the International Graphoanalysis Society.

A lot of her business comes through the mail. "When I give a lecture, there's always someone in the audience who needs my services and writes to me after the talk," she reports. Lillika works from her home, and adds, "Wherever mail is delivered, a person can become a certified graphoanalyst." She and her husband spend a lot of time in Florida, and she brings her work with her.

Besides the initial cost for the correspondence course, you need a couple hundred dollars for printing a brochure and business cards to set up shop. "After all, you're dealing with a pen and paper and a magnifying glass," she says. For document examining, you'll need a microscope and other specialized tools to test for forensic values.

"I love the entertainment value of graphology," she remarks. "It has its fun side, but it's a serious career, too."

HARDWARE STORE

Uncle Wally's Ace Hardware Store

Walter Funk
Strongsville, Ohio

Ease of Startup	Difficult
Range of Initial Investment	$500,000
Time Commitment	Full-time
Can You Run the Business From Home?	No
Success Potential	Moderate

Description of Business: A retail shop that sells hardware and offers repair services to consumers and businesses.

Ease of Startup: Difficult. It's expensive and you need to stock many different kinds of inventory.

Range of Initial Investment: $500,000.

Time Commitment: Full-time

Can You Run the Business From Home? No

Success Potential: Moderate. Success depends on the number of hardware stores already in your area.

How to Market the Business: Advertising, word of mouth, referrals.

The Pros: A hardware store is a happy business: It's easy to run, and you're helping people fix up their houses with supplies and advice.

The Cons: It's easy to be undercapitalized because you need an extensive inventory.

Special Considerations: People who've always tinkered in the basement and who've always had too much of everything in the garage will feel right at home running a hardware store.

For More Information: *Hardware Age*, 1 Chilton Way, Radnor, PA 19089.

Story of the Business

To look at how Walter Funk spends his day, you'd never say he was retired. He spends about 40 hours a week at his 7,000-square-foot hardware store in a suburb of Cleveland, and he still has a full medical practice where he specializes in general surgery.

Dr. Walter Funk has always loved hardware stores, and he's also collected tools. When a couple of patients who owned a hardware store less than a block from his office offered to sell it to him in 1985, Walter jumped at the chance. "I basically bought it for my kids, who were done with school, but I figured it would give me something to do as well," he adds.

It does. After spending the morning in surgery, he spends a few hours at the store. Then he heads for his office, where office hours start at one in the afternoon. After he's done, he goes back to the store and works until closing. "I work until my day is done. That's how I manage everything," he explains. "If there's work to be done, I do it."

Ace Hardware is not a franchise, but a buying cooperative that's a cross between an old-fashioned hardware store and a more modern facility. The store sells lots of prepackaged items, but also nails in bulk. Uncle Wally's also repairs screens and windows, a job Walter particularly enjoys. Do people in town think it strange that the doctor they see in the morning might fix their screen door in the afternoon? "They were a little surprised at first, but it's worked out quite well because I'd been in practice for 31 years. Besides," he says, "I call most of these people by their first names anyway."

He doesn't do much marketing to promote the store, aside from sales circulars that the Ace company puts together. Funk instead relies on word of mouth and people becoming familiar with the store. This is one way Funk's other business undoubtedly helps out.

His initial investment was $500,000; his 1993 gross was $800,000. His three sons and one daughter-in-law enjoy working in the business with him. "It's a natural business for my children and myself," he remarks. "We don't have any real problems, except when the moon gets full and people get cranky. Most of the time, I feel like a kid in a candy store."

Funk says one surprise he didn't expect when he bought the store involves maintaining cash flow. "When we started the business, we set our gross sales goal. We figured if we could sell that much each day, we could make the business work," he indicates. "We're now at seven to ten times that, and we're still struggling. It costs more to run a store now, and they tax you for everything under the sun. We do most of our own maintenance, but it's still more expensive to run than I thought it would be."

For people considering opening a hardware store, Funk advises if they're familiar with the services and skills necessary to run a hardware store, then they should go for it. He adds be sure you have enough money. "We had to borrow from my practice because I was undercapitalized," he recalls.

How long is he planning to continue his double life? "I still have kids in school," he says. "I'd quit medicine today if I could."

HERBALIST

Happy Ventures

Happy Griffiths
Lebanon, New Hampshire

Ease of Startup	Easy
Range of Initial Investment	$100
Time Commitment	Part- or full-time
Can You Run the Business From Home?	Yes
Success Potential	Difficult

Description of Business: Growing herbs to sell in a variety of forms from potpourri to herbal cosmetics.

Ease of Startup: Easy. Many who become herbalists have been growing herbs for a number of years already.

Range of Initial Investment: $100 and up for seeds.

Time Commitment: Part- or full-time

Can You Run the Business From Home? Yes

Success Potential: Difficult. The market if pretty saturated; you'll need to come up with something no one else is doing.

How to Market the Business: Advertising, word of mouth, retail stores, teaching, lectures.

The Pros: You can make money from growing things.

The Cons: It's competitive; you have to come up with new ideas to stay in the market.

Special Considerations: People who love to grow herbs and who love a challenge should give it a shot.

For More Information: *Herb Quarterly*, POB 548, Boiling Springs, PA 17007.

Story of the Business

After her kids graduated from college, Happy Griffiths was looking for the kind of opportunity that would fit her way of life and what she liked to do. She had been teaching a course in herbs at the local community college twice a year. She covered growing, cooking and making potpourri with herbs, but she didn't find teaching satisfying enough.

The director of the Museum at Lower Shaker Village in nearby Enfield asked Happy to teach an herbal class there for area residents. Shortly after her course they offered her the position of resident herbalist, responsible for designing and maintaining an 11,000-square-foot garden in the Shaker style. She accepted the challenge. This eventually led to the establishment of Happy Ventures, which serves as an umbrella business for her teaching, her herbal products and her lectures.

"The job at the museum opened up a wealth of opportunities. I can run with it any way I want to," she says. She began at the Museum in 1986 and relying on help from the Museum's village gardeners program, where people from the community can help out in the garden. Over the years the garden has doubled in size, and the program has grown to 14 community gardeners. "The museum gives me free reign. They provide me with the materials to create a garden that's the envy of the other Shaker communities," she says.

Working there helped build her reputation as an expert, providing a market that recognizes her name when it appears on the products she sells, both at the museum and else-where. It has also helped her become a popular speaker.

Her products include potpourri, garlands, baskets, herbal cosmetics, aroma therapy products and herbs for teas or cooking preparations. She grows the herbs both at the Shaker gardens and in her home garden. Happy admits her own garden takes a back seat, since she spends every morning at the museum during the growing season, which runs from mid-April until mid-October.

Griffiths specializes in packaged herbs because the state of New Hampshire places so many restrictions on home-based food manufacturers that about the only thing she could make without a licensed kitchen is herbal vinegar.

She gives talks to local garden clubs and associations, charging $75 per lecture. "I spend two or three days preparing for the talk because I show a lot of things," she says. "Sometimes I cook and get participants cooking. I like to get people involved." Some weeks she gives two or three speeches; then several weeks go by when she doesn't give any. She prefers to accept only one engagement a week unless the requests are on a similar topic.

Griffiths spends her winters researching different and new aspects of herbs. "The last few winters I've researched aromatherapy, herbal cosmetics and medicinal herbs," she reports. As she researches, she tries to formulate an outline for teaching about these new topics.

It's becoming necessary for Griffiths to branch out; her knees are beginning to show the strain of years of gardening. "My body is telling me I'm overdoing it, and I've had to pull back." she says, "I'd like to increase the number of classes I teach. I enjoy sharing my knowledge with others. The more I learn, the less I know," she remarks.

HISTORICAL IMPERSONATOR

Abraham Lincoln Impersonator

Gerald Bestrom
Middleville, Michigan

Ease of Startup	Easy
Range of Initial Investment	$0
Time Commitment	Part- or full-time
Can You Run the Business From Home?	Yes
Success Potential	Easy

Description of Business: A business in which an individual makes personal appearances acting as a particular historical figure.

Ease of Startup: Easy. All you have to do is learn about the person and his or her ideals. Then put together costumes and start walking around like you are that person.

Range of Initial Investment: $0

Time Commitment: Part- or full-time

Can You Run the Business From Home? Yes

Success Potential: Easy. The business is unusual enough that if you're a dead ringer for someone, you'll have a lot of business.

How to Market the Business: Word of mouth, referrals. ·

The Pros: You'll be a walking history book and help kids learn.

The Cons: You might have to start by making appearances for free to build up your clientele.

Special Considerations: A person who is able to convey the appearance and personality of a much-loved historical figure will do well.

Story of the Business

"I thought you were dead!"

"You're so well kept, Mr. Lincoln!"

These are just a few of the reactions that greet Gerald Bestrom when he appears in full coat and top hat, talking about the principles of early America through the eyes and ears of the 16th president.

Bestrom works full-time as a Lincoln impersonator. He makes appearances primarily at schools and civic events in 20 states across the midwest, the south and the east. He even has a motor home painted to look like a log cabin.

In 1985 a friend told him he looked a lot like Lincoln, even before he grew his beard. "He said it often enough that it registered," relates Bestrom. "I had always admired Lincoln's principles and values. Even though I barely remembered the Gettysburg Address, I could envision myself standing on a stump and giving that speech with the same kind of intensity."

That year he went to an annual event for saw players, which he attended every year. He thought about dressing up like a clown but then somebody—again—mentioned Lincoln. He bought some clothes and rented a stovepipe hat. At that point his beard was only about a month old, so he filled it in with shoe polish. At the event he stood on a stump and gave the Saw Players' Address. Afterwards a woman came up to him to encourage him to do more because she thought he was so believable.

That was the catalyst. Gerald started to do in-depth research on Lincoln. He saw one way in which his own life paralleled that of The Great Orator: neither one had finished high school. While working second shift at a nearby factory, Bestrom got his GED and tested the waters as Lincoln. He got a local directory listing the enrollment and size for all the schools in his area—larger schools would tend to have the budget to hire Bestrom for an afternoon or longer. Then he walked into the offices of some of the schools dressed in his Lincoln garb. "I'm my own best advertisement," he points out.

Teachers and ministers have written letters of recommendation for Bestrom. His fees depend on where he's performing and what the market will bear. In Appalachia he gets $175 for two assemblies and two classroom visits; in the Midwest, he gets $275. In the east, his fee is considerably more. "I ask what their normal fee is," he says. "I don't like to discriminate if they can't afford me, because what I have to say is more valuable than the fee."

In 1992 he did 125 performances in one school year; one week he did 18 and had to take a break after that.

"There's a real longing today for the principles that made our nation strong," says Bestrom. "Nobody embodied that more than Lincoln. If I can get in there and undergird the teachers who still teach absolutes, then I've done my job."

Everything he shares is historically accurate. Bestrom enjoys working with children because he believes he didn't give the time to his own children that he should have.

"A woman told me recently that three years ago her child saw me perform at his school. Ever since, he's been talking about Lincoln. This," he reflects, "is my propelling force. I love it."

HOME JEWELRY PARTY HOST

Lady Remington Fashion Jewelry Representative

Virginia Wilson
Hampton, Virginia

Ease of Startup	Easy
Range of Initial Investment	$195
Time Commitment	Part-time
Can You Run the Business From Home?	Yes
Success Potential	Easy

Description of Business: An individual who holds home shows to sell jewelry and builds a network of others to sell jewelry.

Ease of Startup: Easy. You sign up through another host, order a kit and schedule a party.

Range of Initial Investment: $195 for the kit, which you don't need to pay for upfront.

Time Commitment: Part-time

Can You Run the Business From Home? Yes

Success Potential: Easy. If you're outgoing and love to sell, the potential is there.

How to Market the Business: Word of mouth, referrals.

The Pros: Hours are very flexible; you can work as much or as little as you like. The more people you have working under you, the more money you'll make.

The Cons: Finding a steady stream of new guests to attend parties can be tough; recruiting new hosts can also be challenging.

Special Considerations: People who are fashion-conscious and who love meeting new people will do well as party hosts.

For More Information: Lady Remington Fashion Jewelry, 818 Thorndale Avenue, Bensenville, IL 60106.

Story of the Business

While working as a supervisor at a local social service agency, Virginia Wilson also worked part-time for Lady Remington Fashion Jewelry. She held parties where she could display and talk about the jewelry and scout out recruits who could hold their own parties.

When she first looked for work she could do on the side, Virginia wanted something she could build on once she retired. Her retirement was planned for 1994. In a surprise move, her employer offered her early retirement in 1991. Virginia took it.

Wilson had previously worked for another direct-sales company on the side, so she already knew how to get business and book parties. The Lady Remington Fashion Jewelry line specializes in high-quality fashion jewelry. The company currently has 2,500 sales representatives throughout the United States and other countries.

The jewelry doesn't cost more than $30 for one piece; special discounts and incentives often cut prices in half for guests. Wilson works about 20-25 hours a week setting up parties, scouting for guests and talking with prospective hosts. A recruiter makes a percentage of the sales of the hosts she has signed up.

Virginia has a unique way of approaching new guests. "I'll get dressed up and go to the mall, making sure to wear lots of beautiful jewelry so people can comment on it," she reveals. "I go into a store or restaurant, and someone will say, 'I love your bracelet,' and then I start my spiel. No one compliments me on my jewelry who doesn't get my spiel."

When someone mentions her jewelry, Virginia says, "I'd like you to have a piece just like it for free." Of course, they want to know how. That's when she tells them she works for Lady Remington as an advisor. She offers to conduct a fashion seminar for the admirer and her friends, mentioning that the woman will get a piece of jewelry free just for hosting the party.

Virginia hosts about two shows a week and nets $200 on the average from those shows. Each show lasts about two and a half hours; she spends five hours preparing for each show.

The company makes it very easy to start as a host. They provide a kit with about $700 worth of jewelry and $100 in supplies. You can either pay for the kit up front for $195, or earn it through commissions. The company will also arrange to pay you 15 percent of your total sales and keep the rest until you've paid for the kit. Since she is an advisor for the company, Wilson makes 30 percent on everything she sells; a unit manager—the next level up—can earn 37½ percent from her own sales. Virginia earns 7½ percent on her recruits' sales, and unit managers make more as well.

She holds most of her shows and receives most of her orders from October through December and gets busy in January and again in July, when a new catalog comes out.

Not every show is successful, but Virginia says she still has to get geared up for each show. The company helps out with tapes and literature to help with shows and recruiting new hosts.

"The thing I like about the company is that I can determine my own income," explains Wilson. Lady Remington also offers bonus incentive trips with all expenses paid for top sellers. Virginia is working toward a trip to Switzerland.

HOUSE RENOVATOR

Andy Winskas
Tallahassee, Florida

Ease of Startup	Moderate
Range of Initial Investment	$30,000+
Time Commitment	Part- or full-time
Can You Run the Business From Home?	No
Success Potential	Moderate

Description of Business: Buying and repairing houses to rent or sell afterward.

Ease of Startup: Moderate. You need money and a good eye for a property that needs primarily cosmetic work.

Range of Initial Investment: $30,000 and up, or credit for that amount, depending upon the real estate market in your area.

Time Commitment: Part- or full-time, depending on if you contract out some of the work or do it yourself.

Can You Run the Business From Home? Not unless you want to live there while you renovate.

Success Potential: Moderate. You need a background in construction and real estate, as well as money to invest.

How to Market the Business: Sell or rent the property through newspaper ads or realtors.

The Pros: It's extremely satisfying.

The Cons: It's hard work, and it might take some time to sell or rent the property.

Special Considerations: Keep an eye out for up and coming areas to make the most profit.

For More Information: National Association of the Remodeling Industry, 127 South Peyton, Alexandria, VA 22314.

Story of the Business

Andy Winskas was an electrician in Chicago, when he came down with asbestosis after working with asbestos for 23 years. He couldn't stay in Chicago because the pollution aggravated his condition, so he moved to Tallahassee. He began buying old houses with the intention of fixing them up and then renting them out.

"I had a little cash, so I looked for buildings that had been repossessed by the bank and would offer cash," he recalls. He specifically looked for buildings that weren't falling into the ground; ones that needed cosmetic and perhaps a bit of structural work to get them into shape. Some of the buildings had been on the market for awhile, which made an eager bank more apt to strike a deal. Winskas worked with real estate agents who represented the banks.

He bought three-bedroom ranches in the mid to upper $20,000s, some in the city itself and some on the outskirts. He concentrated on reasonable neighborhoods and tried to stay away from the higher-priced handyman's specials. He did some of the work on the houses himsel, but contracted sheetrock work or anything else that involved heavy labor. He put from $5,000-$15,000 into each house.

At first he thought he'd fix them up and rent them for income, which he did. But then he began to receive Social Security each month, which provided an income. "Also, I couldn't take the stress of renting, so I sold them," he recalls. He's in the process of selling the last few houses now as he can't do the work anymore.

Andy spent four to six months working on each house, though he rarely worked a full day. He'd then put them back on the market for $15-$20,000 more than he bought them for; they'd usually sell within four to six months. He liked the work because the hours were flexible and the work wasn't stressful. "You can play around with it and still make some money."

Winskas believes that to do well in this business one should have a background in real estate or experience in one of the building trades. Then there's no need to contract out a lot of the work. Though Winskas wasn't a tradesman, he did know how to fix buildings. So he had a background in both real estate and renovation.

"Buy it right, whether you want it to be a rental or you want to fix it up and sell it," he advises. It takes some cash to get into the business. A lot of real estate people do this, but many aren't good at fixing up places. If they have to contract it out, that eats into the eventual profit. "It's also stressful if you don't know what you're doing," reflects Winskas.

HOUSE SITTING

Home Sitting

Pat Richardson
San Diego, California

Ease of Startup	Moderate
Range of Initial Investment	$2,000/$8,000+
Time Commitment	Full-time
Can You Run the Business From Home?	Yes
Success Potential	Easy

Description of Business: A specialized agency that hires independent contractors to house- and pet-sit for clients.

Ease of Startup: Moderate. You'll need to develop a roster of on-call sitters and clients simultaneously.

Range of Initial Investment: $2,000 if you do it yourself; $8,000 and up if you buy a distributorship or franchise.

Time Commitment: Full-time; busier during holidays.

Can You Run the Business From Home? Yes

Success Potential: Easy. If you're located in an affluent area where people travel frequently, you'll be quite busy.

How to Market the Business: Brochures distributed to select neighborhoods, advertising, referrals and repeat business.

The Pros: It can be very lucrative in a populated, moneyed area.

The Cons: You can get burned out on dealing with people, both sitters and clients.

Special Considerations: You should enjoy juggling many tasks at once and like to work with a variety of people.

For More Information: *Sit & Grow Rich* by Pat Doyle (Dover, NH: Upstart Publishing, 1993); Pat Richardson, 5851 Antigua Blvd., San Diego, CA 92124; 619-576-4417.

Story of the Business

When Al Sutherland of Denver retired in 1972, he was surprised to find he had nothing to do. He figured there must be a lot of other seniors around in the same situation. He also saw that many retirees no longer smoked or drank and they preferred lifestyles that were largely stationary. So he put two and two together. He started a house-sitting referral agency using only retirees as sitters.

That was more than 20 years ago, and Al is still running Home Sitting from Denver. He's also sold house-sitting distributorships to people all over the country who run thriving agencies in their areas. His niece, Pat Richardson, began working at a San Diego agency run by Al's daughter; she took it over in 1984 after she retired from secretarial work.

Today, in an area with a population of two million, Pat has from 50 to 70 sitters on call. She books anywhere from 350 to 500 sitter days each month. The average length of time her sitters stay at each job is seven to 10 days. The charge for one day is $30, of which the sitter receives 40 to 50 percent, depending upon the difficulty of the assignment. Oh yes, and Pat grosses about $220,000 each year.

Running a house-sitting agency is much like running an employment agency, except it's more relaxed. One minute Pat might be on the phone with a couple who needs a house sitter to come stay for the weekend; when she hangs up, the next call might be from a retiree who saw her ad in the Yellow Pages and is wondering if she's looking for more sitters.

"It's a lot of phone work," she indicates. She prefers to do most of the work at the agency herself; she only has one part-time assistant who comes in for 20 hours a week. "One of the reasons I think my business is so successful is the personal touch: I service them myself," she explains. "People remember that."

In fact, most of Richardson's business comes from the phone book. She's listed in five different books in San Diego County under three different headings, so it's no wonder she spends most of her day on the phone.

When a prospective sitter calls, Pat sends out an application, which has questions about driving and smoking habits, work experience and references. After receiving the completed application, she calls the senior back for an interview, goes over a typical assignment and reviews the agency's policies. "Then I'll start them off with a small job to see how they do, and call the client to see if they're satisfied," explains Pat.

"I also take a new sitter with me when I visit a client, and the client will talk about what she expects from a sitter." House sitters cannot stay away from the house for more than a few hours at a time; they sleep there, and the client provides food for the time they're there.

Besides the phone book, sitters also refer their friends to Pat, and word of mouth is a big part of how clients find Home Sitters as well.

"In the beginning, we rented mailing lists of people who lived in the most affluent zip codes; we sent out thousands of brochures," she recalls. Now she gets a tremendous number of referrals and has a great repeat business. Most of Pat's clients need a house sitter twice a year, and some use her services six times a year. While on the job, a sitter is responsible for pet and plant care. In addition the sitter takes in the newspapers and mail and makes sure the house looks lived-in. As a sideline to Home Sitters, Pat has an eldercare business; she places people in homes to care for the elderly. She provides a variety of services ranging from companionship to preparing meals and doing personal care.

Besides running the agency, Pat also sells distributorships to the home-sitting business. A distributorship is different from a franchise: with a franchise, the purchaser pays a certain percentage of sales for support and advertising; with a distributorship, the buyer owns the business outright. The company sells the concept, an instruction manual, the necessary forms, three days of training and the right to purchase bond and liability insurance, which can sometimes be difficult to obtain when you're just starting out. They also offer continuing support. An agency Pat helped open in the middle of the retirement belt in Florida was going like gangbusters after its first six months.

IMPORT BUSINESS

Folklore Ethnic Imports

Tom Stammer
Port Townsend, Washington

Ease of Startup	Difficult
Range of Initial Investment	$5,000-$10,000
Time Commitment	Full-time
Can You Run the Business From Home?	Yes
Success Potential	Difficult

Description of Business: A business that specializes in bringing products to the U.S. from overseas, selling them wholesale or retail.

Ease of Startup: Difficult. You need to have a specific focus—items you're going to buy—after surveying the market.

Range of Initial Investment: $5,000-$10,000 and up.

Time Commitment: Full-time

Can You Run the Business From Home? Yes

Success Potential: Difficult. It's important to have the contacts set up on both ends before you start the business.

How to Market the Business: It depends on who you're selling your products to. For wholesale you need personal contacts. For retail you will depend on the community and advertising, sales and other promotions.

The Pros: You're helping people in less affluent countries make a living.

The Cons: It's difficult and expensive to deal with customs officials at both ends.

Special Considerations: If you are going to travel to countries yourself, you'd better know the culture and know people there.

For More Information: *Import/Export: How to Get Started in International Trade* by Carl A. Nelson (Liberty House).

Story of the Business

Tom Stammer had no idea when he joined the Peace Corps and traveled to Ecuador to help villagers improve the breed of sheep for wool that he would see the results of his efforts years later when he started a business.

Stammer runs an import business buying items mostly from South America. He focuses on handmade woolens like sweaters, caps, mittens, scarves, hats, wall hangings and tapestries. He travels to South America twice a year; each trip ranges from a week to a month. He buys directly from the people who make the yarn and the garments.

"I've been buying from the same people for 16 years," he relates. "I have lunch with them; they are my friends." The fact that Stammer speaks fluent Spanish helped to pave his entry into the community so many years ago.

"I go to a town and say I'd like 50 of a particular kind of sweater; then I go into the room where they keep all the yarn and pick out the colors." To buy crafts, he visits markets and buys them there. "They know me immediately when they see me," he says. "Sometimes I send a letter ahead of time so they know I'm coming. After all, I'm not the only person buying from them."

On an average trip, he buys 400-600 sweaters, 600 Panama hats and 1,000 wool caps. It's virtually impossible to drive from the U.S. to Ecuador, so Tom flies down and arranges to have the merchandise airfreighted back. "I bring a few things back in my bag if I want to get them here right away," he says, "I also tell them what I need for my next trip so they can have the items already made."

There are no guarantees that what he wants will be waiting upon his return. "I can tell them to make 150 sweaters of a certain kind; sometimes I'll get there and there will be only 80. Other times, I told them aqua, and to them aqua is another color," he warns. Sometimes he has to eat those mistakes, but sometimes he doesn't. "I just tell them I can't buy a sweater, and they're usually able to sell it to somebody else."

Unlike many importers, Stammer prides himself on paying the villagers a fair price for their merchandise. "We don't haggle," he says. "A villager tells me a price and I pay her. She know that if she gives me a fair price, I'll sell her sweaters faster and the faster I'll be back." He also bases the price on the Ecuadorean cost of living. In Quito, the capital, it costs about a nickel to ride the city bus.

Importers must add on the cost of their trip down and the freight. The Ecuadorean government also takes a cut before U.S. Customs gets its share. Stammer has a broker on the American end who helps with the paperwork because the rules are constantly changing.

Tom pays about $15 for a sweater. By the time all the expenses are taken into account, his investment is $20. Traditional markup in retail is 100 percent, so he charges $40 for it in his store. If the importer is a wholesaler, he'll charge a retail outlet $40; that will put it on the rack for $80.

He pays the knitters when he picks up the sweaters. "I go down to buy a lot of sweaters," he says. He pays with a personal check, but both the people and their bank know him.

Today he's seeing the fruits of his Peace Corps labors in the improved woolen goods he buys. "I decided I could continue to play Peace Corps by doing what I'm doing now," he admits. He feels this is the most worthwhile part of the business, which currently grosses $80,000 a year.

Stammer suggests that if importers are going to deal directly with people in a foreign country, they should learn the language. If you want to import to your own retail store, it's best to have a large variety of items.

"There was a store in Denver called Macchu Picchu that just sold Peruvian imports," recalls Tom. "I looked at the store and thought, 'He won't be here in six months.' I was right. It would be like a store selling one kind of tire."

INFORMATION SERVICE

Find People Fast

Jim Laux

St. Louis, Missouri

Ease of Startup	Difficult
Range of Initial Investment	$10,000
Time Commitment	Full-time
Can You Run the Business From Home?	Yes
Success Potential	Easy

Description of Business: A business that sells specific information to individuals and businesses.

Ease of Startup: Difficult. It can be expensive and take time to gather your sources.

Range of Initial Investment: $10,000 and up to set up a database.

Time Commitment: Full-time

Can You Run the Business From Home? Yes

Success Potential: Easy. This is the Information Age. If you are willing to do the legwork and target a specific audience, you'll do quite well.

How to Market the Business: Advertising, publicity, word of mouth.

The Pros: It can be satisfying to help people get the information they need.

The Cons: It's expensive to start.

Special Considerations: If you're good at collecting, organizing and disseminating information, you'll do well if you promote yourself to the right audience.

Story of the Business

In the spring of 1992 Jim Laux was looking for a business to start or buy, when he met Graham Bloy. Bloy was adopted as a child and had tried to find his biological parents a few years before he and Laux met. He succeeded only after many phone calls. In the process, he became aware of the vast amount of data that existed and could be used for a variety of purposes.

When Bloy met Laux, he said he suspected there were a lot of people in his situation: They were looking for someone but didn't know how to go about finding them.

The two men founded the company Find People Fast, which does just what it says it does. People call up with the name and any other identifying features of the person they're searching for. If they're lucky, Find People Fast will provide them with a telephone number and address.

The first thing Laux and Bloy had to do was sift through the available. They decided which sources to acquire and assembled their own database. "There are companies out there that gather this kind of data," explains Laux. Phone directories, direct mail lists and vehicle registrations are sources that are publicly available. Find People Fast makes that information more accessible to the average person.

"There are vast amounts of information out there, but it's not available to the general public," points out Laux. "What we're doing anyone can do with a computer, a modem and a subscription to any one of these databases. Gathering and supplying information is a very exciting business. The twist we've put on it is to act as an intermediary and help a lot of people who either don't have access or are computer illiterate."

Bloy is responsible for the technical aspects of the business, while Laux handles the business end of things. They share the marketing tasks; the primary promotional device they use is radio talk shows. They initially developed a database of radio talk show producers, but later started advertising in a publication called *Radio TV Interview*. When they appear on radio shows, Find People Fast performs complimentary searches for people who call in on the air. The success rate and the excitement this generates has them doing eight to ten radio talk shows a week. They are interviewed around the country from their phone at the office.

Their success rate depends on what kind of information the caller provides them with. If the caller just gives a name, and Find People Fast can locate one or more people with that name, the caller is able to find the person about 80 percent of the time. With a Social Security number, the rate of success increases to 90 percent.

Three different categories of people use the service: people looking for their relatives, veterans tracking down someone they served with, and classmates looking for friends from high school or college. People often call back to report about the people they've found, which is a side benefit of the business.

Laux and Bloy spent $300,000 for computer equipment, software, resources and marketing to set up the business with the help of outside investors; they have added more resources over the years. They've also developed some quality software programs for the business.

Laux suggests that people interested in starting an information service should research existing services and their charge. "Gathering and supplying information is a very exciting business," he reports.

INSURANCE AGENCY

New York Life Insurance Agent

Harry Campbell
Falls Church, VA

Ease of Startup	Easy
Range of Initial Investment	$2,000 and up
Time Commitment	Part- or full-time
Can You Run the Business From Home?	No
Success Potential	Moderate

Description of Business: Selling a variety of insurance—from one or from several companies—to individuals and businesses.

Ease of Startup: Easy. Start out by representing one company.

Range of Initial Investment: $2,000 and up.

Time Commitment: Part- or full-time

Can You Run the Business From Home? No

Success Potential: Moderate. Focusing on a community or a particular audience will help.

How to Market the Business: Direct mail, personal contacts and referrals.

The Pros: Most people carry several kinds of insurance; the need is out there.

The Cons: Insurance is an intangible product, and it may be difficult to convey its importance to a potential client.

Special Considerations: Insurance is basically a sales business; you should decide if you want to handle the ups and downs and constant rejections.

For More Information: Independent Insurance Agents of America, 127 South Peyton, Alexandria, VA 22314.

Story of the Business

When Harry Campbell retired from the military as an active duty Navy officer at the age of 43, he knew he wanted to put a solid 20 years into his next career. He looked at a number of franchise opportunities. He started with a New York Life franchise in August 1989 because they didn't require him to commit large amounts of money up front. In fact, Campbell paid no franchise fee, and the company even provided him with modest office space so he could start out. He went through training with the company, took and passed the state exam for his insurance license and bought a computer, which the company financed.

"I started by asking myself who I already knew who could use my product," he recalls. Six months later, having exhausted this list, he began to send out direct mail literature that boosted his contacts.

Campbell focuses on selling life and health insurance. "I made a commitment to work 15 hours a day on this from the beginning," he explains. "For someone who's making the transition from a military career, these hours are not news."

The business offers Campbell a constant challenge because there's always room to expand and improve what he does. As he's built up his customer base, he's gotten into areas that were new to him like estate planning. "I could expand into management with the company, but I'm leaning more toward continuing as an agent because of the independence it offers."

Harry is quick to mention that insurance sales is not for everyone—a fact that the company realizes as well. "There's a process every insurance company puts prospective agents through that helps both of them decide whether this is a good match or not," he explains. The first step is a career profile administered by the company. Campbell believes this is an accurate indication of a person's ability to succeed as an insurance agent. If you qualify and want to pursue the franchise, they train you and help you set up an office.

The most difficult part of the business can be dealing with the public. "It can be frustrating," remarks Campbell. "A person may say one thing and then do another. Or they'll decide to buy insurance; then they talk to Uncle Fred who says, 'You did what?' Even though he isn't familiar with the business, the rug is pulled out from under your deal. This just comes with the territory."

Campbell employs a full-time secretary. As he expands, he might need to hire more help. The first year of his business, he grossed $75,000; he reached $125,000 in 1993. One advantage of being an insurance agent is the ability to buy your own insurance at wholesale. "I'm one of my own best clients," he says.

Campbell could have started his own agency from scratch, but chose a franchise because he likes the idea of something proven. "I can go out there and people already know what it is," he explains.

Campbell is satisfied with the business he chose, even though frequently people aren't interested in talking with him about their life insurance programs. "I'm improving people's lives and their financial well-being," he says. "I'm dealing in an intangible product. That sometimes makes the value difficult to convey, but overall there's a lot of satisfaction."

INTERIOR DESIGNER

Tersa Agard
Boca Raton, Florida

Ease of Startup	Difficult
Range of Initial Investment	$20,000
Time Commitment	Full-time
Can You Run the Business From Home?	Yes
Success Potential	Difficult

Description of Business: An individual who consults with residential and commercial clients decorating their homes and offices.

Ease of Startup: Difficult. You have to go to school and become certified. It then can take a year or more to get your first client.

Range of Initial Investment: $20,000 for schooling and initial promotion.

Time Commitment: Full-time

Can You Run the Business From Home? Yes

Success Potential: Difficult. The great majority of Americans don't hire an interior designer. The field is saturated in many areas.

How to Market the Business: Publicity, word of mouth, referrals.

The Pros: If you like to decorate your home, working with other people to design their homes will be great.

The Cons: The business is highly competitive and jobs can be scarce.

Special Considerations: People with sufficient retirement income who can invest the time for school and getting the business off the ground are the best candidates for starting an interior design business in retirement.

For More Information: American Society of Interior Designers, 608 Massachusetts Ave. NE, Washington, DC 20002.

Story of the Business

"Everyone's convinced she has good taste, but of course that's impossible. Most people have to be guided by someone else," says Tersa Agard, an interior decorator who specializes in residential clients. "To be a good designer, you have to bypass trends and avoid tackiness. A good client/designer relationship uses their creativity to help the client design a place with their own distinct stamp."

Agard became a designer after working as an account executive and advertising manager for years. "I'd always decorated my friends' homes because they asked me to, and one day I figured, why not do it professionally? So I went back to school."

She concentrates on jobs where the client has a moderate budget. This gives her a bigger field to work with, since most decorators aim for the big-budget jobs. "I like to create, but I resent spending a fortune on something that's mediocre," she says.

Working three jobs at a time amounts to full-time work. Agard prefers to have only two jobs running at once. First, there's the consultation. "I speak with a client just enough to tell her what I do, but I've learned not to tell her too much," indicates Agard. "In the beginning, I told too much: they were able to go out and do it themselves." She discusses their budget, draws some floor plans and picks the fabric, which sets the color scheme.

Some clients hire her to do one room at a time or one room each year, while others have her redecorate their entire homes. After they select colors and decide on a floor plan, Tersa chooses furniture at showrooms and stores. "I go in advance and make a few selections and bring the client in to approve them," she says. "I'm selling a look, though, not individual pieces."

If she can't find a particular item she's looking for, like a wall unit or kitchen cabinets, she designs it and contracts it out. Such pieces can be made in eight weeks or less. Furniture ordered from a showroom can take 10 weeks to come in. "Sometimes a project can be completed in six months to a year. I can complete three rooms in the same time it takes to do one," she says. "Most of the time is spent waiting for everything to come in."

She prefers to avoid fads and trends, even though her clients may request them. "As soon as someone says something is in, I reply, 'Then it's going to be out.' I try to make my designs timeless."

Sometimes semantics get in the way, "For instance, a client tells me what she wants. I'll think she means one thing when she really means something else. Frequently, I take a magazine or book with me and ask the client to point out what she likes."

Agard makes some money from charging a retainer, which covers the cost of doing a floor plan. She makes the bulk of her fees from a percentage of what she buys for a client. For instance, if she buys fabric worth $1,000 at retail, she gets it at wholesale for $600. She then charges her client $800—making $200—and they both come out ahead.

"It's slow when you're first starting out. It helps to do your first job for free so people will hear about you," she advises. "Even then, it can take a long time until you get your first client."

INVENTOR

The Squirrel Stumper

Joseph Burleigh
Franklin, New Hampshire

Ease of Startup	Difficult
Range of Initial Investment	$20,000
Time Commitment	Part- or full-time
Can You Run the Business From Home?	Yes
Success Potential	Difficult

Description of Business: An individual who develops an idea and presents it to industry, retaining the rights of creation.

Ease of Startup: Difficult. You need a patent attorney to take you through the steps, which can be expensive.

Range of Initial Investment: $20,000.

Time Commitment: Part- or full-time

Can You Run the Business From Home? Yes

Success Potential: Difficult. It's very difficult and time-consuming to bring an idea to industry.

How to Market the Business: A contact at a manufacturer can help pave the way to final acceptance of your idea.

The Pros: It can be lucrative and pay off for many years.

The Cons: The competition is fierce, and there are no guarantees.

Special Considerations: A person who has an idea for an improvement on an existing product, or something entirely new and the patience and stamina to attempt to bring it to market may succeed as an inventor.

For More Information: National Inventors Foundation, 345 W. Cypress Street, Glendale, CA 91204. *Marketing Your Invention* by Thomas Mosley (Dover, NH: Upstart Publishing, 1992).

Story of the Business

"My business card reads 'Designer of bird feeders,'" says Joseph Burleigh, who developed and perfected a bird feeder that squirrels cannot penetrate. "I've been feeding birds since I was a child; wherever I've lived, I've had a bird feeder. Somewhere along the line I started thinking I could improve upon the bird feeders I bought, because I always found fault with them." In fact, he hasn't bought a bird feeder in more than 15 years since he started to make his own.

When he retired from the consumer electronics field, Burleigh had a lot of time on his hands. He had built a couple of bird feeders that were functional; but they weren't too attractive, so he built a few more.

When designing a product that could eventually end up on a store shelf manufactured by someone else, there's a certain procedure an inventor must go through. Even after the inventor thinks it's perfect, the manufacturer gets involved and often finds a fault.

"First I come up with an idea of how to improve a feeder's efficiency, then I construct a prototype and put it outside my window to see if it works," he explains. "If it does, then I go back to see if it can be manufactured and how. Then the manufacturer does its own independent testing, so I have to build several prototypes."

After Burleigh completed the prototypes, the manufacturer sent them to the ornithology department at Cornell University for further testing, which took a full year. "I had to make some changes because their squirrels were bigger than my squirrels," laughs Burleigh. "Then they sent some of them out to the West Coast for testing—where they have huge squirrels—and further modifications had to be made."

When he first came up with the idea, Joseph wanted to protect his design, so he went to a patent attorney with one of his working prototypes. Once the patent process was complete and the feeder had a patent pending on it, he began to approach manufacturers. Several were interested, but he chose a company called Hyde.

When Hyde became interested in the Squirrel Stumper, they asked for an option on the product. An option is an agreed-upon length of time for the manufacturer to do the research and testing necessary before going ahead with production. "It took a lot longer than I had expected," he recalls. "I thought it could be done in three months, and it was 15 until they accepted the design."

The full cost for retooling a machine to produce a new product is $50,000. With a catalog, packaging and distribution, the manufacturer is spending about $100,000 before the feeder even reaches the store shelves, so the company needs to be confident the product will sell. Even during the production process, Burleigh worked closely with the company because of flaws that may become apparent late in the game.

Burleigh thought about making the feeders himself, but he decided against it when he figured out the money necessary to hire employees. "Between benefits and taxes, you have to add 50 percent to an employee's salary," he explains. "I don't know how businesses do it."

He could have presented the idea to industry without a patent, but he chose not to. "I needed to patent it because it is unique. Without patent protection, anyone could make it," he points out.

With a successful product, the inventor is guaranteed a steady royalty income over the life of the patent that normally runs 17 years. Burleigh's royalty on the Squirrel Stumper through Hyde will range from three to ten percent, based on a negotiated unit price, which rises with inflation and volume. Royalties are paid quarterly. Burleigh estimates that if Hyde sells 10,000 feeders a year, he'll earn about a dollar on each feeder.

He advises prospective inventors to learn about what products already exist and research a patent thoroughly. "Though it's possible to get a patent without a lawyer, your chances of having the patent accepted improve by having a lawyer," he remarks. For the Squirrel Stumper, Burleigh says he's spent about $20,000 on legal and U.S. Patent Office fees.

"To be an inventor is a pretty hard term to define," he says, "There are more opportunities in inventing than people realize."

JEWELRY DESIGNER

Sandra Bunnell
Ann Arbor, Michigan

Ease of Startup:	Moderate
Range of Initial Investment:	$500-$1,000
Time Commitment:	Part- or full-time
Can You Run the Business From Home?	Yes
Success Potential:	Difficult

Description of Business: A business in which a person makes custom jewelry pieces for stores and individuals or designs pieces contracts the work and wholesales them.

Ease of Startup: Moderate. Design and make a few sample pieces and then take them around to local stores on consignment.

Range of Initial Investment: $500-$1,000 for materials.

Time Commitment: Part- or full-time

Can You Run the Business From Home? Yes

Success Potential: Difficult. This is a very competitive business. Your work needs to be different from what's already out there, and you need contacts.

How to Market the Business: Sales reps, shows, retail stores, word of mouth, referrals.

The Pros: Making jewelry probably won't seem like work. If your pieces are in demand locally, you'll be able to handle the business yourself.

The Cons: Around the holidays, you might need to work around the clock to meet deadlines. Also, the business is very competitive.

Special Considerations: To run a successful one-person operation, push the fact that you make your jewelry by hand.

For More Information: Jewelry Industry Council, 8 West 19 Street, 4th Floor, New York, NY 10011.

Story of the Business

After 20 years in the public relations business—five of which she spent running her own agency—Sandra Bunnell was looking for something new. "I wanted to do something where I wouldn't be so stressed out," she relates. Then she went to an antique show, bought a button she liked, took it home and made a necklace out of it. A friend bought it from her, and a light bulb went off in her head. "Maybe I could do this," she thought.

Bunnell took an afternoon off from running her agency to take a bead-stringing class at a local bead shop. "I got hooked," she recalls. That was in 1984. Bunnell began to invest in beads; then she began to sell her jewelry to friends and family. She now has a collection worth $5,000 of beads from all over the world.

In the beginning of 1993 she retired from her last PR job and began to make jewelry full-time. Throughout the nine years she made jewelry on the side, she concentrated on custom work and small runs that she could handle herself. Her jewelry is shown at four galleries in the Ann Arbor area, and she sells some pieces wholesale to a local shop. She also works with a clothing designer and has a client list of 2,000 that she sells to directly.

Now that she has more time, she's introducing a new product that she plans to wholesale nationwide. "The custom business is fun, but it doesn't sell in enough volume to support me," she explains. With this new venture, Bunnell will serve as the designer of a piece that will be manufactured by outside workers. She teamed up with a partner who has experience in the jewelry business and will rely on reps to sell her line to department stores.

Bunnell's already sold her work at Saks Fifth Avenue, where she gave her first show in the early '90s. She's found it's a tedious process to apply to sell a product at a high-end department store, and it may not be profitable. "First you visit their buyers and apply to become a vendor. They check you out and look at your work before placing an order. I wasn't happy about how I was promoted; I do a much better job," she says.

Bunnell says her biggest challenge is meeting deadlines, which she finds difficult because she works out of her home. "It's easy to get distracted, and my private life tends to intrude when I'm living and working in the same space," she relates. "Especially when I'm doing it all myself. That's why I'm glad to have a partner; it keeps me on track. This is the kind of business that once you get into the market, you have to be ready to fly."

If one of her reps visits a store that places an order for several hundred pieces, she has to be ready to get the jewelry out to them, or else they lose interest. One technique she has used is to assemble a case of about 30 sample pieces and visit the stores. If they place an order she does a limited run for the holiday season, handling it herself without contracting out the work.

Bunnell buys her materials wholesale from several trade shows where suppliers from all over the world come to sell their materials. She also buys stones and beads from mail-order catalogs. She would eventually like to go directly to countries like India and China, but it's not necessary because things are very accessible through direct mail and the shows.

The piece she's planning to make for a nationwide distribution costs between $10 and $20 in materials, and it takes about an hour for her to make one piece. She plans to wholesale it for $70, and a store will sell it for twice that. Even if her business grows, she'll still do any custom work herself, since it has her name on it. She uses semiprecious gemstone beads, shells, pearls, and crystals; she occasionally adds amber or wood. "My work is very organic looking," she remarks.

Bunnell grossed around $8,000 a year on her custom work when she was working full-time and only making jewelry five or ten hours a week. Once the wholesale business gets going, she expects to gross $70,000 the first year.

"It's more fun than marketing," she says of her business. "Sometimes it feels like I'm playing all day."

LAND DEVELOPER

The Farms at Quincy

William G. Crawford
Quincy, Florida

Ease of Startup	Difficult
Range of Initial Investment	$50,000+
Time Commitment	Part-time
Can You Run the Business From Home?	Yes
Success Potential	Difficult

Description of Business: Buying a plot of land and selling parcels, with or without houses on them.

Ease of Startup: Moderately difficult. You need to pass zoning and environmental restrictions if they exist in your area.

Range of Initial Investment: $50,000 and up, depending on the land and the area.

Time Commitment: Part-time

Can You Run the Business From Home? Yes

Success Potential: Difficult. With a real estate slump, this can be a very risky business.

How to Market the Business: Advertising, word of mouth, referrals.

The Pros: In the long run, land development can be a very profitable business if you've bought low in an up-and-coming area.

210

The Cons: It can take years to sell all the parcels. Local governments can be very picky in what they'll allow you to do.

Special Considerations: Real estate investors in it for the long haul can make a good investment.

For More Information: Realtors; local zoning boards; bank-owned property.

Story of the Business

"If I were starting out today, I probably wouldn't start," says Bill Crawford, a licensed real estate broker and certified building contractor who bought 535 acres of abandoned tobacco plantations in 1979 that he is still trying to sell off in parcels.

Quincy is 20 miles from Tallahassee, in a county that was strictly agricultural up until the mid-70s. Crawford bought two adjacent farms because one of them was directly across from a well-trafficed country club, which helped establish the style and tone of his development. In addition, he made an arrangement with the club so everybody who bought a parcel at The Farms at Quincy automatically receive a membership to the club.

One of the farms had nine barns, fourteen tenant houses and three farmhouses in all degrees of disrepair. He dismantled most of them, salvaged a few and converted two of the farm's irrigation ponds to swimming ponds.

Back then, the county was happy to have his business and was very supportive of what he planned to do with the land. Restrictions were few. Even so, Crawford placed basic restrictions on The Farms, since he'd seen other farms that had been developed where the land was badly abused.

"If you're going to develop a quality piece of land, you have to protect your buyers by establishing certain covenants," he says.

The zoning restrictions in the county stiffened considerably in the early '90s. Now there are environmental regulations and water management codes that developers have to meet. A new planning and zoning director was hired who is very concerned with a complex conservation plan handed down by the state. "There's one thing after another," says Crawford, "but I've gotten it to the point where the land is already over a lot of hurdles, and it's all ready to go."

His development contains both restrictive and protective covenants. Each buyer is restricted in what she can do with her land, but she's also protected by knowing her neighbors are restricted, too. Crawford sells nothing less than one acre, and some parcels go up to 30 acres. "Land is very expensive to develop if it's a very large piece and you have over fifty parcels," he remarks. "Then, you have to register with the state land board, unless you have a final plan that's already been accepted by the county."

He builds houses on some of the parcels, and prices them from $80,000 to $250,000. The land varies throughout the development; some parcels have open fields, while some have heavily wooded areas.

He originally bought the land for $760 an acre, and he sells a plotted and recorded acre for $3,500 to $6,500. In another part of the property, he's put in a water system; acres in this section can go for up to $12,000. Today, farms in the area go from $1,200 to $4,000 an acre, depending on the location.

Crawford markets the land by a little advertising and word of mouth. He also benefits from the development's location across from the country club, which has brought in a number of buyers of all ages.

"In a relatively undeveloped area, you can't forecast the growth," he indicates. "You can in a place like Miami, where you know where you'll be in three to five years. People who are looking to get into the business better be sure they know real estate first."

LANDLORD

R & L Enterprises

Ray Daniels
Boulder, Colorado

Ease of Startup	Difficult
Range of Initial Investment	$10,000+
Time Commitment	Part- or full-time
Can You Run the Business From Home?	Yes
Success Potential	Moderate

Description of Business: Buying houses and apartments to rent out. The business can also manage propertics for other landlords.

Ease of Startup: Difficult. You have to go through the red tape and legality of buying property, preparing it for rental and finding suitable tenants.

Range of Initial Investment: $10,000 and up, depending on the purchase price, the down payment and the condition of the house.

Time Commitment: Part- or full-time

Can You Run the Business From Home? Yes

Success Potential: Moderate. In a growing or well-populated area, your vacancy rate will be low.

How to Market the Business: Advertisements and referrals.

The Pros: Tax benefits are favorable to landlords. The more units you have, the benefits rise exponentially.

The Cons: Tenants may be unreliable; sudden repairs can be expensive.

Special Considerations: Buying and renting properties is a good investment. If you don't want to deal with tenants, you can hire a manager to collect rents and handle complaints.

Story of the Business

One of the best ways to have a steady income, build up an investment and reduce your tax bill without much effort is to become a landlord. That said, anyone who's ever been a landlord is well aware of the downside of renting out property. Tenants often pay rent late or not at all; there's an increased amount of wear and tear on the building; and there are unexpected bills from plumbers and electricians.

Ray Daniels of R & L Enterprises has renting down to a science. He started investing in property around Boulder back in the early '80s. He and his wife were working at IBM, and they were looking for a place to invest their money. They started with a single-family home in town. They accumulated several more over the next 10 years. When he took early retirement from IBM in 1991, Daniels decided to build upon his initial real estate portfolio.

In 1993 he owned 15 houses and three condominiums for rental, and he's looking to expand even more. Daniels doesn't want to rent apartments, since an on-site maintenance person is usually required and adds expense. Plus, he finds people who rent apartments tend to be more transient.

Daniels says that one of a landlord's most important responsibilities is to screen tenants carefully. "Houses tend to attract a more professional and responsible person," he indicates. "People who rent houses are usually more committed to the community." He finds out about how long they've been on their jobs, verifies their income and references from past landlords. "If I get good reports," he says, "then I'll rent to them."

His rule of thumb in renting to prospective tenants is that single professional men are best. He ranks married couples next, then married couples with a small child, single professional women and finally students. He chooses not to rent to students. "Students tend to party a lot, and there's more wear and tear on the house," he explains.

"In a college town like Boulder, I set up all my leases to go from September to September each year. When college students come back in the fall, they take up all the apartments and a lot of landlords jack up the rent," he says. "People in the categories I prefer don't have as many apartments to choose from."

Daniels also manages several properties in town for other landlords, for which he receives seven to 12 percent of the rent. He's developed a network of support people—plumbers and electricians—and over the years he's learned which ones are reliable and which aren't. Daniels doesn't have a superintendent. Instead, he sends out a letter with the names and numbers of these support people to each tenant. Whenever a tenant has a problem in a house, they call one of the names on the letter. Since Daniels has already established a relationship with the plumbers and electricians, they know they're going to get paid.

He says he only spends about 10 or 15 hours a week managing his property. "Once you get it set up, it pretty much runs itself."

When he bought his first house—an 1,100-square-foot, two-bedroom ranch house, he paid $32,000. In 1993 similar houses were selling for $125,000 and up. He's still buying houses because the rent can run from $1,000 to $1,200. "Because I have houses with positive cash flow, I can carry some houses with negative cash flow for long-term investments and writeoffs," he remarks. Daniels says the business grosses approximately $180,000. He still remembers buying the first house.

"It was a big hurdle for me to buy that first house because I didn't have any experience, and without knowledge there's perceived risk," he remarks.

"Spend some time talking with people who already own properties to find out which parts of town are the growing areas. Buy a small house on a side street in a neighborhood that's pretty nice, learn how to screen tenants and look at it as a long-term investment," Daniels advises.

LLAMA RAISING

Pleasant Bay Llama Keep

Joan Yeaton
Addison, Maine

Ease of Startup	Moderate
Range of Initial Investment	$100,000
Time Commitment	Full-time
Can You Run the Business From Home?	Yes
Success Potential	Moderate

Description of Business: Llamas are a popular, versatile animal that require a minimum of attention. You can sell their fleece, use males for stud service, sell young llamas and breed females or use them for trekking.

Ease of Startup: Moderate. If you already have sufficient land—three to fours llamas per acre is average—all you need is to buy the llamas and build a shelter.

Range of Initial Investment: $100,000 if you already have the land; you need a minimum of ten animals to get into breeding.

Time Commitment: Full-time

Can You Run the Business From Home? Yes

Success Potential: Moderate. The bigger the herd, the better. This allows you to concentrate on more than one specialty.

How to Market the Business: Advertising, brochures, word of mouth, agricultural shows and fairs.

The Pros: Llamas are intelligent, loving animals—they only spit at each other.

The Cons: Llamas range from $500 to $5,000 for males and from $4,000 to $11,000 for females. Fancy llamas can cost $50,000. With high prices on a nonessential item, your income can be sporadic.

Special Considerations: Most people aren't familiar with llamas; llama breeders and sellers have to act as ambassadors to the public.

For More Information: International Llama Association, 2755 Locust Street, Suite 114, Denver, CO 80222; 303-756-9004; *Llama Banner Magazine*, 714 Poyntz, Suite B, Box 1968, Manhattan, KS 66502.

Story of the Business

Joan Yeaton and her husband, Lee, were living in Exeter, New Hampshire. He had an insurance agency, and she had a real estate firm, 10 llamas and not enough time for any of it. "Wouldn't it be nice," they thought one day, "to have enough time to enjoy them and not have to go to an office?" They began to think about how they could pull this off. Before they knew it, the Yeatons had sold everything except their llamas and furniture and were building a house on the seacoast of Maine, less than an hour from the Canadian border.

Joan had been exposed to llamas when she was in Peru years earlier, and she fell in love with them. "I loved the idea of raising llamas because I didn't have to slaughter or eat what I raised in order to make a living from it," she says. "Because you don't have to kill them, you can put a huge emotional investment in them, and it pays off."

In Exeter, she started with two animals and grew from there. Today she has around 30 llamas at any time; 15 to 19 of them breeding females. People bring their llamas to the Yeaton's farm to be bred; stud fees range from $600 to $1,000. Joan sells females and males; their prices depend on their color and blood lines. Young males go from $500 to $1,500, while proven males—those who have fathered—sell for $2,000 to $5,000. Females that haven't given birth cost $4,000 to $5,000; Joan sells topflight bred females—sold when they are pregnant—for up to $11,000. She guarantees a live birth with her bred females. If the baby dies, she will breed the mother again for the customer for no charge. The Yeatons chose to specialize in selling llamas in the $5000 to $10,000 range because they didn't have the money to invest in expensive llamas. They also thought there would be more demand for moderately priced llamas. "We were targeting people like ourselves," remarks Joan.

Joan also runs a three-room bed & breakfast out of her home that looks out onto Pleasant Bay and says she frequently sells llamas to guests who visit the B & B. "Many come to the B & B not knowing what to expect from the llamas, but they'll go out for a walk with the llamas and come back a convert," she reports. "We just sold a llama to people who came to the B & B four years ago. It's amazing how something I did a few years ago will come to fruition. In a business like this, you're in it for the long haul, since the lifespan of a llama can range from 15 to 30 years."

Though there are more people raising llamas today than when she started in 1988, the prices have leveled off. This has allowed many people to buy llamas who couldn't afford it previously.

Joan advises people who are interested in raising llamas to start slowly and expect to work hard. Some weeks she works 35 hours. She spends several hours a day with the llamas; then she does peripheral things like working in the barn and mending fencing. On some days she spends all day with the animals.

She suggests people visit a variety of llama farms to pick the style that would fit them best. "It depends on what you think you can live on," she indicates. "If we thought we needed $100,000 a year to live on, we wouldn't be able to support ourselves. Instead we sold our businesses, took a low mortgage and planned to live relatively simply. We put our money into the buildings and increasing the herd." The Yeatons also grow their own food and try to be as self-sufficient as possible.

Besides the B & B, potential customers find out about Pleasant Bay through advertisements in local papers and local trade publications, but most of their business comes through word of mouth and referrals. Maine has its own association for llama breeders, which has 35 members. They meet for a potluck supper several times a year, sharing stories and advice. The group also has a field day every June where the general public is invited; thousands of people attend.

The Yeatons gross anywhere from $20,000 to $35,000 a year from their breeding services. "You can't expect to make a killing in llamas," advises Joan. "we look at it as more of a lifestyle."

MAGAZINE PUBLISHER

Choices Magazine

Gloria Bursey
Grand Rapids, Michigan

Ease of Startup	Moderate
Range of Initial Investment	$3,000+
Time Commitment	Full-time
Can You Run the Business From Home?	Yes
Success Potential	Difficult

Description of Business: A publication on a specific topic that appears anywhere from biweekly to quarterly.

Ease of Startup: Moderate. If you have a desktop computer system, you can write, lay out and print an issue in a short period of time. Distribution—free or paid—frequently requires outside help.

Range of Initial Investment: $3,000 and up.

Time Commitment: Full-time. Many publishers focus on editorial and production, hiring an outside sales staff for advertising.

Can You Run the Business From Home? Yes

Success Potential: Difficult. Many magazines are unable to draw the amount of advertising and/or subscribers necessary to cover costs.

How to Market the Business: With sufficient distribution, trades with radio stations, promotional and event tie-ins with other businesses and a quality publication.

The Pros: You're viewed as a voice of the community.

The Cons: It's hard work. Collecting money from advertisers can sometimes be difficult.

Special Considerations: In the last decade, magazines have become more narrow. Find a topic and an audience that's not being addressed.

For More Information: *The Magazine: Everything You Need to Know to Make it in the Magazine Business*, by Leonard Mogel (Globe Pequot); Magazine Publishers of America, 575 Lexington Avenue, New York, NY 10022.

Story of the Business

When Gloria Bursey decided to stop publishing a regional women's magazine called *Glory*, she told herself she never wanted to publish another magazine as long as she lived. Then she became a widow. She had no choice but to start looking for work, keeping her promise to herself in mind. "I was known as a writer in this area, but no one wanted to hire me," she remembers. "It seems they would rather hire somebody younger, to whom they didn't have to pay as much money."

At the same time she looked around for advice about retirement and aging issues but didn't have much luck. "What I saw out there didn't tell me very much," she recalls, "and people are living longer and have much more retirement time than before." She thought about breaking her promise.

Bursey began by talking with seniors around town to find out what they would like to see in a magazine geared toward them. She also met with prospective advertisers. She wrote up some columns and features and designed the layout on a Macintosh computer—when she published *Glory*, she had to rely on typesetters. Before she knew it, she was publishing another magazine.

Choices is a 16-page monthly newsmagazine printed on paper that's higher quality than newsprint. She prints about 23,000 copies each month and has a circulation of about 40,000, due to people lending their copies to others. Most of her sales staff of five are retired, and she pays them a 23 percent commission.

Though Bursey still writes the editorial and an occasional article, she relies on outside writers to fill the pages. She's never had a problem finding reliable writers, since people will write or call to suggest stories. "*Choices* has a mix of columns and features," explains Bursey. "We recently featured Ms. Senior Michigan, who's in her 70s." The magazine also includes a financial column, a travel story, a health column and stories geared towards singles. Though she is starting to include some controversial stories in the magazine—about hospices and Medicaid—she tries to keep the tone upbeat. "I think too many papers are negative," she points out.

There's also a calendar of local events and a column by a local man who's 93. She pays her writers $25 for a column, $35 for a short article and up to $125 for a long story.

Each issue is free. Bursey distributes the magazine in over 200 places within a 60-mile radius, including grocery stores, department stores, restaurants and senior centers. Even though it's a free publication, she still strives to make the cover inviting. It started out in black-and-white and is now four-color.

"I started the magazine because I'm a writer," she says, but admits she was a little bit ahead of herself when she started the magazine because businesses weren't used to gearing their advertising toward people over 50. Now they're used to the idea. The magazine has a 50-50 advertising to editorial ratio: each page contains half ads and half editorial. In general, the smaller the publication is, the more you have to load it with advertising. "As it gets larger," Bursey points out, "you make more money and you can have more editorial."

Advertisers are billed when the issue comes out. Some take a while to pay, however, and she turns some over to an attorney for collection. "Our policy is if they don't pay by the second ad, they can't place another ad until they've paid. If it's a new business, I suggest we get payment ahead of time."

Bursey also writes a column for a local newspaper, which she is trying to syndicate to more mainstream area papers. She also does some photography for the magazine, working out of her home. She's looking into the possibility of expanding *Choices* to cover the entire state, but then she'd have to approach a completely different type of advertiser to make it fly.

"I love publishing because it keeps me active in the community," reports Bursey. "I'm in the center of everything because I'm the media."

She thinks magazine publishing would be a great business for a couple to run, with one keeping the books and the other selling ads. "Even if you aren't a writer, you can always find people to write for you. After all it's impossible to do everything. People are aging more slowly these days—I call it Star Trek time, or time that we didn't think we'd have. But I meet editors who do everything, and I don't know how they do it."

MAIL-ORDER FOOD BUSINESS

The Extended Family

Gretchen Cryer
New York City

Ease of Startup	Difficult
Initial Investment	$300,000
Time Commitment	Full-time
Can You Run the Business From Home?	No
Success Potential	Moderate

Description of Business: Selling food through the mail.

Success Potential: Moderate. It's necessary to set yourself apart from the thousands of other mail-order food companies.

Ease of Startup: Difficult. Since you're conducting interstate commerce, you need to work with the Department of Agriculture for approval.

Range of Initial Investment: At least $300,000 for a major business.

Time Commitment: Full-time

Can You Run the Business From Home? No.

How to Market the Business: Through publicity, direct mail, some advertising and word of mouth.

The Pros: It can be very rewarding.

The Cons: It's expensive, takes time to get established and will consume all your time.

Special Considerations: If you can find a niche not being filled in the specialty food business—whether it's a regional specialty or a certain audience—and can persist for several years, you'll do well.

For More Information: *From Kitchen to Market* by Stephen Hall (Dover, NH: Upstart Publishing, 1992); Mail Order Association of America, 1877 Bourne Court, Wantagh, NY 11793.

Story of the Business

A few years ago Gretchen Cryer's parents became ill. They were in Indiana, and she was in New York, where she's had a successful career as a playwright and actress, her most significant credit was the musical *I'm Getting My Act Together and Taking It on the Road.* She was able to manage occasional visits to her parents every two months. Her brother was taking care of her parents, but wasn't a very good cook. As a result, their appetites were flagging. They were losing weight since they couldn't go to the store by themselves and couldn't cook. Gretchen responded by cooking for them herself and shipping the food to them via Federal Express.

"I cooked about two weeks' worth of meals in one weekend, froze them, packed them in dry ice and sent them out. It changed their lives," she recalls. "The psychological effect was as important as the nutritional effect."

She'd been cooking for them for almost nine months when her mother suggested she turn it into a business. Other people echoed her mother. One Christmas, while she was cooking for her parents, Cryer cooked up similar packages for friends. One gave her package to an aunt, another gave hers to a daughter who'd just had a baby.

The Extended Family was born after a long gestation period, and not without a lot of headaches. Cryer needed to build a special kitchen according to USDA regulations. Everything—from each recipe to the label—had to be okayed by a representative of the department. The bureaucratic red tape, in itself, took months. Then she had to raise enough capital from banks and private investors to fund the project. The 3,200-square-foot building cost $225,000 to build; the land was $28,000. By the time the first batch of meals was prepared by a crew of two in June, 1991, two years had elapsed.

The first month, The Extended Family had 50 customers who purchased packages that cost $95 and included seven full meals for two people. Each meal includes an entree, two side dishes, dessert and bread. The entrees range from chicken pot pie to beef stew to flounder stuffed with crabmeat—"comfort food" as Gretchen describes it.

Why did she choose to invest so much money from the beginning only on projected sales? "I knew if we started with a small kitchen and grew quickly, we'd be lost. I decided we needed to start with a larger facility," she explains. By Christmas of 1992 the kitchen was turning out 1,250 packages a month.

From the beginning Cryer put much of her effort into building the market. "After all, this is a new idea. There was no one else in the country doing this, so we've gotten a lot of press in major newspapers and magazines," she reports.

But there have been problems. The first week the kitchen was in operation, half the packages were spoiled because they weren't insulated well enough and there was a massive heat wave.

Cryer also thought the business would grow more quickly than it has. "I thought if people started with us, they'd order every single week," she indicates. Instead, her market has consisted more of people who give a week of meals to somebody else for a special occasion. As a result, she's had to go after first-timers more aggressively, due to the lack of repeat business.

She markets primarily through publicity. At the beginning she hired an independent consultant who was just starting her career, so her price was lower than established PR firms. Cryer, who has spent her life in the theater as a playwright and performer, was familiar with the media. Her son, John Cryer, is an investor in the company; as an actor he has a certain visibility, which she says has been another factor in getting exposure.

She's also considering other strategies, like placing advertising in major newspapers, using direct mail and placing an ad in the AT&T 800 phone directory. Her biggest challenge is getting the volume up to a steady level year-round. Winter is a busy time for The Extended Family, because gift certificates are being redeemed and more people are house-bound. In April business starts to drop off until September, when it picks up again.

The business grossed $700,000 in 1993, serving approximately 100,000 meals. There are now 20 employees in all, with 15 in the kitchen.

Cryer eventually wants to expand to other areas of the country. "It's very rewarding to get letters from people thanking us for being here," she relates. "This is a growing segment of society. I'm helping people stay independent as long as they possibly can."

MASSAGE THERAPIST

Ginny Keith
Scottsdale, Arizona

Ease of Startup	Difficult
Range of Initial Investment	$5,000
Time Commitment	Part- or full-time
Can You Run the Business From Home?	Yes
Success Potential	Moderate

Description of Business: An individual who offers massage through other businesses and through private practice.

Ease of Startup: Difficult. You need specialized training that can take 18 months or more.

Range of Initial Investment: $5,000 for training and equipment.

Time Commitment: Part- or full-time

Can You Run the Business From Home? Yes

Success Potential: Moderate. Your chances are better in an urban area.

How to Market the Business: Advertising, word of mouth, referrals.

The Pros: The opportunities are unlimited in most areas of the country.

The Cons: Business can be sporadic. Few people feel they require a weekly massage.

Special Considerations: If you're physically strong and enjoy contact with other people, this is a good business.

For More Information: *Massage Magazine*, POB 1500, Davis, CA 95617.

Story of the Business

Ginny Keith was living in California and had been working in insurance for 20 years. She was bored. In 1988 she was involved in a serious car accident that turned her life around. "I had chiropractic treatment, and my chiropractor suggested massage to me," she recalls. "It was so beneficial that I took an introductory class, and there was no turning back."

Licensing requirements vary from state to state, and even from one town to another. The town where she lived in California when she attended massage school required 500 hours of classroom training, while others only required 100. In fact, since she's been living in Arizona, the requirements in Phoenix have gone from 100 to 500 hours. Before moving to Arizona, Keith completed the program at the Monterey Institute of Technology in Carmel Valley in just over 15 months. She attended part-time. Even if she hadn't needed the 500 hours to become certified, Ginny would have taken the full course anyway. "I needed to know more," she relates. "I didn't want to be a run-of-the-mill massage therapist."

Keith does both massage therapy and neuromuscular massage. "With regular massage, you can pretty much do what you feel, it's very intuitive," she indicates. "Neuromuscular massage is both more technical and specific, since I'm working with injured people."

She does primarily neuromuscular therapy at a medical clinic three days a week where she works in conjunction with other therapists. She spends one day a week doing massage for visitors to an area resort spa; she also has a number of clients in private practice. She earns $26 a session at the clinic; $12 an hour at the spa; she charges $40 for a private session with her own clients; if she travels to their home, she charges $55.

"It's more practical to have my own clients so I can work smarter, not harder," she says. She's drawn up a brochure and a business card, which she distributes wherever she can. She recently bought a condo and sent out a letter to her neighbors. "When I was in insurance, I did telemarketing. I was used to selling the product, but it's really hard to sell myself." She grosses about $25,000 a year from her work. Her goal is to work shorter days and still keep her income at the same level.

Ginny says the opportunities for a massage therapist are unlimited. A therapist can go anywhere with the training. "I moved from California to Arizona, knew nobody here and went right to work," she says.

She advises aspiring massage therapists to take as much training as possible and to be willing to market themselves. "You need to be physically strong, have a nurturing attitude and a desire to help other people," she adds.

"When I first started my training, the energy and contact with other people is what I particularly liked. I get as much from giving a massage as the clients do in receiving. It's a wonderful feeling to make people feel good, and it's so different from insurance."

MOVING SERVICE

The Golden Touch

Renee Bressler and Sandra Russell
Birmingham, Alabama

Ease of Startup	Easy
Range of Initial Investment	$1,000
Time Commitment	Part- or full-time
Can You Run the Business From Home?	Yes
Success Potential	Easy

Description of Business: Helping people move by performing services from lining up a moving company to unpacking and decorating the new home.

Ease of Startup: Easy. Line up services and suppliers to help you do your job, market yourself, and you're in business.

Range of Initial Investment: $1,000.

Time Commitment: Part- or full-time

Can You Run the Business From Home? Yes

Success Potential: Easy. With America's mobile population, and people who hate to deal with moving, this business is in demand.

How to Market the Business: Advertising, publicity, word of mouth, referrals.

The Pros: It's satisfying; people are grateful for the help.

The Cons: Moving companies frequently break items; handymen and other help can be unreliable.

Special Considerations: People who are organized and detail-oriented and who like to help people are good candidates for this business.

Story of the Business

In 1988 Sandra Russell's mother was moving from her big family house into a two-bedroom apartment in a retirement community, and she needed some help. So Sandra and her friend Renee Bressler decided to take matters into their own hands from start to finish.

"First we had to get rid of a lot of her stuff because it wouldn't all fit in her new place," reports Bressler. "But more importantly, it was vital that her mother feel comfortable and happy where she went."

So Bressler and Russell made all the arrangements. They found a moving company, took some of her things to a consignment shop, hired a decorator and filled out change of address cards. "The most important thing was to bring her into an apartment that was decorated, ready to live in and filled with the things she wanted to have with her the most," relates Bressler.

Russell's mother told everyone what the two women had done. It wasn't long until one of her friends asked the two women to provide the same service for her. "From that point, it was all word of mouth," says Bressler. In the beginning they moved a woman who had no children living in the area, and her family was grateful for the help.

"The business amounts to a lot of phone calls and footwork," indicates Bressler. "We're like surrogate children, and we hold their hands through the whole thing. We arrange for them not to be there for the move. When they come into their new place, everything is arranged, and they don't have to do a thing."

Most of the people the women deal with either don't have children living in the area, or the children don't want to be bothered. Sometimes their children are too busy working and raising their families to be able to handle a move. Some of their clients make their own moving arrangements, but The Golden Touch has people available to do everything from wrapping china to arranging the closets.

Bressler and Russell each put up $1,000 to get business cards printed and to handle the expenses on the first job before they were paid by the client. They now take a deposit at the beginning and list the tasks they'll handle on a contract. "We try to base our charge on an hourly rate. We keep it as reasonable as we can because many people are living on fixed incomes," explains Bressler. "It also depends on how much work is involved, but generally our time is worth $50 an hour. The average job comes to about $2,000." The busiest time of year is spring and fall, when they're swamped.

Bressler and Russell make the initial arrangements over the phone with a client. The actual work is done within the course of one week. They also do a follow-up the week after the person is settled.

When a person is moving to the area from far away, they make the arrangements through the retirement home. "On the first visit, we'll take the client around and show them the best places. Then the client contacts us and we arrange to do everything once all their stuff is moved here," says Bressler. "We set up the telephone and appliances. If they have a huge TV and need a smaller one, we go out and get one for them."

The biggest challenge of The Golden Touch is dealing with people who have a hard time parting with anything. "They're moving into tight quarters, but it's hard to convince them to pare down their possessions."

They've been called about franchising their service, but they don't want to get any larger than they are now; they gross about $60,000 a year. "I think a lot of people should be doing this. It's a very useful job to do for people, and it's very satisfying," remarks Bressler.

MUSIC HALL

Bargemusic

Olga Bloom
Brooklyn, New York

Ease of Startup	Difficult
Range of Initial Investment	$100,000
Time Commitment	Full-time
Can You Run the Business From Home?	No
Success Potential	Difficult

Description of Business: A business—sometimes nonprofit—that presents musical concerts and recitals.

Ease of Startup: Difficult. You need a lot of money up front, permits from your city and lots of time to build your reputation.

Range of Initial Investment: $100,000 and up.

Time Commitment: Full-time

Can You Run the Business From Home? No

Success Potential: Difficult. If you offer something different from what's already out there, you'll have a chance. Otherwise, attendance can fall in a poor economy.

How to Market the Business: Advertising, publicity, word of mouth, referrals, direct mail.

The Pros: It's fun and enjoyable to stage performances and make people happy with music, especially in an unusual location.

The Cons: It's very expensive, you have to meet local building codes, and it can be difficult to organize the musicians.

Special Considerations: If you love music and have deep pockets, it can be a thrill to stage live performances.

Story of the Business

Olga Bloom says the idea for Bargemusic began the day she was born, but quickly amends that to the age of four when she took her first violin lesson. She became proficient in the instrument, winning several scholarships. She managed to carve out a career as a professional musician in the days when live music was more prosperous in New York.

"In the arts section of the newspaper, there would be three or four pages of recitals and concerts, like the apartment rental section today," she recalls. "Those pages have vanished because people in the business found that having a handful of electronic instruments played by people who may be sincere—but not necessarily skilled or classically trained—is better for the bottom line."

She started Bargemusic—live music performed on a barge anchored right under the Brooklyn Bridge with a fabulous view of lower Manhattan—as a revolt against the burgeoning trends in music. Bloom makes it sound like starting Bargemusic was easy. "I went to Jersey and bought a barge," she says. "I've always been a musician. I'm happy I was able to make enough money to buy a barge." She bought a coffee barge for $10,000; it was one of several that had been retired-before its time. "But I wasn't so charmed in the beginning when I was sweeping out coffee beans," she adds.

When she first acquired the barge, it did not occur to her to get permission from the city to anchor it. "I'm one of those people that goes forward with the conviction that in due time, everything will be revealed to me and an answer will be found," she remarks. "They came after me, of course, and they still do." Bloom had to bring the barge into compliance. This involved providing toilets with wheelchair turn-arounds, a sewage treatment plant, a sprinkler system and two fire exits. "We are now an exemplary example of what city planners call floating structures," she explains. Every two years, she has to bring the barge into drydock for maintenance and inspection.

Where did she get the idea for Bargemusic? "Like any idea, it doesn't come from carrier pigeon," she says. "Rather, it grew out of the experiences of my life. I grew up in Boston and was very aware of the pull of the sea."

Two performances a week are held year-round. Bargemusic has 130 seats, and an annual budget of $600,000. She has a music director who finds musicians for the various performances. "Musicians who play here have a great deal of happiness," says Bloom. "All have competed in world competitions, and they perform with relatively few rehearsals." Olga has run Bargemusic since 1977; she finds the musicians give their utmost to a receptive audience.

Bargemusic is a nonprofit organization. Bloom spends a lot of her time fund-raising. She sends a calendar of upcoming concerts to a mailing list of 14,000 every season, and she holds candlelight supper concerts once a month to raise money for the foundation. She also offers the premises to other groups who need a place to meet. "This has endeared us to the community, and because we're concerned for them, they're concerned for us," she adds. She's also planning to establish an endowment.

The musicians enjoy performing in an unusual setting, though sometimes they have a hard time maintaining their equilibrium when another boat goes by and a surge occurs. "Nobody ever stopped playing. Once it was so severe that the piano rolled into the lap of the pianist," she recalls. "But this is the touch of terror that reigns here."

MUSICIAN

Grayson Babcock
Fort Atkinson, Wisconsin

Ease of Startup	Difficult
Range of Initial Investment	$0
Time Commitment	Part- or full-time
Can You Run the Business From Home?	No
Success Potential	Difficult

Description of Business: A professional musician performs solo or travels with bands locally and nationally.

Ease of Startup: Difficult. Unless you've been playing for years and have many contacts, forget it.

Range of Initial Investment: $0.

Time Commitment: Part- or full-time

Can You Run the Business From Home? No

Success Potential: Difficult. Extremely competitive; even if you're good, there are no guarantees.

How to Market the Business: Word of mouth, referrals, getting an opportunity to play.

The Pros: Getting paid to play music is a dream.

The Cons: Because it's a dream, there are frequently hundreds of people vying for one spot.

Special Considerations: If you love to make music, have the talent to back it up and are willing to make endless contacts in the business, give it a shot.

For More Information: Musicians National Hot Line Association, 277 E. 6100 South, Salt Lake City, UT 84107.

Story of the Business

After he spent 35 years as band director at Fort Atkinson High School, Grayson Babcock retired to focus on what had been a sideline during all the years of his "regular" job. He began playing the saxophone, flute and/or clarinet in various combos and dance bands year-round—just on the weekend or during school vacations.

"I probably play more now because I can travel, but music has been both my hobby and my vocation all my life," he remarks. Babcock's played with several big-name swing, jazz and big bands like Guy Lombardo, Ken Garber and the Russ Morgan Orchestra. In 1992 he spent almost half the year on the road. He enjoyed it, but he's very happily married and wants to stay so. "Being on the road is not conducive to a happy marriage," he reports.

The three factors that have helped him succeed are knowing the right person, being in the right place at the right time and being able to do the job. "Some of the opportunities came my way because of a substitute who sat in a band I played in; he frequently played in other bands and liked what I was doing. He recommended me to another band-leader he worked with," Grayson recalls. "At my level, I could get on the phone and call a lot of different directors, but that doesn't mean much. It works when someone recommends me and the director has respect for their judgment."

Babcock has friends all over the country who play in bands. "I consider myself a people person. I can get along with anyone for at least a short period of time. People who do the hiring like the fact that I'm not a prima donna or a troublemaker," he reports.

He receives offers for more work than he can handle. "A lot of times, bands call when they need a sub at the last minute," he adds. Babcock is primarily a sax player. He is also proficient on the alto, tenor and baritone sax; many sax players just specialize in one. He also plays clarinet, bass clarinet and flute. The variety of instruments enhances his opportunities for work. He turns down a lot of work because he limits his travel or because he already has another job scheduled.

Since his retirement, he goes on the road with a band for a week or two; sometimes his wife accompanies him. Most of the time, the band he's playing with plays at a different place each night. "We stay in a different hotel or motel every night. Sometimes we do what we call a hit-and-run; we pack down after the show and head for the next town, which may be 400-600 miles away," he says. Some of the buses have bunks so the musicians can sleep.

In 1993 alone Babcock played with 12 different bands. He says the music isn't challenging, but trying to stay healthy on the road is. "We often go without eating before we play because we arrive late," he reports. "It's not an easy life."

But that doesn't seem to dissuade people from wanting to live it. Ironically, the more famous the band, the worse the pay. Babcock has played with the Glenn Miller Band, which gets more bookings than any other big band because of its nostalgia value. "But they also pay the worst," he says, citing the value of having the name on your resume. "If you complain or do something wrong, they have a line of people a mile long who'd be happy to take your place.

"The music schools are putting out people left and right, and there are no opportunities for them," he continues. "These people want badly to play, and there are so many of them that the bands don't have to pay much." Substitutes get paid more than regular members, and some bands pay travel time and car expenses. Babcock gets paid an average of $150 for one night's work, which consists of a three- or four-hour job with a couple of breaks. Some bands pay for lodging; others deduct $12 a night from a member's paycheck.

You don't do it for the money. There are no medical or dental benefits, and the conditions are frequently hard. Why does Babcock stick with it?

"I love doing it," he says. "It's a way to keep doing something I thoroughly enjoy and make some money at it, besides."

MYSTERY NOVELIST

Chet Oksner
West Bath, Maine

Ease of Startup	Difficult
Range of Initial Investment	Negligible
Time Commitment	Part- to full-time
Can You Run the Business From Home?	Yes
Success Potential	Difficult

Description of Business: Writing mystery novels sold in the U.S. and overseas.

Ease of Startup: Difficult. Have you ever tried to write a novel?

Range of Initial Investment: Negligible if you already have a computer.

Time Commitment: Part- to full-time

Can You Run the Business From Home? Yes

Success Potential: Difficult. This an extremely hard-to-break-into business.

How to Market the Business: You'll need a literary agent to sell your work, since most major publishers do not look at unsolicited manuscripts.

The Pros: It's extremely satisfying if you make it.

The Cons: You may never make a penny. The competition—even among published writers—is fierce.

Special Considerations: If you have a wild imagination and love to write, give it a shot; but don't expect it to sell.

For More Information: Mystery Writers of America, 17 E. 47th St., 6th Floor, New York, NY 10017.

Story of the Business

Just the way Chet Oksner, author of two published mystery novels, answers a simple question makes it obvious he's a great storyteller.

When asked how he started writing novels, he responds that he got fed up with practicing law and decided to take a year off. "My wife, Dorothy, quit her job as a bank officer in Santa Barbara, where we lived, and we drove to Florida and bought and fixed up a boat," he says.

"During this sabbatical on a boat, I was going to write this great novel, and by the time I got home, I'd send it off and see what happened. Then I'd go back to work. By the time we got back 18 months later, I hadn't written more than a paragraph. I discovered you can't take care of a boat and write at the same time because the boat is a full-time job."

When they returned to California, there wasn't too much left of his law practice, so Dorothy went back to work. They bought a small cottage. Chet stayed home to write the book and remodel the cottage so they could sell it.

Having been on firm land for awhile, Oksner wrote the book; he also finished the house and sold it at a profit.

"Then we went cruising again," he recalls. "Again, 18 months later, I still hadn't written a word. So we rented a house in Florida for six months and I wrote the second book." Somewhere in the middle of writing the second book, the first one sold through his agent.

After Florida, Chet and Dorothy moved to Maine, where they rented a house and he sat down to write his third book.

The most common question asked by many would-be novelists is how to get a literary agent, since most publishers won't even look at a novel unless it's been submitted by an agent. Oksner responds: "When I finished the first book, I sent out query letters with some sample pages. I got rejections from them all saying, 'This is pretty good, *but.*' There were a couple of agents who never responded. I was angry because I felt I was entitled to a response."

Oksner wrote a nasty, sarcastic letter saying 'Please check one of the following boxes: Never received it, We threw this garbage in the trash months ago, Whatever.' He got a letter back from one agent telling him that they'd never lost a manuscript, but they found his in the corner of a closet. The agent took it home, read it, thought it was great and decided to represent him.

It took the agent six months to sell Oksner's first novel, *Punitive Damage*, to William Morrow; it was published in 1987. The second book, *Burdens of Proof*, came out in 1990, and Oksner said he beat Scott Turow on the title by about six months.

The advance against royalties that he received on the first book was $10,000, minus his agent's commission, which is usually 15 percent. Foreign rights were sold to Japan, Italy and Germany. The total of foreign sales turned out to be more than the initial advance. He figures he grossed just under $60,000 for the book.

For the second novel, Oksner was supposed to receive $25,000, but the publisher went out of business shortly after his novel was published. He only received $15,000 of the advance.

Oksner says he spends about four or five hours a day working on his writing. "In the beginning, when I'm trying to figure out plot and character, it's so difficult that I can't spend longer than three hours on it," he says. "I'm solving problems and making everything credible in advance. Once I get what I think is a credible outline, I can write for longer periods of time. At the end, I might be writing six to eight hours a day, six days a week." He averages about five pages a day.

Oksner says that writing mystery novels is hard work, but it's very satisfying. "Compared to practicing law," he says, "it's like being God. In real life, courtroom trials are all very problematic. When I'm writing a courtroom thriller, when I want a witness to lie and get caught, I catch him. If I want a judge to rule in my favor, he does. It's a lot of fun."

He's not crazy about the money, which is frequently both erratic and low. "I get paid a modest amount, and then there are periods of nothing," he says. Also, publishing is very unpredictable. "Before the contract for my third book was signed, the holding company said they were going out of business, so the publisher decided they didn't need the book.

"Realistically, fiction writers should realize this may never earn you money, or at least not enough to make you a living," he reports.

NEWSLETTER PUBLISHER

Booktalk

Ron Rich
Lakewood, Colorado

Ease of Startup	Moderate
Initial Investment	$500
Time Commitment	Part- to full-time
Can You Run the Business From Home?	Yes
Success Potential	Easy

Description of Business: A regular publication sold by subscription that focuses on a very specific field.

Ease of Startup: Moderate. You need one sample issue to start.

Range of Initial Investment: $500 if you already have a computer.

Time Commitment: Part- to full-time

Can You Run the Business From Home? Yes

Success Potential: Easy. If you fill a niche that nobody else is addressing, it's easy to succeed if you have the marketing plan to back it up.

How to Market the Business: Direct mail, publicity, conferences, lectures, advertising.

The Pros: It's satisfying to have people pay for what you have to say.

The Cons: Sometimes it's difficult to get subscribers to renew.

Special Considerations: Newsletter publishing is for people who have a particular interest and are able to address it in very specific ways.

For More Information: *Publishing Newsletters*, by Howard Penn Hudson and *The Newsletter on Newsletters*, available through The Newsletter Clearinghouse, POB 311, Rhinebeck, NY 12572; 914-876-2081.

Story of the Business

Ron Rich had been an elementary school teacher and principal for 30 years. He had developed a reputation as an expert in children's literature and frequently gave talks on children's books in his classrooms.

He took early retirement in 1990. At first he didn't know what he was going to do. When he voiced his concerns to a friend, the friend replied, "I'm sure it will have something to do with children's books." He turned out to be right.

"I wanted to publish a newsletter about books geared toward kids from kindergarten through the eighth grade." recalls Rich. The result is *Booktalk*, an eight-page newsletter containing reviews of recently published books. When he started the newsletter in 1991, Rich initially geared it toward teachers and parents. He quickly discovered librarians are the ones who have the money to buy the books and who want to know what's new in the field, so he began to promote *Booktalk* to them.

He publishes the newsletter monthly from September through June and charges $32.50. School districts frequently pay for the subscriptions. In 1993 he had 100 subscribers, but hopes to increase his circulation to 500. He reinvests all the money he receives back into promotion and direct mail.

To market the newsletter, Rich sends flyers to school librarians. He attends state book conferences, frequently as a speaker. Another service he's developed is a program for kindergarten through 6th grade called Let's Read A Book. He visits school classes and reads to the class in 30-minute sessions. In 1992 Rich conducted 20 such sessions.

Rich works as the Children's Reading Specialist in the local Barnes & Noble bookstore; he also manages the children's department, with over 12,000 titles. He likes working at the bookstore particularly because he has access to any book he'd like to read. He often is visited by subscribers to his newsletter.

He spends about 20 hours a week working on the newsletter. Since he already had a computer, he spent very little on the first issue. "I started with 500 names; they were names of acquaintances, people I was working with and people at school districts. I sent each a copy of the first issue, which I mailed first class," he recalls. Half of his subscribers live in Colorado, with the rest scattered throughout 29 other states.

"It's a one-person business, and I do it all myself," he remarks. "This is not stressful, it's real enjoyment." The only downside is that with a subscription-only publication, many people don't renew. "I have to constantly campaign about my cause to replace the readers who don't renew," he indicates. Every year the number of those who do renew is increasing.

Currently Rich is exploring how to expand the newsletter to include parents who don't have the funds to buy new books that librarians do, since the average children's book costs $15. "I think some parents who subscribe to *Booktalk* use the newsletter to identify certain books, and then check them out of the libraries," he says.

Ron gets his books from the news releases and review copies that publishers send him; he also reads new titles from the store.

"Publishing the newsletter gives me a lot of personal satisfaction and forces me to keep on top of things," though he admits with 5,000-6,000 new children's books published each year, it can be difficult. "Be prepared not to make a lot of money in the beginning," he advises. "Do your homework in identifying your audience, because if this is going to be a retirement career for you, make sure it's going to be fun and profitable."

NEWSPAPER PUBLISHER

Out West

Chuck Woodbury
Grass Valley, California

Ease of Startup	Moderate
Range of Initial Investment	$500 -$5,000
Time Commitment	Full-time
Can You Run the Business From Home?	Yes
Success Potential	Moderate

Description of Business: A newspaper published weekly, monthly or quarterly, focussing on a particular community or area.

Ease of Startup: Moderate. You need to publish a sample issue to demonstrate your newspaper's focus to advertisers and readers.

Range of Initial Investment: $500 -$5,000.

Time Commitment: Full-time

Can You Run the Business From Home? Yes

Success Potential: Moderate. This can be successful if there's no competition or if you're addressing a niche that's not being filled.

How to Market the Business: Radio ads, event sponsorships, adequate distribution, reader contests, publicity.

The Pros: Publishing your own newspaper is a way to become the voice of a particular community.

The Cons: Advertisers sometimes pay late or not at all; readers will frequently cancel for frivolous reasons.

Special Considerations: For a person with experience in journalism, publishing a newspaper is a power trip. It will get into your blood.

For More Information: Newspaper Association of America, 11600 Sunrise Valley Drive, Reston, VA 22091.

Story of the Business

Like many people, Chuck Woodbury didn't like his job. But unlike the rest of them, he quit, took his savings and decided to take two years off from the real world to travel around the western United States in an RV. His most pressing decision was whether to turn left, right or go straight at a congruence of dirt roads out in the middle of nowhere.

He had been working in public relations on a freelance basis for 10 years when he decided it was time to bail out. He also had a small monthly newspaper he was publishing which he sold to finance his bare-bones living expenses for a couple years.

Somewhere in the middle of Wyoming toward the end of the first year he thought of combining his two passions—traveling and writing—into a business he could run himself. Woodbury came out with the first issue of *Out West* barely six weeks later. Today *Out West* is a quarterly, 40-page newspaper filled mostly with stories about the places he visits and the people he sees.

In the beginning, the paper was 24 pages and he had 25 subscribers—mostly family and friends. After the first issue was published, he sent copies out to the press. Shortly, the news media started calling. A few months later, he appeared on "World News Tonight," and the subscriptions started to pour in.

Despite the power they wield, many members of the media are as unhappy with their jobs as the rest of the world. Chuck feels that the media responded so enthusiastically to *Out West* because there were many journalists who would love to do what he was doing. They naturally felt a lot of their readers would feel the same way.

"I was doing something I loved. I was able to make a living from it, but went into it on a shoestring," he says. "Also, I was free. That's why the media wrote about me so much, and that's why people subscribe."

To do the research for an issue, Chuck spends about a month on the road with his wife, Rodica—who serves as associate editor—and their young daughter, Emily. They decide to cover a certain area before they leave; they stick to the less-frequently traveled roads and avoid the interstates.

He writes and designs the newspaper with a Macintosh and a laser printer. He uses a laptop computer on the road, importing the data into the Macintosh when he gets home. One reason he started the newspaper is because he thought it would be fun; he has to work really hard to keep the business part of the paper under control. "I've been tempted a few times to increase the frequency of the paper to bimonthly, but then everything would become a chore," he says. "Besides, I don't want to hire anybody because then I'd be a boss. I'm more concerned about putting out a good product than spending a lot of time promoting the paper. By putting out a quality product, it promotes itself."

He still sends news releases and sample copies to the media. He does radio talk shows over the phone while he's traveling and when he's at home. "I do about four or five shows a month on big-city radio stations. I phone in from wherever I am. It's a good source of new subscriptions."

Out West accepts advertising, but he doesn't do much to solicit new ads; as a result, the ratio of editorial to advertising space is about nine to one. The paper grosses about $100,000 a year from subscriptions and ancillary products like a videotape and a book Chuck wrote for a major publisher. He'd like to spend more time increasing the renewal rate, which stands at 60 percent, but he can only send out a few renewal notices. "I don't like to play that game," he indicates, but many people won't renew until they get a fifth notice, so he's added another mailing.

He writes and lays out the paper before sending it to the printer, who then passes it along to a mailing service. He maintains his own mailing list. "It's important to keep your overhead really low," he warns. "Don't get carried away with equipment, even though it's easy to become addicted to the new technology."

For people who are thinking about starting their own newspaper, he suggests: "Find a subject that's of burning interest to you. With the new technology, it's very easy and affordable to get the word out."

NONPROFIT ORGANIZATION— ENVIRONMENTAL GROUP

The Arise Foundation

Edmund Benson
Miami, Florida

Ease of Startup	Difficult
Range of Initial Investment	$30,000
Time Commitment	Full-time
Can You Run the Business From Home?	Yes
Success Potential	Difficult

Description of Business: An organization raising funds to increase public awareness of a particular facet of the environment.

Ease of Startup: Difficult. You have to narrow your cause and then apply for nonprofit status, which can take more than a year.

Range of Initial Investment: $30,000.

Time Commitment: Full-time

Can You Run the Business From Home? Yes

Success Potential: Difficult. The environmental field is glutted. It takes awhile to establish a nonprofit.

How to Market the Business: Publicity, word of mouth, referrals.

The Pros: It's very rewarding to be devoting your retirement to helping environmental causes.

The Cons: It's expensive to fight big business. Sometimes it can be hard to make your voice heard.

Special Considerations: People who believe in a cause passionately and have the energy and endurance to back it up will love running an environmental nonprofit group.

Story of the Business

"We're making the world safe for children," are the first words out of Edmund Benson's mouth when you ask him what he does. He institutes a variety of environmental programs geared to the local school system. His concerns began because of something much closer to home.

In 1982 he retired and sold his furniture leasing company; he was beginning to enjoy retirement while he waited for his wife to retire too. They were living a mile and a half from the largest incinerator in the world, and it was affecting his wife's health. They called it Miami Snow, since a fine layer of white ash was covering their home and yard. "She asked me if there was anything I could do," says Benson, and he was off.

"I began to realize that the environment was in horrible shape, and we were going to be leaving our children a horrible mess," he remembers. He began a fight against Dade County that not only resulted in a massive curbside recycling program in the city and schools but also in the county spending $100 million to fix the incinerator.

The next problem he tackled was poor nutrition in the schools. "My wife, who was a teacher, brought home meals from the cafeteria. We called the meat 'mystery meat' because we couldn't figure out what it was," he recalls. He petitioned the school to start a nutrition task force. The meals are now held up as a paragon of what schools can do to improve the nutrition and health of their children.

Benson formally founded the Arise Foundation just before the nutrition task force went into effect. He now oversees a variety of far-reaching programs in schools both in Miami and around the world. The Foundation sponsors Lead Awareness Week and water conservation programs. They run a special program for second to fifth graders called the Envirocops, where every second grader in the county is sworn in as an Envirocop every November. In 1993 there were 225,000 Envirocops: Each was given a membership card and a coloring book.

A related program is called the Environmentors. High school and college students spend an hour each week in an elementary school classroom teaching the kids about the environmental facts of life. The Environmentor program has spread to states that include Pennsylvania and Oregon and around the world to Ecuador and Moscow. Edmund would now like to start an Envirocops day camp for underprivileged children in Miami. He's also started "See a Gun, Dial 911" week in Miami.

Benson has no employees, an annual budget of $200,000, and not enough hours in the day. He started the foundation in 1986, but had been hard at work since he retired. He believes it's easier to work within the system than to stand outside, complain and picket. "People in government and the school system are receptive to those who really want to help," he says. "We've never had a no. If you want to be a changemaker, the best way to do it is from the inside."

He warns prospective nonprofit entrepreneurs not to be swayed by the nonprofit label. "A nonprofit foundation is still a small business," he explains. "There are too many nonprofit foundations that receive a grant, and the first thing they do is build an overhead with it, which is why so many of them don't succeed. It's really important to be very conservative with your expenses and overhead."

NONPROFIT ORGANIZATION— INTERGENERATIONAL COMMUNICATION

The Listening Post

Mabel Barth

Denver, Colorado

Ease of Startup	Easy
Range of Initial Investment	$0
Time Commitment	Part- to full-time
Can You Run the Business From Home?	Yes
Success Potential	Easy

Description of Business: An organization placing adult mentors in the schools to foster communication among students.

Success Potential: Easy. This is an idea whose time has come.

Ease of Startup: Easy. Contact the schools and find listeners, and you can start.

Range of Initial Investment: $0.

Time Commitment: Part- to full-time

Can You Run the Business From Home? Yes

How to Market the Business: Publicity, word of mouth, referrals.

The Pros: You'll be helping students open up to impartial adults; the adults benefit as much as the kids.

The Cons: There's almost no money involved.

Special Considerations: This "business" is for men and women who want to reach out to kids.

Story of the Business

Picture an older man and a woman sitting at a table covered with a strip of calico cloth. A bowl of fruit sits in the center and is surrounded by peanuts in various stages of dis-shell-ment on the table, on the floor and even on the people sitting at the table.

Nobody much cares about the way it looks. Young students—from elementary school through college level—are talking to the man and the woman, who are listening to them carefully.

The kids are speaking so passionately because they know the adults are there to listen. They also know they'll be there the same time the next week and the week after that.

Mabel Barth started The Listening Post as part of a graduate school project at the University of Denver, where she was working on a Masters degree in interpersonal communication. "I always thought the world would be a better place if we listened to each other," she remarks, "and what better place to put it into practice than an urban campus with 25,000 people?"

She specifically designed The Listening Post so students would find it acceptable. She thought carefully about each element. "The fruit attracts attention," she says. The unshelled peanuts give people who are under stress something to do with their hands while they talk and help slow down the communication process. The cloth communicates that it's not an academic setting, so it makes people feel more comfortable. With the peanuts messy all over the place, it's easier for people to talk because it's not formal. If a person is failing a class or their marriage is in trouble, it's easier to sit down at a messy table and start to talk." Each Listening Post is in a busy, noisy area, like a student center or cafeteria, so students don't feel their conversation is being overheard.

Barth ran the organization for 10 years before she formed a nonprofit organization in 1989. Most of that time, she paid the expenses out of her own pocket. She wrote a handbook geared toward people who want to begin their own Listening Posts; it sells for $32.50, plus postage and handling. She also has a video available for $10. The fees help cover her costs.

Her primary expenses are for stationery, phone bills and reprinting the handbook. She writes a lot of grants, receiving eight in 1993 from local foundations and public service companies. Her annual budget ranges from $20-25,000 a year, enough to pay for three part-time contract workers. She doesn't pay herself a salary by choice.

Most of her volunteer listeners are seniors. She finds them by talking at luncheons and placing notices in church newsletters. When she has enough listeners, then she'll approach a school.

"One man has been a listener for 10 years," she says. "The students love it. They look forward to seeing the listeners each week."

A Listening Post can be started for virtually nothing. The main cost is for fruit and peanuts, which the school pays for. In 1993 there were 110 Listening Posts in the U.S. and Canada.

Barth personally trains each volunteer before they go out to serve as listeners. They're also instructed to refer people to community organizations in cases where someone is suicidal, a drug abuser or has a serious problem.

"I want whatever happens at the Listening Post to be very professional," indicates Barth, "but I'd never want it to look that way."

NONPROFIT ORGANIZATION— URBAN BOOSTER

Big Apple Greeters

Lynn Brooks
New York, New York

Ease of Startup	Difficult
Range of Initial Investment	$20,000
Time Commitment	Full-time
Can You Run the Business From Home?	Yes
Success Potential	Difficult

Description of Business: A non-profit organization that works within city government to improve the image of that city.

Ease of Startup: Difficult. You need to form a nonprofit, which can take a year or more, and gain support in the meantime.

Range of Initial Investment: $20,000 at least.

Time Commitment: Full-time

Can You Run the Business From Home? Yes

Success Potential: Difficult. You need contacts, determination and a clear vision to convince others of the necessity for your business.

How to Market the Business: Publicity, word of mouth, referrals.

The Pros: It's extremely satisfying to watch your altruistic vision fly.

The Cons: It can be tough to make that first contact. Fundraising concerns are never far away.

Special Considerations: Running a nonprofit is for a person who believes in a cause and is willing to do anything for it.

Story of the Business

Lynn Brooks had been thinking about her idea for years before she started it. It marinated during the years she spent working at nonprofit organizations, particularly in her job as dean at a university, where she founded a center on volunteerism.

"I was very frustrated when I traveled," she remarks. "Whenever people asked me where I was from and I told them, they'd say, 'Oh, what a terrible city. People get shot there.' I'd heard bad things about New York for years. I'm a New Yorker, and I love New York. I believed there were a lot of people who felt the way I did. I started thinking about how I could communicate this to the rest of the world."

Brooks thought about doing something to save the city herself, both for the people who live there and for people who come to visit. Then, luck struck: she was out of a job.

"I thought, if I didn't do something about it now, I'd never do it," she recalls. Brooks started Big Apple Greeters, which was her way to promote the city worldwide. "I was sure there would be lots of volunteers in the city who loved the city and wanted to share it as well as meet visitors coming to New York, and I was right."

She began the non-profit in her living room in 1991. Before she made her first match between New Yorker and visitor, she needed to set up the organization, make contacts with people who could help her promote it and start to raise money. "So I wrote to Ruth Messinger, the Manhattan borough president, and asked to meet with her to tell her about my idea," remembers Brooks.

"When I got there, she had several people with her. They were all waiting for me to give my presentation, which I wasn't expecting," she recalls. Brooks talked about her program. On the spot, Messinger gave her a desk, a phone, a computer to use and the support of her office—but no money. Brooks immediately began to work. She wrote letters to people and foundations requesting funding; she also gathered a committee of influential people in the city. Brooks spent eight months working full time before she received her first grant.

"I had originally wanted to work only three days a week, but very quickly, I was up to five," she remembers. Her initial funding came from grants from *New York Newsday* and *The New York Times*. A small story in the travel section of the Sunday *Times* calling for volunteers brought a huge response, and she had a waiting list of people.

Brooks also went after hotels by delivering a flier aimed at tourists about her service. The business caught on quickly. In the first 18 months of Big Apple Greeters, more than 2,500 tourists were matched with New Yorkers. Brooks had been able to raise close to $300,000 in the same period.

Tourists who hear about the organization call or fax the office to say when they'll be in town and what they'd like to see. The volunteer director takes the information, checks the database for suitable volunteers and makes a match. The volunteer director then notifies the tourist and the volunteer. Each meeting of volunteer and tourist averages about four hours.

Meanwhile, Brooks is ecstatic that her idea has taken hold. She's thinking about expanding her services to the disability community.

"It's bigger and better than I ever imagined," she remarks. "We've even gotten calls from other cities and countries that want to replicate it. We've gotten more publicity for the city of New York than we ever imagined."

NONPROFIT SOCIAL ORGANIZATION

The Giraffe Project

Ann Medlock
Langley, Washington

Ease of Startup	Difficult
Range of Initial Investment	$10,000
Time Commitment	Full-time
Can You Run the Business From Home?	Yes
Success Potential	Difficult

Description of Business: A not-for-profit service that relies on foundation grants and donations from individuals and members for its income.

Ease of Startup: Difficult. You need an attorney and accountant to set up as a nonprofit; it also takes time.

Range of Initial Investment: $10,000 and up.

Time Commitment: Full-time

Can You Run the Business From Home? Yes

Success Potential: Difficult. It's difficult to get the attention of foundations in the beginning, so sufficient money for the first couple of years is a necessity.

How to Market the Business: Publicity, direct mail, grant writing.

The Pros: You don't need to show a profit. Having big corporations give you money because they believe in what you're doing can be very satisfying.

The Cons: It's easy to become discouraged in the beginning.

Special Considerations: For a person who believes in a cause to the point of distraction, setting up a nonprofit is a great source of satisfaction.

For More Information: Society for Nonprofit Organizations, 6314 Odana Road, Suite 1, Madison, WI 53719; *A Working Guide for Directors of Not for Profit Organizations* by Charles N. Waldo (Quorum Books).

Story of the Business

Ann Medlock runs an unusual business from a small office on an island in Puget Sound, population 800. She describes The Giraffe Project, which she started in 1982, as "a nonprofit press service for heroes." She relies on a nationwide network that nominates people who become known as Giraffes—or people who stick their necks out— once they are selected by a jury.

Medlock started the organization as a continuation of a project she'd been working on at a magazine that since went under. She's honored more than 700 Giraffes in all parts of the country. They've included a former Wells Fargo bank officer who has worked without pay for three years to open a socially responsible bank, a man in New York who opened a can redemption center geared towards the homeless—both as customers and as staff, and a woman in Los Angeles who rescues wild and exotic animals from people who thought they would make good pets but found out otherwise.

After the jury approves the Giraffes, the wheels of the project begin to turn. "We contact the Giraffe's local media as well as the national press," explains Medlock. "The idea is to seed the media. It's not just good news we're trying to spread, we want to draw attention to someone who's making headway and show people they can do something like it, too."

She chose nonprofit status for several reasons. "We could have been a traditional, for-profit business, but I didn't want to be in the business of selling people's stories. It felt better to be a nonprofit," she remarks. "I also knew my peers in the media well enough that if I was a business they'd be less inclined to listen to me. Since we're a nonprofit, their dukes go down and they're all ears."

People thought she was crazy when she announced she was going to start the project—whose motto is "Nobis est," or It's up to us"—including the owner of the magazine who started the original Giraffe program. "I negotiated with the owner to keep it going as it was, but we couldn't pull it off. We had to give up the graphics, the name, everything. We had to start from scratch."

So determined was Medlock to make it that she maxed out her credit cards and her savings to pay the printers for the initial press mailings. "My first donor was someone I know who figured if I was that crazy, I needed some help. He invested $11,000 and helped me to set up as a nonprofit," she recalls.

"I remember getting this book, *How to Write a Foundation Grant*. I worked without pay for two and a half years. I figured I had to do it that way, because I couldn't see working another job and doing this a few hours at a time." she adds.

Since she wrote her first grant application, over 41 foundations have donated money to The Giraffe Project. Medlock also offers Giraffe memberships that include a newsletter, buttons and bumper stickers as part of an annual membership.

"The key was enlisting the right talent," she says. "It's very important to draw on the good will of people around you who also want to see the project work. One of the classic mistakes entrepreneurs make is to hire someone exactly like themselves. You've duplicated the talents instead of bringing in the skills that are missing."

Ann hired a person who's good with details and at making things happen. "I'm not like that," she reveals. "I come up with 12 ideas an hour."

To recruit members to The Giraffe Project, Ann tried direct mail, but it didn't work. "We rented a mailing list, designed fliers and sent out 65,000 pieces of mail. Unfortunately, they all arrived on the day of the stock market crash," she recalls. "We took it as a cosmic warning that we weren't cut out for this type of marketing." Since then, members have signed up mostly by word of mouth.

A spin-off of the Project is a children's curriculum called Standing Tall. "It takes kids through this process," she says. "They hear about our Giraffes, they find Giraffes and then tell their stories."

Medlock's newest foray is television, doing Giraffe segments on "Good Morning America" with Spencer Christian in 1994. Through it all she never doubted she could make The Giraffe Project work. In fact, she says, it's simple.

"You need to find the work you want to do and put yourself in a position where nobody can tell you to stop doing it."

NOSTALGIA COMPANY

BiFolkal Productions, Inc.

Lynn Martin Erickson
and Kathryn Leide
Madison, Wisconsin

Ease of Startup	Difficult
Range of Initial Investment	$10,000
Time Commitment	Full-time
Can You Run the Business From Home?	Yes
Success Potential	Difficult

Description of Business: A business that sells historical and educational "kits" to schools and other organizations.

Ease of Startup: Difficult. To provide a multimedia presentation, you have to arrange for music, scripts and collect the materials to complete each kit.

Range of Initial Investment: $10,000.

Time Commitment: Full-time

Can You Run the Business From Home? Yes

Success Potential: Difficult. It's an unusual business, and it may be difficult to convince people of the need for it.

How to Market the Business: Advertising, publicity, trade shows, word of mouth, referrals.

The Pros: You're helping people reminisce about good times in their lives and helping students learn about history hands-on. It's fun pulling everything together.

The Cons: It involves a lot of detail work. Gaining acceptance by nonprofit organizations—a primary market—can take a long time.

Special Considerations: People who enjoy history and educating people about it will enjoy running this business.

Story of the Business

Lynn Martin Erickson and Kathryn Leide run an unusual company engaging the tendency of people to look back on their lives and the events that shaped them. They produce kits geared toward a specific theme and era that consist of scripted skits, music tapes, slides and items from the period ,like a mah jongg set. They market the kits to libraries, schools and nursing homes, allowing individuals to benefit from the materials.

They began BiFolkal Productions as a project at the Madison Library School at the University of Wisconsin in 1975. Their assignment was to design a service for a specific group of people. They geared their presentation to nursing home residents, presenting a show about Halloween with slides, poetry readings and tricks they performed—and then demonstrated—for the residents.

The residents and directors at the home loved it. This success led to a grant from the Wisconsin Division for Library Services for the two women to develop three more kits over the course of a year. They presented their kits at a special preconference of the American Library Association; other librarians asked how they could get copies of the kits, and BiFolkal Productions was born.

"We didn't consciously think we were going into business," recalls Erickson. "It was more like we were making materials available to people."

268 · 100 BEST RETIREMENT BUSINESSES

Erickson writes all the skits and songs, while Leide concentrates on gathering and producing the visuals for the kits. Though the women initially geared their product toward older adults, they discovered the kits were also ideally suited for intergenerational sharing. This helped broaden their audience. Today they market the business by using their in-house mailing list, producing a quarterly newsletter and by exhibiting at trade shows. Frequently they are invited to speak at training workshops and conventions. While they're on the road, they keep their eyes out for additions to current or future kits.

"We do some research before the trip to see what photographic collections and other resources might exist in that particular region," reveals Erickson. They had an easier time getting memorabilia for the kits in the beginning. "When we were only putting out eighteen of one kit, we could go to an antique shop and buy a mah jongg set and have enough," she points out. "Today it's more difficult, as we've already gone through all our family and friends' attics."

BiFolkal sells about 700 kits a year, with 60 percent of their sales to libraries and 25 percent to nursing homes. School districts and their community education programs make up the rest of their business. The company is nonprofit. This provides certain advantages: "It makes us eligible for grants and other funding. It also gives us a better bargaining position for photo fees, since the fees for nonprofits are lower," Erickson explains. "Our mission is to encourage reminiscence, not make a profit."

NURSERY

Alpine Gardens

Ron Backhaus
Bethel, Vermont

Ease of Startup	Moderate
Range of Initial Investment	$1,000+
Time Commitment	Part- or full-time
Can You Run the Business From Home?	Yes
Success Potential	Moderate

Description of Business: A specialized nursery that sells trees and contracts custom landscape work.

Ease of Startup: Moderate. You order the plants, set them out and wait.

Range of Initial Investment: $1,000 and up for trees and plants.

Time Commitment: Part- or full-time

Can You Run the Business From Home? Yes

Success Potential: Moderate. Demand for a specialized nursery stock is less than for conventional nursery stock. It can take years before trees are mature and ready to sell.

How to Market the Business: Advertising, word of mouth, referrals.

The Pros: You can time things so that you start the nursery before you retire; then when you've left your job, the trees will be ready to sell.

The Cons: It takes time to build up a clientele, especially with unusual kinds of plants and trees.

Special Considerations: A nursery will work for people who love to dig in the dirt and don't need immediate income.

Story of the Business

Ron Backhaus has an unusual nursery in an area that's not noted for its delicate plant life. Alpine Gardens specializes in dwarf conifers, small varieties bred from needle-leaf trees like pine or spruce. Ron became interested in dwarf conifers at his previous home in Long Island, where a neighbor grew and sold them.

"I liked their style and the life that goes with it," he explains. "It's not like perennials where you have to cut them down every year."

When he moved to Vermont in 1985 Ron supplemented his retirement income by mowing lawns until the business got established. Like a winery, the trees need time to mature. Dwarf conifers can take a lot longer than many wines to mature: Some varieties take from five to seven years.

He set aside three of his 10 acres for the nursery. There are about 1,000 trees planted at any one time. Now that there are a number of mature trees to sell, he plants new trees every year to replace the ones bought by customers.

In spring Backhaus cleans up the gardens that have been damaged by winter and fertilizes the soil. In May and June, the cuttings he ordered over the winter arrive and are put into the ground. People come to buy trees for their gardens, or sometimes they contract Backhaus to design and plant a dwarf conifer garden for them.

In the summer, people have done their buying until fall, but Ron has to weed and mulch the garden. In September and early fall, he plants again to replace the trees he's sold. In October he starts to prepare the nursery for winter, which he sees as his time off. "Catalogs come in by the millions then. If I want cuttings for spring delivery, I order them in December," he says.

Spring and fall, Ron spends six hours a day, seven days a week outside working in the nursery and planting clients' gardens. "It's a long day, and it's not easy work," he says. "You have to do lots of cultivating, you have to weed, and the weather can be a problem. I want to make my nursery a showpiece, so I put in my own dwarf conifer gardens as a display."

Backhaus has done some local advertising in weekly papers. A couple of articles in local papers have boosted his business. "I don't have large quantities of trees. My trees are relatively more expensive because it takes so long for them to become a salable item," he says. His trees sell from $25 to $150, depending on their age.

He wants to keep the nursery as a manageable retirement business. "A specialized nursery is good for me because I'm not interested in getting much bigger," he remarks. "This is a very selective, small market. If I were younger, I think I'd be more diversified and have other plants to sell that are compatible with dwarf conifers."

Since dwarf conifers are not well known, Backhaus's biggest problem is teaching people what dwarf conifers are. "Most people are used to doing a lot of fertilizing. Dwarf conifers just don't need it," he says. "Some people think dwarf conifers are just plants that haven't grown up yet."

ORCHID GROWER

John McKinnon
Apalachicola Federal Forest, Florida

Ease of Startup:	Moderate
Range of Initial Investment:	$2,000
Time Commitment:	Full-time
Can You Run the Business From Home?	Yes
Success Potential:	Moderate

Description of Business: Selling orchids through the mail and to walk-in customers.

Ease of Startup: Moderate. Most orchid growers begin growing as a hobby, so they already have the skills and the contacts.

Range of Initial Investment: $2,000.

Time Commitment: Full-time

Can You Run the Business From Home? Yes

Success Potential: Moderate. Orchids are easy to raise, and they have a cult following. It may take time to build up a customer base.

How to Market the Business: Advertising, direct mail, word of mouth.

The Pros: Many gardeners dream of making a living from their avocation.

The Cons: The field is competitive. Unless you specialize in a certain area, it's difficult to expand the business.

Special Considerations: If you want to start a business working with orchids, go ahead; but it's a lot different than hobby growing.

For More Information: American Orchid Society, 6000 S. Olive Avenue, West Palm Beach, FL 33405.

Story of the Business

John McKinnon and his partner, David Horton, began dabbling in orchids in 1972. They started a business in 1982 and discontinued it seven years later. To this day, John refers to himself as an orchidoholic, even though he doesn't grow the flowers anymore.

"You buy a few and it's like drinking," he remarks. "You can't stop. The sheer beauty and number of different kinds of orchids is just overwhelming. Our business was a hobby that ran wild."

They belonged to the local orchid society. They got more involved each year until they were grossing $20,000 a year from just their mail-order operation. They sold 10 different varieties of orchids.

Both were self-taught and talked with other people who knew about orchids. John tended to take some of the advice with a grain of salt. "I had to have a good instinct for who to listen to and who to ignore," he explains. "There's a lot of information out there about orchids, but a lot of it is just false. I learned to read between the lines."

Though orchids are very forgiving plants, they need a greenhouse—even in Florida—which protects them from the cold in the winter and helps keep them cool in the summer. "We could go away for a couple of weeks, and the orchids would be fine," he remarks. "You couldn't do that with a house plant."

But they rarely left the plants. As David joked, they spent 80 to 90 hours a week on the business. They sold both plants and seedlings. They cross-bred orchids to attain a certain size, shape and color. Their orchids were sold mostly through the mail to a list generated from an ad in the American Orchid Society bulletin. Their own mailing list consisted of about 600 names.

"We'd also give talks at local garden clubs and we usually brought plants to sell. This brought people out to the greenhouse," points out John. This was important to the business, because chances are they wouldn't have stumbled upon it themselves. "We're 30 miles from the closest freeway, and we pick up our mail 12 miles away," explains John.

They concentrated on the orchids, but they also sold potting mix and supplies. Orchids ship very easily and tend to arrive in good shape.

When they started the business, they lacked capital. They bought the orchids they liked, about ten varieties in all. "In that way, we started with the high hurdles, since we ended up with most of our money tied up in orchids that were not of hybridizing quality, along with a limited stock," he said. "Had we been more selective in buying the plants, we would probably still be in business.

"If we were starting out now, we'd start very differently," explains John. "We'd focus on one aspect. We'd probably choose to grow seedlings, because that's what we did the best. We didn't have the money to go ahead with other products. We either had to get bigger or get out, so we got out."

He also believes that if the greenhouse was more centrally located, the business would have done better. "We hung ourselves by coming to such a remote area," he says.

Today, they are raising parrots and rheas, South American flightless birds. "A market is developing in this country for meat, feathers and hide," explains John. "The strip of fat on the back of the birds has properties that medicine is using to treat arthritis and take out wrinkles. We're just getting up the breeding stock now. We're not interested in a farm; we breed in incubators."

Maybe this will be another hobby that runs wild, but at least they've learned from the mistakes they made in their orchid business.

PAINTER

Ruth Block

Grand Rapids, Michigan

Ease of Startup	Moderate
Range of Initial Investment	$500
Time Commitment	Part- or full-time
Can You Run the Business From Home?	Yes
Success Potential	Difficult

Description of Business: Creating paintings for sale either on speculation or on commission.

Ease of Startup: Moderate. You need supplies, examples of your best work and a lucky break.

Range of Initial Investment: $500 for supplies.

Time Commitment: Part- or full-time

Can You Run the Business From Home? Yes

Success Potential: Difficult. It's a difficult business to break into; you need both contacts and talent.

How to Market the Business: Shows in restaurant and other public areas, galleries, word of mouth.

The Pros: Painting is restful and creative.

The Cons: It can be difficult to sell your work. Painting can be an isolating and confining art.

Special Considerations: People with a talent for art and self-promotion will have a better shot than others.

For More Information: *Art Business News*, POB 3837, Stamford, CT 06905; local galleries.

Story of the Business

Ruth Block's story is painfully common. She began to paint when she was very young, and she wanted to be a professional artist. But first she got married, had eight children, and her art was, by necessity, pushed aside.

When her first husband was dying of cancer, she met Clem Block at the hospital. His wife was also dying of cancer. A few years after their spouses had died, Ruth married Clem and started to paint again.

"I took some art classes and workshops. Then I began to show my paintings at local galleries and malls," she relates. Ruth sold her first painting at an art show. Because her paintings were so popular—she concentrates on landscapes—she began to make and sell prints of her more popular paintings.

She does mostly commissioned work. She frowns on art shows, but they're a good way to get started. "Art shows are very hard because there's a lot of lifting. When you have glass and prints, they're in danger of being broken," she says.

Ruth tries to make her paintings quiet and restful. She wants them to be "something you can live with." Her commissions tend to be more unusual than the paintings she does on her own. "I work in different ways," she explains. "Sometimes a customer will bring me several photographs and ask me to make a composite. Other times they'll tell me to do whatever I want. One man was moving from a house he had lived in for 35 years, so he asked me to paint a picture of his backyard with a squirrel, raccoon and some birds. I try to please the person I'm painting for."

Block got her first commissions a few years after she began to paint professionally. The commissions keep her busy, but sometimes she starts a painting of her own choosing. She works on canvases that are seldom smaller than 20 x 24 inches, and occasionally they're much larger. She prefers acrylic paints, since she's allergic to oil paints. Her commissions take anywhere from a few weeks to a few months to complete. Though she's sold her work for as much as $1500, Ruth says $250 is more typical. "Everyone says I price my things too cheaply, but most people don't have a lot of money. I don't want to cut out any sales," she says.

In the last few years, she's begun to make prints of her more popular work. She sells them—matted—for $85. She takes the paintings to a printing company. They take a picture of the painting and reproduce it in different sizes. Usually Ruth orders 25 prints at a time. This ties up a great deal of money, but it allows her to display them in many different places. "We decide to make a print of a certain painting when someone requests it," she remarks.

Block prefers to keep her business at its present size; this allows her to spend a few hours each day painting. She has some advice for people who are thinking about selling their paintings: brush up with a few classes, read some books, join a club and get involved with other artists. "You must set up a studio with good lighting, otherwise you can't really commit yourself to your work," she believes.

She likes painting because it relaxes her and takes her out of herself. "I can totally forget everything around me when I really get into it," she adds.

PERSONAL FINANCIAL CONSULTANT

Arthur Lieb
Falls Church, Virginia

Ease of Startup	Difficult
Range of Initial Investment	$3,000+
Time Commitment	Part- to full-time
Can You Run the Business From Home?	Yes
Success Potential	Easy

Description of Business: Advising individuals about financial issues including tax preparation, long-term saving plans, insurance, stock sales and estate planning.

Ease of Startup: Difficult. You have to become certified to be a financial planner; you also need to take courses and become licensed to sell stocks and insurance.

Range of Initial Investment: $3,000+ for the initial study and certification, plus overhead.

Time Commitment: Part- to full-time

Can You Run the Business From Home? Yes

Success Potential: Easy. The more services you can offer, the better. It helps if you're located in an affluent area.

How to Market the Business: Pro bono cases in the beginning, referrals, ads in the phone books and local newspapers.

The Pros: Clients place their trust in you.

The Cons: People can be very secretive about their money.

Special Considerations: You need to be a people person. Others need to feel comfortable in your presence, or else they won't trust you with their money.

For More Information: Institute of Certified Financial Planners, 7600 E. Eastman Avenue #301, Denver, CO 80231

Story of the Business

The seeds for Arthur Lieb's personal financial consulting business were planted when he was at his last job as Executive Officer of the Library of Congress, where he worked from 1964 until his retirement in 1989.

"The impetus came in the early '70s, when I was asked to serve as the director of the Library's federal credit union, which was a volunteer position," he said. "I knew absolutely nothing about finances, and I became immensely interested in them. Soon, I became the most active person on the board."

Lieb's position led to a general interest in consumer finance and financial planning. He passed five required courses while still at the Library and became certified in 1983. He took the self-study courses through the College for Financial Planning in Denver, an association that also granted him certification in the field. This requires proficiency in taxation, retirement and estate planning, investments and insurance.

In the beginning, just to get some clients, Lieb performed pro bono work for a few people, some of whom he still works with. Soon he began working with his first paid hourly clients, but they were slow in coming. "At first I thought I would do a lot of hourly work, but then I discovered there was great consumer resistance to paying somebody money to get advice. I did what a lot of people do: I passed the exam to become a stockbroker two years later," he reports.

A few years later he became licensed to sell insurance. Lieb also earned a Virginia real estate license because he frequently advises his clients about real estate, though he doesn't sell property. "I'm like a full-service bank and can offer many things to my clients," he says.

"I don't promise my clients instant wealth, because I think that takes more luck than ability. I'm a long-term planner and basically conservative by nature," he remarks, adding that he enjoys the work. "It's also important that people find you comfortable to work with. I can't emphasize that enough. My first client told me I was the first person who took the time to explain complex financial matters to her, and I thought I should use the fact that I listen carefully and answer questions as a marketing tool."

When Lieb meets a new client and they ask about his services, he tells them he's not going to drop an 80-page report that's just been pulled out of a computer and leave them to fend for themselves. Instead, he gives them a short article about one type of financial issue, and they go over it together because he wants them to have a basic understanding of what's going on.

He works from an office in his home; this allows him to have time to practice for his other career playing piano at restaurants and special functions. "When I'm in my office and have dead time, I can practice the piano for an hour," he says. His home office also makes it easy for clients to see him in the evening and on weekends.

Lieb says he grosses from $40,000 to $50,000 each year; this includes commissions from his consulting work and from stocks and insurance practices. He works with 200 clients; some clients are very active, others come in only once a year. He places a small ad in the Yellow Pages, which he says just about pays for itself. "Virtually all my clients come from referrals or from people I meet," he points out. "Referrals are the best kind of clients because they come to you and already have some confidence in you."

PET GROOMING

Shampoo*Chez

Anne Singer
Santa Cruz, California

Ease of Startup	Moderate
Range of Initial Investment	$30,000
Time Commitment	Full-time
Can You Run the Business From Home?	Yes
Success Potential	Easy

Description of Business: A shop that offers personalized grooming services, a self-service dog wash area and a variety of pet supplies and foods.

Ease of Startup: Moderate. You should attend grooming school before setting up a facility.

Range of Initial Investment: $30,000 for school and equipment.

Time Commitment: Full-time

Can You Run the Business From Home? Yes

Success Potential: Easy. People do more for their pets than they do for themselves or their children; for many, grooming is a necessary luxury.

How to Market the Business: Advertising, word of mouth, referrals, publicity.

The Pros: People are happy to leave their pets with you; people who own pets tend to be more giving than people who don't.

The Cons: Grooming is hard physical work.

Special Considerations: For people who love animals and have an artistic bent, pet grooming will be an enjoyable business to run.

For More Information: Anne Singer, Shampoo*Chez, 1380 Soquel Avenue, Santa Cruz, CA 95062.

Story of the Business

After running a nationally known pet grooming center for close to 10 years, it's difficult to believe Anne Singer spent most of her life being afraid of dogs.

"My mother had been bitten by a dog, and I was always petrified of them," she says. It took a daughter home from college with a puppy named Avery to convince Anne otherwise.

"For the first six months, I didn't go near that dog," she recalls. "Then all of a sudden, I fell in love with her and she became the most important thing in our lives."

That was in 1970. Singer and her family moved to Santa Cruz a few years later. A year after they arrived, Avery died from a vet-prescribed mixture of cortisone and heavy-duty pesticides to treat a flea problem. Anne went out and got two more dogs. She had to wash them often in the backyard because of the fleas, which frequently turned into an exhausting ordeal.

"One day, I told my husband if there was some place like a car wash for dogs, I'd be willing to take the dogs there," she remembers. "That thought just stuck in my head and wouldn't go away. Even as a little girl, I wanted to have my own business, so I mentioned the idea of a self-service dog wash to my friends and family. They thought it was such a good idea, they all offered to loan me money to open the business."

A year later she found a suitable location and opened the store. The first day the shop was open, 33 dogs came in. Shampoo*Chez was written up by a columnist in the *San Francisco Chronicle*; the local paper and TV station did features on the shop. It's been busy ever since.

Three groomers are available for people who don't want to wash their dogs themselves. A retail shop carries over 1,500 pet supplies, some with the Shampoo*Chez label. The grooming charge depends on the breed of dog. Cocker spaniels are $25 and up, while poodles range from $24 to $29. A self-service wash costs $11 for the first 20 minutes and a dollar for each additional five minutes. A self-service drier is also available.

"I believe you must give back to the community which gives to you," asserts Singer. She sponsors essay contests in the schools to help kids develop a humane attitude toward animals. She also gives a coupon for a free self-service wash to people who adopt a dog from the local SPCA; she's given away more than 3,000 in only a few years.

Anne sends out a bimonthly newsletter to customers. She publishes a "petalogue" four times a year that features Shampoo*Chez products and a variety of useful items. She has a mailing list of 20,000 names nationwide and is busy expanding this part of the business. She has also franchised the business: There are two franchises running successfully in California.

Anne suggests that potential groomers go to school, as some states require. She adds that most grooming shops also sell some products to increase profits. "You can start out easily by grooming from your garage, or you can go to people's homes and groom their pets."

"You have to love animals, because it's not a pleasant job," she adds. "You also have to have some artistic and creative ability. I've found that the really good groomers are better with animals than they are with people."

PHOTOGRAPHER

Photographs by Dike Mason

Dike Mason
Wiscasset, Maine

Ease of Startup	Easy
Initial Investment	$5,000
Time Commitment	Part- or full-time
Can You Run the Business From Home?	Yes
Success Potential	Moderate

Description of Business: A professional photographer shoots special events and everyday subjects as well.

Ease of Startup: Easy. You need skill and some adequate equipment.

Range of Initial Investment: $5,000.

Time Commitment: Part- or full-time

Can You Run the Business From Home? Yes

Success Potential: Moderate. If you limit your work to specific kinds of photography while you're building a business, you will limit the number of jobs. Later on, it helps to specialize.

How to Market the Business: Advertising, publicity, word of mouth, referrals.

The Pros: If you've always been a hobbyist, it's very satisfying to make a living from photography.

The Cons: It's very competitive; there are a lot of amateur photographers who call themselves professionals.

Special Considerations: You have to be as tireless in running your business as your are pursuing great photos. If you don't want to promote yourself, it'll be hard to succeed.

For More Information: Professional Photographers of America, 1090 Executive Way, Des Plaines, IL 60018.

Story of the Business

"I'm really an entrepreneur pursuing my hobby, and I get other people to pay for it," reveals Dike Mason, a professional photographer who had dabbled in photography during his professional career as a mechanical engineer at General Electric and an officer in the military. "Some people say, 'What a great photograph!' and write out a check. Others say, 'What a great photograph!' and don't want to pay for it. The truth is I do better quality work if I'm getting paid, because if someone's paying me I try to do the best job I can."

Mason has been carrying a camera with him since the 1930s, when he spent a vacation hiking the Appalachian Trail. "I started taking photos of children, and I've been doing it ever since," he recalls.

Dike's work has been displayed in shows organized by the Photographic Society of America. He doesn't shoot for weddings or graduations except for relatives. He focuses on theatrical photography for local dramatic groups, which he says is dramatic, fun and requires a few technical tricks. "I work at dress rehearsals; I shoot three or four rolls of film, take the best six and blow them up to put in the lobby," he says. "The cast loves to have their photos, and I make extra prints for them." He does his own developing at home.

Most of the groups are local nonprofit repertory companies. He rarely charges for his time, only for materials. But since many of the actors order extra prints, Mason can make up to $200 from one shoot.

To get other work, he runs a small, one-inch display ad in a local weekly paper, the *Maine Times*. The ad reads: "Photographs by Dike Mason. Practice limited to subjects of interest." It then lists his phone number. "I get a lot of calls from that ad because so many people see it," he says. "I took out the ad because a friend who's also a freelance photographer told me that if you're going to take up photography, you must have a local ad appear regularly. That way you can get professional prices without a fight." The ad provides him with instant credibility, which has been its biggest utility. The rest of his business is generated through word of mouth.

He says advertising also brands you as a professional in the darkroom. Without that distinction, people are always comparing your prices to the 35-cent print they can get at the drugstore. "The small prints will kill you," he says, referring to 3 x 5 and 5 x 7 prints. "An 8 x 10 isn't any more work than a 5 x 7, but you make twice as much money, and the increased cost of materials is negligible.

Mason says that if you're going to go into the business seriously, quality equipment is essential. "You need at least a couple of cameras and some darkroom equipment to get started," he reports. "I started with used equipment and have used it for a good part of my life. I've also been able to get some new equipment; that's the good thing about making some money from photography." Three or four cameras and a dozen lenses add up pretty fast, though he says a professional photographer doesn't need this kind of equipment to start out.

"I think of my camera as expendable," he remarks. "They do wear out. I spend a lot of time sailing in the salt air with them." Work is pretty steady throughout the year, though sometimes a few weeks will go by without any jobs. Then all of a sudden, five jobs will come in that all need to be done at once.

Mason also does some video work, mostly for local cable channels and documentaries. The work is fascinating, but it's difficult to make any money from it.

"Video's hard, because it's difficult to get people to pay for considerably better quality," he indicates. "They feel they can do it themselves for free, even thought they don't do a great job. I don't see a great future in it."

"I carry my camera everywhere I go," he says. "It makes me look at things I never would have thought of looking at. They come out of the blue, and when they come, I'm available for them."

POTTER

Great American Wheelworks

Trudy Litto
New Baltimore, New York

Ease of Startup	Moderate
Range of Initial Investment	$5,000
Time Commitment	Full-time
Can You Run the Business From Home?	Yes
Success Potential	Difficult

Description of Business: Making pottery and traveling to regional craft shows to sell it.

Ease of Startup: Moderate. You need adequate equipment and time to build a following.

Range of Initial Investment: $5,000 for potter's wheel, kiln, clay and other materials.

Time Commitment: Full-time

Can You Run the Business From Home? Yes

Success Potential: Difficult. You need to have skill and products that stand out, especially if you're interested in juried shows.

How to Market the Business: If you concentrate on shows, the promoters will market the shows. It doesn't hurt to develop your own mailing list.

The Pros: Potters love their work.

The Cons: It's hard work lugging the pottery around to shows, and it's very time-consuming.

Special Considerations: For people who've always dabbled in pottery and wanted to turn it into a business, start with nonjuried shows.

Story of the Business

Trudy Litto has always been involved in art in one form or another. Her background was in painting—she earned a BFA from Syracuse University—but she always dabbled in pottery. Then, when she realized she wasn't going to make it in painting, she took graduate courses in art education "because that would be a practical skill to have," she says.

She started teaching, then went back and got her masters. One day at a teacher's convention, she saw there was a fabulous potter speaking and demonstrating. She fell in love with pottery all over again. She continued to teach, but started to do pottery on the side.

"The closer I got to retirement, the more time I spent at the wheel; finally I realized this is what I was going to do," she recalls. Before she retired, she started to sell her work at craft fairs and had begun to build up a clientele. "When I retired, I was delighted to be in the studio full-time, since I've been playing in the 'mud' since the early fifties."

Trudy makes what is called minimum production pottery; these are utilitarian pieces of high-fired stoneware with an emphasis on the functional. She sells some of her pieces—ranging from a $10 vase to a complete set of dishes for $1,400—to galleries and museum shops and a few to wholesale accounts, but she concentrates on the craft fairs.

Litto likes to do about 20 shows a year. She concentrates on those within a seven-hour radius of her home, including Boston, Rochester, Maryland and Vermont. Her busy season starts at the beginning of May and runs through mid-December. She doesn't like to clump the shows together, preferring to schedule them so they fall every other weekend. She works at the wheel in the weeks between shows as well as during the off-season.

Her biggest challenge is finding the right show, and thus, the right market, for her work. "We're always picking and choosing. We try different fairs to see which ones work," she reports. "I'm also continually working to upgrade the quality of the fair I get into. This involves refining my work and getting really fine slides of my work to submit to the panels." She doesn't do flea market shows where anyone can get in; instead she sends her slides to the judges and often faces really stiff competition.

Her other requirements for selecting a particular show include the need for a 10 x 10-foot space. "We use a rigid structure that opens to those dimensions. If they don't have the space, I generally won't do the show," explains Trudy.

Booth fees range from $250 to $500 for shows that last two to three days. She prices her pieces according to what the market will bear, so they're consistent with what other people are charging. For special pieces, she raises the price. She also considers the time it takes her to make the piece and the amount of space it takes up in the kiln. "If I think I can get what it's worth, given my time and the kiln space, then I'll charge it," she explains. "If I can't get enough money to make the piece, then I'll drop the piece from my line."

Litto keeps a book at her booth so people can put their names and addresses on her mailing list, already up to 1,500 names. She sends them a calendar postcard that shows the full spectrum of the pottery she makes and the dates of her upcoming shows. "I mail them out to my good customers twice a year, letting them know when I'm going to be in their area," she reports.

Though she likes to do shows because she loves meeting the people, Trudy says the setup and teardown work at the shows is probably more difficult for a potter than for any other craft. "There are other crafts where you can make a lot more money and have an easier time producing the work and lugging it around than pottery," she says.

It's also expensive to get started. Trudy set up her studio gradually because of the expense. A potter's wheel can cost $800, building a kiln can run $2,000 to $3,000 while an electric kiln costs from $500 to $1,000. You also need adequate studio space.

"Unless you've been doing it for awhile and love doing it, pottery is very difficult work," she remarks. "We're going to be cutting back on it because I want more time for myself. My husband is very involved in the business. Unless you have someone who is supportive of the business, it's almost impossible to do."

PROFESSIONAL GOLFER

Bob Betley
Las Vegas, Nevada

Ease of Startup	Difficult
Range of Initial Investment	$1,000,000
Time Commitment	Full-time
Can You Run the Business From Home?	No
Success Potential	Difficult

Description of Business: An individual who competes in professional golf tournaments.

Ease of Startup: Very difficult. You have to have decades of play under your belt. Even many professional athletes let themselves go once they hit 50.

Range of Initial Investment: $1,000,000 for training, course fees and equipment over the years, plus $75,000 a year for travel expenses to and from the tournaments.

Time Commitment: Full-time

Can You Run the Business From Home? No

Success Potential: Difficult. The field is extremely competitive; most of the players competed on the regular PGA Tour.

How to Market the Business: Talent and skill.

The Pros: Getting paid to play golf is a dream for most golfers.

292

The Cons: You'll probably never make it that far.

Special Considerations: You need to be extremely talented and persistent to qualify for the Senior PGA Tour, so don't hold your breath. Becoming a club pro might be more within your grasp.

Story of the Business

Be forewarned: if you spend any amount of time in the pursuit of golf, the following story will turn you green with envy.

At the age of 28, Bob Betley discovered golf. On one of his days off from his job as police officer, his two brothers and a friend picked him up to spend the day golfing. "I'd never played before, but I immediately fell in love with the game and was pretty good at it my first time out," he remembers. "The next day, I went out and bought clubs, shoes, everything. I was hooked."

Two years later, he quit the police force and turned pro, working as assistant club pro at the Desert Inn Country Club, where he worked for three years. He then began playing regularly in state tournaments and mini-tours. In 1976 he left to play for two years in Asia and New Zealand. When he came back, he played on the PGA Tour from 1978 until 1981. He then returned to small-circuit play—frequently called the Grapefruit Circuit—competing in any tour he could get into. In 1990 he joined the Senior Tour, where he qualified after 22 tries.

"Every golfer on the Grapefruit Circuit who's getting close to 50 has the Senior Tour in the backs of their minds," says Bob. "I frequently get calls from people who want to know what it takes to get on the tour."

He believes the key to qualifying for the tour is to stay in shape. "Many golfers lack physical and mental conditioning," he explains. "They played when they were younger, but they let their physical selves go, and they got quite heavy and out of shape. Then when they get out on the course, they're not at all competitive."

To prepare for tournament play, Betley spends six to nine hours a day working out. He practices putting or driving outside or he exercises in his home gym. When he's on the road, the Tour provides a workout trailer for the players. Even though he stresses physical conditioning, that's only part of his routine. "After you get the physical work done, you have to concentrate very hard on your mental game. I work very hard at that as well," he reports.

Despite his conditioning, injury is always a possibility. In 1991 Bob had surgery on his shoulder and was off the Tour for eight months; he played only seven tournaments in 1992.

In 1993 he played 22 tournaments in a row, and he also won his first tournament, the Bank of Boston Classic. Thirty-five tournaments are planned for 1994, and he is going to try to compete in all of them.

Tournaments in the Senior Tour last only three days. With the exception of a few tournaments, there's no cut: every player earns some money, even the one in last place.

Betley enjoys the Senior Tour more than his earlier golfing jobs. "The guys on the Senior Tour are a tighter knit organization," he says. "They've already made their millions, so they're not fighting tooth and nail to make money. They're a lot more fun to be around." In 1993—a very good year—he grossed $390,000 from the Tour, while shelling out around $70,000 for travel expenses.

He's not sure if being club pro helped him get where he is today. "The big thing about being a club pro is that it allowed me to play in a lot of tournaments," he remarks. "The key to playing in any of the tours is having your game in excellent condition. It's probably the best feeling in the world to play golf and get paid for it," he relates. "It's something I love to do. I feel very lucky."

PUBLICIST

Adrienne Creative Images

Louise Cotter
Orlando, Florida

Ease of Startup	Easy
Range of Initial Investment	$500
Time Commitment	Part- or full-time
Can You Run the Business From Home?	Yes
Success Potential	Easy

Description of Business: A business that promotes businesses by getting them mentioned in the media or in their own trade magazines.

Ease of Startup: Easy. You might have to start with small projects before a business hires you for a complete campaign.

Range of Initial Investment: $500.

Time Commitment: Part- or full-time

Can You Run the Business From Home? Yes

Success Potential: Easy. Publicity is on the increase as a marketing tool.

How to Market the Business: Through referrals, pro bono work, existing contacts, and word of mouth.

The Pros: Publicity is fun, and it provides a rush when you get a placement.

The Cons: Dealing with the media sometimes may be difficult and discouraging. You have to keep coming up with new ideas.

Special Considerations: A person who is creative, good on the phone and can come up with as many persuasive angles as a lawyer will do well in publicity.

For More Information: The Public Relations Society of America, 33 Irving Place, 3rd Floor, New York, NY 10003-2376.

Story of the Business

If you earn a reputation doing publicity, the only place you won't have to do much marketing at all is for yourself. If you're good at getting people and businesses written up in the media, they will find you.

That's how it is with Louise Cotter, who runs her public relations firm—Adrienne Creative Images—from Orlando. "I'm scared to ask for work because I'm afraid I'll get it," she reports. "I'm overloaded already. I want to be able to leave my desk and go to the beach occasionally, so I only take what I believe I can do."

Cotter worked as the editor of a beauty trade magazine in New York for 10 years. Before that, she was a cosmetologist. After she retired from the magazine and moved to Florida in 1986, her former contacts at cosmetic companies, trade shows and other businesses contacted her to do freelance work as a media consultant. They wanted help marketing themselves to other media in the field.

In fact it was publicity that established her in her own PR business in the beginning. "When I first left the magazine, the new editor ran a half-page story about what I was doing. A lot of readers called me," she explains. "Several manufacturers and distributors called and asked if I wanted to work for them."

She hit the ground running. To maintain her contacts, she stayed involved in the National Cosmetology Association as a freelance style director and editor after she moved to

Florida. The director of the largest annual beauty trade show in the world, the National Beauty Show, asked Cotter to do the publicity for the show from that year on.

A publicist gets clients into the media by making initial contact with a press release and then following up with a phone call. Having a lot of contacts helps because editors and producers already know the publicist. They know she's done her homework about whether or not the client would be good to include in their publication or on their show. A publicist suggests specific story angles as well.

Through Cotter's connection with the National Cosmetology Association—she writes a bimonthly newsletter for the Association's student membership—a number of salons have hired her to do some publicity for them. She's also responsible for designing, writing and placing their ads for radio and newspapers. For this work, she charges a flat fee. However, she's cut back on the amount of work she chooses to do for small businesses. "They're used to having an employee do the marketing who has no background at all," she explains. The small companies often balk at her fee and at the costs for a photo shoot. She now concentrates on large corporations that are used to working with public relations specialists.

Cotter works with companies in three ways. For $500, she meets with a business and suggests ways they can get some press attention. They write their own letters and press releases, which Louise then edits. She charges $1,000 for a predetermined number of writing and placement tasks. She also works on a monthly retainer of $2,500 and up. She usually works in this way for national clients who can afford the fee and recognize the importance of public relations.

Cotter likes doing publicity because she finds it extremely stimulating. "I'll sometimes talk with people in four or five states in one day. I think it's the most interesting business anyone could be in because it's so diversified," she explains. "You have to like people and what you're doing. If you don't, the people you're contacting in the media will catch on very quickly, and your placements will decline."

REAL ESTATE AGENCY

Heritage Realty and Investment

Ozzie Geiger
Tallahassee, Florida

Ease of Startup:	Moderate
Range of Initial Investment:	$20,000
Time Commitment:	Full-time
Can You Run the Business From Home?	No
Success Potential:	Moderate

Description of Business: A firm that sells commercial and residential property and land.

Ease of Startup: Moderate. You need to work as a salesperson first, then become a broker. Each involves required courses and examinations.

Range of Initial Investment: $20,000.

Time Commitment: Full-time

Can You Run the Business From Home? No

Success Potential: Moderate. It takes awhile to get established. If you can survive the first two years, your chances are good.

How to Market the Business: Through advertising, word of mouth, referrals, the Chamber of Commerce, getting out there and meeting people.

The Pros: You'll meet a lot of different people and see many types of housing.

The Cons: Income can be sporadic; deals can fall through at the last minute.

Special Considerations: For people who love houses and chaos and work well with people, real estate is a good business.

For More Information: Institute of Real Estate Management, 430 N. Michigan Avenue, Chicago, IL 60611; National Association of Real Estate Brokers, 1629 K St. NW, Washington, DC 20006.

Story of the Business

The hardest thing Ozzie Geiger had to face—when he first decided to get into real estate after retiring from the Air Force in 1977—was working for somebody else.

"When I first started out as a salesperson, it was hard," he remembers. "In the Air Force, I had 20 people working for me."

He stuck it out for a year—Florida real estate law dictates that you work as a salesperson for a year before you can become a broker. He worked for 18 months for that first agency, then he got his broker's license and opened his own firm. He had to do it all himself, but he was happy, even though the first year was lean.

He's been running Heritage Realty since 1979. His 10 salespeople handle both commercial and residential property, land sales, property management and real estate investments. Geiger says he spends only about 10 percent of his time selling property; the rest managing the office. "It's better not to compete with your own associates," he suggests. "This way, you're always free if they need advice. Besides, I supervise all the salespeople very closely because the real estate laws are so complex now that I have to make sure they're doing everything right to avoid lawsuits."

Some of his salespeople work full-time, but one woman works only one day a week, making up to $12,000 in the course of a year. "Personality is the most important part of being in real estate," reports Geiger. "You have to be a listener and be empathetic. If you have that and an average education, I think you could be a very good real estate agent." In fact, he's seen some agents who've scored very high on the real estate exams totally bomb as salespeople because they lacked the personality.

To become a real estate salesperson in Florida, it's necessary to take Course I, which consists of 63 classroom hours, and pass the state exam. The entire process takes several months. "Florida is one of the toughest states in which to get a license, along with California," says Ozzie. "There's a lot of property sold here, and the state requires that it be done correctly." Many people buy retirement homes in Florida, which helps increase the market.

To receive a broker's license, the salesperson must pass Course II, which takes another 72 hours of classroom time. Once you pass the course, you're eligible to take the state exam. In addition, in Florida you have to have a clean record, with no arrests or convictions. They even fingerprint you when they give you your license.

Geiger suggests people contact their local board of realtors for the requirements in their state. It's a good idea to join the board of realtors after getting your broker's license. It serves as an entree to local and state seminars and classes that will enhance your knowledge and increase your business. In addition, the board offers classes for appraisers and for real estate land managers on commercial and residential leases.

Ozzie estimates that a broker's first year gross could range from $12,000 to $50,000, depending on the area you're in and what the market is like. "Little towns might be harder," he says, "but in little towns you know more people."

Knowing the minute a new property goes on the market helps create a successful investment in real estate, whether for a rental or for yourself. "You get to know where the good buys are," indicates Geiger, "A lot of people get into real estate for that reason alone."

If you want to exercise what you've learned, you need a lot of contacts. Geiger suggests you join a civic club, become active in the PTA and your homeowners' association and at church. "Then you hear about people moving in or out," he says.

A person must promote themselves and their services. Geiger suggests that any real estate broker or agent spend 10 percent of their income to advertise through pictures in the newspaper, fliers and business cards.

You can also open your mouth. Geiger tells of one instructor he had in a real estate seminar who explained how he sold a house. "He was going through a bank drive-through window. When the teller took his deposit, he asked her if she was interested in buying a house. She said she was. He gave her his business card, and she ended up buying a townhouse from him."

RESTAURANT

Brannon's

Nancy Brannon
Cody, Wyoming

Ease of Startup	Difficult
Range of Initial Investment	$50,000
Time Commitment	Full-time
Can You Run the Business From Home?	No
Success Potential	Moderate

Description of Business: A seasonal, limited-menu restaurant that's open only two nights a week.

Ease of Startup: Difficult. It takes money, vision and persistence.

Range of Initial Investment: At least $50,000 to start; it's easy to spend $200,000 and up if you purchase the property.

Time Commitment: More than full-time in season.

Can You Run the Business From Home? No

Success Potential: Moderate. If you stress quality and atmosphere in an area where these things are rare, you'll build a following.

How to Market the Business: Publicity, advertising and attention to the community will create word of mouth and regulars, the lifeblood of a restaurant.

The Pros: Every evening, the curtain goes up: you and the food are the stars.

The Cons: Be prepared to work twice as hard as you think you need to.

Special Considerations: If you limit your restaurant to a couple of nights, or one meal, two people can handle it by themselves. Beyond that, you have to hire help.

For More Information: The National Restaurant Association, 1200 17th St. NW, Washington, DC 20036; *The Restaurant Planning Guide* by Peter Rainsford and David H. Bangs, Jr. (Dover, NH: Upstart Publishing, 1992).

Story of the Business

Nancy Brannon—an expatriate from Columbus, Ohio, and the advertising business—had been living in Cody, Wyoming, for a short time when, in the space of two months, she met a man, married him and bought an abandoned lodge 3-1/2 miles up a remote dirt road. While they were on their honeymoon, they planned what would become Brannon's, a gourmet Italian restaurant that serves an eight-course Italian feast on Friday and Saturday nights, March through October.

"A honeymoon is the perfect time to come up with something like this because you're floating three feet off the ground," relates Nancy. Reality struck when they got back. They started removing the masses of garbage from inside and out of the main lodge, repairing the burst pipes and broken windows and replacing the roof. Her sister, who had lived in Cody for a few years longer than Nancy, thought she was crazy. "The forest service even had plans to burn the building, it was so bad," Nancy admits.

That was in 1983. Today, Brannon's has served people from 28 countries and all 50 states, and it's necessary to make reservations three to four *months* in advance. The restaurant has been written up in *Bon Appetit, Family Circle* and many other publications. Nancy has published two cookbooks and is working on two more. She also has a line of specialty foods that sells in stores throughout the region.

What happened to make Brannon's such a desirable restaurant? Endless hard work, along with a special vision about exactly what people are going to get from your restaurant: The food, the service and the atmosphere are equal partners. Nancy prepares and cooks all the dishes, while her husband, Dave, serves.

"We decided on the feast format because you can prepare many dishes in advance," says Nancy. They chose Italian because it's a limitless cuisine. "We figured if we didn't get bored, our guests wouldn't either. If I had to stand here and slap tomato sauce on everything that left the kitchen, I'd be bored to tears."

The menu changes frequently; Nancy relies on her collection of more than 300 Italian cookbooks for inspiration. She also subscribes to Italian food magazines and has learned enough Italian to read the recipes. "We gear it toward foods that are seasonal," she indicates. "We start with two entrees on each menu and build the feast from there."

There is only one sitting each night because the feast can last more than four hours. There are intermissions between a few of the courses called *pausas*; guests can take their wine and wander outdoors by the creek or in front of the fireplace. The atmosphere is in keeping with the theme. Italian music and wine complements the feast and the lighting is provided by kerosene lamps. Brannon's only books a maximum of five tables per night.

Nancy estimates she spends 50 hours a week working at the restaurant part of the business, She does some food preparation on Wednesday and spends all day Thursday on prep. Then on Friday and Saturday, she easily works 14-hour days. There are five cabins where guests can stay overnight. In the morning, Nancy has a breakfast basket waiting for her guests. The baskets are filled with pastries, fruit, juice, coffee and flowers.

The price tag for spending the night at Brannon's is not cheap. The feast is prix fixe at $49 per person; wine and beverages are extra. A cabin starts at $75 per night for a couple. In the beginning, even though there were many nights when there were only one or two couples for dinner, they knew the restaurant would eventually succeed. An article in a Montana newspaper put them on the map that first year; since then, word of mouth has carried them.

"Don't do it unless you love the work and long hours," advises Nancy. "You really are married to the business."

Today Brannon's grosses about $100,000 each year, with food costs hovering around 27 percent. But it hasn't been easy.

"The night before we opened, we were still hanging pictures," remembers Nancy. "When we had finished, we turned on the music, lit the lamps and just stood there and cried. It wasn't just what we had envisioned, it was better. When our guests go home, they write us thank you notes and send us gifts. And of course, they come back."

SECOND-HAND CHILDREN'S CLOTHING STORE

The Children's Exchange

Linda Rogers

Bergenfield, New Jersey, with two other locations

Ease of Startup	Easy
Range of Initial Investment	$4,000-5,000
Time Commitment	Full-time
Can You Run the Business From Home?	No
Success Potential	Moderate

Description of Business: A shop that stocks used children's clothing, toys and equipment, which are purchased outright and are not on consignment.

Ease of Startup: Easy. Put the word out that you're looking for used children's clothing, and you'll be mobbed.

Range of Initial Investment: $4,000-5,000 for clothes and rent.

Time Commitment: Full-time

Can You Run the Business From Home? No

Success Potential: Moderate. You need attention to detail and quality clothing to keep people coming back.

How to Market the Business: Newspaper advertisements, special sales, brochures around town, buying clothes to display that make the store look great but probably won't sell.

The Pros: It's easy to start.

The Cons: It's hard work. You have to turn down clothing from people who may not understand.

Special Considerations: Obviously, you must like children—lots of them—parents and clothing, all in equal measure.

For More Information: National Association of Resale and Thrift Shops, 153 Halsted, Chicago Heights, IL 60411; 1-800-544-0751.

Story of the Business

Linda Rogers loves what she's doing: the tone in her voice and the stories she tells give her away. A lot of people have opened up used-clothing stores for children because they thought they would be easy to run—it's happened in Rogers' own backyard. When reality sinks in, they call Linda up—tail between their legs—asking in a small voice, "Can you buy up my inventory? I'm going out of business."

It's the details that make the three Children's Exchange stores in Bergen County gross $325,000 each year for Linda and her partner. Linda displays Nina Ricci dresses she knew would never sell; they sell only sturdy strollers and clean toys at the reasonable prices; and the shops look like boutiques. But what really sets Rogers apart is the service.

For instance, customers come into the shop looking for equipment all the time. "It's hard to keep enough equipment in the store," she remarks. "We started to keep a book where people wrote down what they were looking for. When that piece came in, we'd call them. People love that. They're just looking for a little bit of attention."

In fact, *Entrepreneur* magazine mentioned Linda Rogers in the same breath as Eddie Bauer in a story the magazine ran on service. People come back for good service as well as for the OshKosh and Health Tex clothing in all sizes. The Children's Exchange also carries expensive European children's clothing by major designers like Dior and Jordache.

Rogers opened her first store in 1988. She had spent the previous year planning the shop and buying clothes. She and her partner went to church bazaars and garage sales. They bought all the quality items they felt would still be stylish a year later when they opened the store.

"We stored the clothes at our houses. We cleaned them up, sized them and put them away in boxes," she recalls.

Then they started looking for a store to rent. "We were picky about the way we wanted the store to look, as well as where it was," said Linda. She and her partner picked a 700 square-foot storefront on a major bus route. Then they spent two months fixing it up. "We didn't want too much space because we wanted to get the most merchandise in the least amount of space in order to make it look good so it would sell."

In the beginning, they sold clothes on consignment but soon changed their policy. "It's much more efficient to buy the clothes outright," explains Linda. About six to eight people a day bring in clothes by appointment. Linda examines them under fluorescent light to check for flaws or stains.

The markup on the clothes can range from 100 percent to 600 percent and more. Linda buys a pair of pants suitable only for the sandbox for a quarter before pricing it at $1.50. "But at that rate, you have to sell a lot of pants before you can pay your rent. That's why we're much more interested in high-end clothes," she explains.

The store took off. People came through word of mouth and because they had seen ads in small neighborhood newspapers—particularly a local paper geared toward families. Their publicity, particularly the story in *Entrepreneur*, was very effective. Ten months after the first store opened, another store in what Linda calls a "magical location" became available. They grabbed it. After running the two stores for 18 months, they found a third shop in another part of the region. With the three stores, Linda feels they cover the county.

"Some people have invited us to open a store in a mall, but then we'd have to hire a real manager to handle it all," says Linda, who adds that she loves working with a partner. "You could do one store alone, but you couldn't do two," she remarks. Between the three stores, The Children's Exchange has six permanent, part-time employees. Twice a year, in summer and winter, the stores hold a major sale to clear space for the next season's inventory. Every piece of clothing is marked down 50 percent or more. What doesn't sell is donated to charity.

The peak months are September and October, when customers are buying fall and winter clothes, and March and April, when they're buying for spring and summer. "The clothes just fly out of the stores," reports Linda.

SECOND-HAND CLOTHING STORE

Patricia Owens

Pat Owens
South Strafford, Vermont

Ease of Startup	Easy
Range of Initial Investment	$0-$2,000
Time Commitment	Full-time
Can You Run the Business From Home?	No
Success Potential	Easy

Description of Business: A shop that sells quality used clothing for women acquired through consignment and outright sales.

Ease of Startup: Easy. There's more clothing out there—and people who want to sell it to you—than you'd imagine.

Range of Initial Investment: $0-$2,000. Fixing up the space can cost a few hundred dollars. If you only sell clothing on consignment, your inventory will cost you nothing.

Time Commitment: Full-time

Can You Run the Business From Home? No

Success Potential: Easy. You'll do well if you're selective about the clothes you choose to sell, making sure they're fashionable and clean.

How to Market the Business: Through your own house-generated mailing list, word of mouth, a little advertising.

The Pros: Perfect for people who love clothes.

The Cons: You'll spend a lot of time cleaning and mending clothes before you put them out to sell.

Special Considerations: It's important to have a theme to your store; this is what will impress customers and bring them back.

For More Information: National Association of Resale and Thrift Shops, 153 Halsted, Chicago Heights, IL 60411; 1-800-544-0751.

Story of the Business

When a chance to "leave the establishment," as she puts it, came around, Patricia Owens packed up and left, lock, stock and barrel, for the sticks of Vermont. Although she had previously worked developing educational programs for the Red Cross in Connecticut, she and her husband jumped at the chance to shed their lifestyles and fancy clothes to live in a cabin with no heat or electricity on 40 acres in Vermont.

"It was wonderful," she said of that first year, "I thought, I'm going to do this for the rest of my life." But soon, she got restless doing nothing, and she started to look for a job.

Instead, she found a flea market in nearby West Lebanon, New Hampshire, that rented space to vendors for $14 a week. "I came home, went to my closet and saw this fabulous wardrobe from years of working in the corporate world. I'll sell my clothes," she decided. The clothes were snapped up, and people asked for more. Since she had exhausted her original supply, she started going to thrift shops and yard sales; she could buy any size she wanted. Soon she expanded to five booth spaces and was buying from wholesalers.

"I didn't like not being able to be in the space after 5 P.M., so we started looking for a space of my own," she recalls. They found an old general store in South Strafford, Vermont, about 30 minutes from Hanover, New Hampshire, and

Dartmouth College. "It's in the middle of nowhere," Owens admits. They began to renovate and decorate the space. Upstairs there were two apartments to rent out, which helped keep the overhead low.

"A lot of people say my choice to be in this town was pure folly, but I came here because of the vision I had in my head: I wanted to play house," she remarks. "I wanted to have an enchanted Alice in Wonderland place, and I needed space I could afford."

Indeed, Owens' store looks like a fashionable Victorian grandmother's attic, with clothes that are classic and in style. A selection of vintage clothing for men and women is in the basement. The two dressing rooms once served as meat lockers.

"In the beginning, I picked what I liked, but I learned as I went along," she says. She spends at least one full day on the road looking for clothes for the shop, hitting junior league shops in Connecticut for cashmere sweaters and other consignment shops in Massachusetts and southern New Hampshire.

"Sometimes I buy things that will look wonderful in the store, and not because I think they'll sell," she says. And sometimes they don't. She keeps clothes in the South Strafford shop for six weeks; if they don't sell, she brings them to the West Lebanon flea market, where she has a huge first-floor shop. If they don't sell after a few months, she gets rid of them. "Sometimes clothes get tired and stale, and there's no more room for them. In that case, you have to be ruthless and get rid of them," she indicates. She bags them, donates them to the many thrift shops she buys from and prays she doesn't buy them again.

After she had been in business for awhile, she began to take clothes on consignment. The consignor gets 50 percent of the retail price; both locals and visitors bring in clothes. She pays for consignments once a month if they sell more than $30 and lets it accrue if they sell less. She also offers a running credit. "Consignors are my partners," she says. She had to learn how to say no nicely when a consignor brings in clothes that are not appropriate for the store. She puts consignor money into a separate account; she knows of some shops that have gone out of business because the owners have spent the money owed to consignors.

She personally handles every piece of clothing she accepts, doing whatever's necessary to make the item presentable before she prices it, which includes cleaning, mending and ironing. "I've had people come in and buy back their clothes because they got washed, ironed and depilled. They said it didn't look like the same piece of clothing," reports Owens. "Part of my business is just that: making something awful look good."

Even though the store is distant, the ride is pretty. "People do exactly what I thought they would do," she says. "Women or couples come here for a jaunt. Some come regularly from 90 minutes away." She limits the hours of the store to give her time to travel looking for clothes. "I didn't want to be in a store all the time," she adds.

"You don't have to have something for everybody," she advises. "Go with your own sense of how you like it. Do what's fun for you. I've found that the more I do what seems right to me, the better I do."

SEMINAR LEADER

Marty McGee
Santa Fe, New Mexico

Ease of Startup	Easy
Range of Initial Investment	$500
Time Commitment	Part- or full-time
Can You Run the Business From Home?	Yes
Success Potential	Difficult

Description of Business: Conducting seminars, workshops and lectures on a specific subject to a paying audience, either locally or nationally.

Ease of Startup: Easy. You can print up a brochure—stressing your credentials—and promote the event to a particular audience.

Range of Initial Investment: $500 for promotional materials.

Time Commitment: Part- or full-time, depending upon how many seminars you lead each year.

Can You Run the Business From Home? Yes

Success Potential: Difficult. You must be an entertainer in addition to a teacher to succeed. It's difficult to find both in one person.

How to Market the Business: Direct mail to your own house list and additional rented lists, advertising in trade publications and with the assistance of your host, if you have one.

The Pros: It can be extremely lucrative. You'll be considered an expert in your field and in demand.

The Cons: Promotion must be relentless. Traveling all over the country to give seminars can be exhausting.

Special Considerations: For people who love to help people, who know a subject inside out and who have a healthy ego, this is a perfect business.

For More Information: International Association for Seminar Management, POB 5223, Washington, DC 20015-0223.

Story of the Business

Marty McGee spent the first years of her career as a captain and lieutenant in the army, where heavy-duty structure is the rule. After she left the service, she began to raise llamas. She was a spinner and a weaver and wanted to use the animals for their wool. Once she had a few animals, she began to train them and develop a mail-order business selling equipment to other llama aficionados across the country. Then she started writing for the llama trade magazines on training techniques. In one article, McGee wrote about Linda Tellington Jones, a horse trainer who uses unorthodox training methods. Marty advised her readers how to adapt Jones' methods to llamas. Soon she was in demand as a trainer, hosting clinics across the country.

Here's how it works. A llama breeder who reads about McGee decides to host a clinic. People who are interested in llamas sign up for the clinic through the farm; each clinic averages between 15 and 20 people.

McGee offers a basic two-day clinic. She covers llama behavior and human interaction, haltering, how to set up a barn, shearing, teaching the llama to wear a pack and how to get the animal to walk through obstacles. Marty often customizes a clinic depending on the number and type of people who are coming and whether they already own llamas or are interested in learning more about them.

The host farm solicits participants through its own marketing efforts. This may include direct mail, local advertisements and talking with people who have bought llamas from the farm. Marty charges the farm $60 per person for each day of the seminar; the host usually adds $15 to $20 on top of her fee.

The hosts supply the pens, collect the money, arrange for lunch and round up animals with a variety of behavior problems. In exchange for their labor, they receive free training for their animals and staff, increased visibility and traffic to the clinic that will help sell their animals.

Marty averages at least $600 for each day of the clinic, though it can range from $300 to $1,000. "I do the workshop even if not enough people show up because it tends to come out in the wash," explains McGee. "I also pay my own travel expenses. I think there is the possibility of bad relations with the hosts if they question your expenses."

She doesn't make the hosts guarantee a minimum number of people for the clinic; it depends on the cost of the airline ticket. "We'll look at the registration figures two weeks before the seminar. If 10 or 12 people are signed up, I feel comfortable buying a ticket because there's usually a lot of activity in the last 10 days."

McGee conducts between 20 and 30 trainings a year. Most farms that have hosted her clinics run one every year or so, depending upon the density of the llama population in their area. The money can be very good, but she sometimes works 16 hours a day. She also spends an incredible amount of time on the phone with her travel agent. So why does she do it?

"I love what I impart to the people and the satisfaction I see them get from this," explains Marty. "I also enjoy seeing the changes. I'll take an animal that's had problems dealing with people his entire life, turn him around in one weekend and make his owner ecstatic. That's very satisfying."

The biggest challenge she sees in her business is the need to reinvent herself constantly so that people want to come back. It's also important to keep herself interested in her subject. "You have to be good at something, and you have to be entertaining," she remarks. "I consider myself as much a performer as a trainer. I'm funny, and I think that's a big reason why people come back. You have to be as concerned about your presentation as you are about your material."

Many seminar leaders start their businesses on a local basis, but McGee had to go national from the beginning because llama people are so farflung.

"Come up with a flier with hot graphics, put yourself out there to clubs and groups and keep your expenses really low as you test the water," she advises. "Doing weekend training seminars is a great way to make money from something you do well. You can work as little or as much as you want, and it doesn't take a lot of money to get started."

SMALL SCALE FARMING

Darby Brook Farm

Howard Weeks
Alstead, New Hampshire

Ease of Startup	Easy
Range of Initial Investment	$100-$300
Time Commitment	Minimal to full-time
Can You Run the Business From Home?	Yes
Success Potential	Moderate

Description of Business: A single-product or multiproduct farm of 10 acres or less that can be adequately handled by one or two people with a minimum of outside labor.

Ease of Startup: Easy. All you need are some seeds and determination.

Range of Initial Investment: $100-$300 for seeds and hand-tools, if you already own the land. If not, the cost of land varies widely and depends on where you live.

Time Commitment: Minimal in winter; full-time in summer

Can You Run the Business From Home? You'd better.

Success Potential: Moderate. The more products to fall back on, the better, given the vagaries of climate and consumer demand.

How to Market the Business: It's important to stay local. Word of mouth, roadside stands, restaurant accounts, gourmet and tourist shops, farmer's markets.

The Pros: It's extremely satisfying.

The Cons: You won't get rich; you might break even. Farming is hard work.

Special Considerations: For weekend gardeners who've always wanted to spend the summer in the garden, this is a perfect business.

For More Information: Local agricultural extension offices; Natural Organic Farming Association; *The New Organic Grower* (Chelsea Green) by Eliot Coleman; *Organic Gardening Magazine*.

Story of the Business

Given its short growing seasons, northern New England might not seem the ideal place to go into business as a farmer. However, the condensed time frame and a few acres make a perfect retirement business for someone who enjoys gardening and wants to turn it into a part-time livelihood.

Howard Weeks, 67, has been farming a two-acre plot in the southwest corner of New Hampshire for 11 years. He cultivates assorted vegetables like broccoli, cabbage and eggplant. He also has pick-your-own strawberry and raspberry patches. A 10-acre hayfield provides extra income. Locals come to the house and buy produce directly from him. He also sells produce once or twice a week at a farmer's market in Keene, 10 miles south. To provide extra income and to make productive use of his 10-room 200-year-old farmhouse, he also runs a small bed & breakfast business in the summertime.

"Things all fall together in your life sometimes," says Weeks, explaining how he moved to New Hampshire and started farming. "I'd been working as a furniture designer in New York, where I grew up, but I spent my summers here in New Hampshire on a farm my father bought in 1929. In 1981, my brother and I inherited the farm, but since he didn't want it I bought him out and moved here full-time."

Once he left New York, Weeks attended horticulture classes at the University of New Hampshire for two years before he began to farm. "Since I had inherited the farm, I felt I should learn something about taking care of it. I used some savings to go to school. It was very beneficial."

Even though he had kept a garden when he lived in New York, it was only after attending UNH that Weeks felt he knew enough to start. He started out small. First he put in the apple orchard, which wouldn't bear fruit for several years. Then he put in the raspberries; they began to generate income the first summer. Then he put in the vegetable garden. Two years ago he started selling at the farmer's market; he usually sells everything he brings. "I don't hire people to help me because my operation is too small," he explains. "Then I'd have to pay worker's compensation and taxes, and that's a little overwhelming. One of the reasons I don't expand is because the farm isn't big enough. Besides I can handle everything by myself." He does, however, hire a helper four hours a week to clean the house when the B & B is in operation.

Off-season Howard designs the garden and starts seedlings in his tiny A-frame greenhouse. He also makes furniture and does cabinetwork for local people. Last winter he built a barn to store hay. In-season between the farm and the B & B, Weeks keeps busy. Work on the farm naturally spaces itself out. "I'm pretty busy from May until October; at least the fruits and vegetables are harvested at different times." The orchard is harvested late in the season. Weeks turns most of the apples into cider, which he sells from his house.

He has experimented with some marketing techniques to increase business, but is quick to discontinue them if they don't pan out.

"I tried a roadside stand, but it didn't seem to work—the produce wilted as it stayed out there all day. Anyway, people know to come to the farm if they want vegetables because I'll pick them right here.

"Last year, I tried providing specialty crops for neighbors. People came here every week to get vegetables. I would pick root crops like carrots for them. I'd dig them up every week and have them ready for pick up. People liked that, so I'm planning to promote that more this year."

His marketing is on a small scale. There's free publicity in local newspapers, by word of mouth and at the farmer's market. He is thinking about building a larger greenhouse to increase the length of his growing season. "For now, plastic covers extend the season, and plants tend to survive longer. A larger greenhouse would be a plus because I could get started sooner and set my prices lower because my volume would increase.

"But if you're looking for a business to retire and make a lot of money, this isn't it," warns Weeks. "It's a lot of work. If you have a feeling for plants and like to work outdoors, it's a great business. It's exciting when something you've planted comes up, and it's also a pleasure when you can eat something you've grown. My aim is to supply the needs of local people."

The pluses? If you already have the land, the initial investment is low. "If you can just buy the seeds, you can start," indicates Weeks. He spends about $100 on seeds every year, and another $100 to replace the raspberry and strawberry plants. "I do almost everything by hand because I stay small. Buying a lot of equipment can kill you."

But so might the gross, which Weeks estimates to run from $1,500 to $2,000 a season. His farm is certified organic by the state, but his small size might interfere with his rating. New Hampshire is planning to change the rules in 1994, denying certification to organic growers who gross less than $5,000 a season.

But that doesn't bother Weeks. "Neither the B & B nor the farm could supply me with a living alone, but for people who want to live in the country and work outdoors it's a great way to live. I'm 67 and wondering how long I'll be able to farm. Even though I'm retired, I feel it's important to keep productive."

SPECIAL INTEREST NETWORK GROUP

Celibate Wives' Network

Joan Avna

Ashville, North Carolina

Ease of Startup	Easy
Range of Initial Investment	$500
Time Commitment	Part- or full-time
Can You Run the Business From Home?	Yes
Success Potential	Easy

Description of Business: A business that offers support to a specific audience through information and seminars.

Ease of Startup: Easy. You'll need to focus on your audience and then use marketing to reach them.

Range of Initial Investment: $500 for stationery and mailings.

Time Commitment: Part- or full-time

Can You Run the Business From Home? Yes

Success Potential: Easy. Pick an audience that's not being addressed, conduct appropriate marketing and people will hear about you.

How to Market the Business: Advertising, word of mouth, publicity.

The Pros: You'll be providing a service people need.

The Cons: It takes time to build your mailing list and your reputation.

Special Considerations: This is a good business for someone who feels passionately about a subject that's not being addressed and who has the stamina and empathy to do something about it.

Story of the Business

It all started one day when Joan Avna was in a woman's support group; the topic of celibacy within a marriage came up. "One woman spoke up and said that she'd been living in a celibate marriage for years," she recalls. "Then three others in this group of nine women said that they were living the same way. Each of them thought they were alone."

The next day, Joan met with a friend and told her what had happened in the group the night before. Her friend acknowledged she, too, was living in a marriage without sex. "The both of us said, 'Let's write a book.' We came easily to the decision, but it took us a year to understand exactly what it was we had to do," recalls Joan.

They learned how to write a book proposal. Then they met with several literary agents, one of whom signed the book. The book was sold, written and published in 1993. Then the floodgates opened: Joan discovered how many women there were out there who were looking for the information she and her partner were providing in their book.

"The mail started coming in. Most of the women asked if I knew of anybody in their area they could talk to about this. The next logical step was to form a network," she adds. They formed Celibate Wives' Network—CWN for short. They wrote and designed a flier, which they sent out to the women who had written to them. Their early plans were to conduct weekend workshops women could attend to learn how to start a celibate woman's group in their own town. The problem with this was many women were too embarrassed to attend a workshop. As a result, only four women showed up for Avna's first workshop and the weekend became more of a personal counseling session than a network. Avna's partner had bailed out just before the workshop.

Avna switched gears and decided to explore other ways she can help the women who wrote to her. She's publishing a newsletter. She's also investigating the possibility of holding workshops in specific areas of the country from which a number of women had written to her, like Kansas City and St. Louis. "I'd contact all the women in one area, gather them together and go there and lead a workshop," says Joan. Most of all, she's looking for the one thing that she's sure will boost her cause.

"If I could get a celebrity to say she was celibate, then other women could feel they have permission to admit they're celibate too," she believes. "It's a very hard thing for people to take that first step, and the need is obviously there."

Other avenues are already opening up without much effort on Joan's part. "I recently received a call from a counselor. She wanted to get a copy of the book so she could start a group of her own," she says.

CWN has gotten a lot of publicity because her network is the first of its kind. Joan made a big initial effort, took a break and is planning more specific publicity campaigns for the future. "I'm planning a trip to Florida. I have a list of every single radio and TV station in the major towns along the way," she mentions. "Before I leave, I'll send them information, tell them I'm coming through and ask to schedule a show."

She's gotten enough letters for a year's worth of columns in her newsletter. Whenever she sees a new magazine on the newsstand, she contacts the editor. "It's very important for me to distribute information so people can help themselves and feel less isolated," she says.

SPECIALTY BOOKSTORE

Your Idea Bookstore

Janine Weins
Lebanon, New Hampshire

Ease of Startup	Difficult
Range of Initial Investment	$100,000
Time Commitment	Full-time
Can You Run the Business From Home?	No
Success Potential	Moderate

Description of Business: A bookstore that goes after one specific market segment—from travel to children to self-help.

Ease of Startup: Difficult. You need to either buy inventory outright, which is expensive, or build up credit with publishers, which takes time.

Range of Initial Investment: At least $100,000 for inventory.

Time Commitment: Full-time

Can You Run the Business From Home? No

Success Potential: Moderate. It's important to fill a niche that no one else in the area is addressing.

How to Market the Business: Word of mouth, radio ads, print ads, publicity.

The Pros: If you love books, it's a dream business.

The Cons: Building a following takes time. Over 40 percent of the American population doesn't buy a book in a year.

Special Considerations: A bookstore owner finds out more about the people in the community than almost anyone else. It takes a lot of time, but doesn't put you at physical risk.

For More Information: *Publishers Weekly*; American Booksellers Association, 122 E. 42nd St., New York, NY 10168; Association of American Publishers, One Park Avenue, New York, NY 10016.

Story of the Business

In 1990 Janine Weins was facing a divorce, didn't have a job, and needed something to do. She had been a patent lawyer working in her soon-to-be-ex-husband's private practice and was in the habit of recommending books to clients. She took this one step further and started a bookstore that carried the books she had been telling her clients about.

June 1990, the depths of the recession, wasn't the best time to start a business, but Janine went ahead anyway. "I started by choosing a very small selection of books for the focused audience I was familiar with," she recalls. "In a very short time, I realized that wouldn't be sufficient, so I quickly expanded the number and types of books I sold to expand my business and income." She started by buying books from publishers and paying in advance, which helped her build up credit. Today, she still buys all her stock and has bought the building where the bookstore is located.

Today, Your Idea specializes in selling books that help people help themselves, though Weins also carries some fiction. In the beginning she marketed the business by word of mouth, print ads—which she didn't find successful—and by giving talks to local groups. But her best marketing technique is a morning radio show she hosts live from the store Monday through Friday for a local talk radio station. She got the position when she started advertising on the station and cut her own spots. "Customers told me they liked my voice, which reminds them of Julia Child, and they told the radio station, which happened to be looking for a talk show host at the time," she relates. "She has a different guest visit each morning and uses the show to tell the audience about books in the store that are related to the morning's topic.

"The biggest challenge is getting the word out, and the second is getting people to connect with the product," reports Weins. "I've learned that the diversity of people is even greater than I had thought." People will often come in and say they're looking for a book. They'll tell Weins the author and title, but she'll discover that it doesn't exist. "When I do find the correct title or author, they seem completely oblivious to the fact that they missed it in the first place," reports Janine. "People's confidence in their knowledge often exceeds their knowledge."

A bookstore is one of the best places to meet people. Since she started Your Idea, Janine has learned about the vast number of people who are dealing with emotional problems and addictions. "Books that help people deal with personal growth and show them how to improve themselves are our biggest sellers," she says. The store stocks books on business, gardening, construction, auto repair, health and fitness, in addition to popular contemporary titles.

Weins adds that a successful bookseller must be willing to get out into the community and talk with anybody at any time about books. The advantage to a self-help bookstore is that much of the product doesn't go stale; this is an important point when the inventory must be purchased upfront. "Some books we buy with an option to return for a credit on future purchases," she says. But gardening books, for instance, do not go stale.

She orders from over 200 suppliers. These include publishers, wholesalers, agents and sales reps; and they often have different policies. At one, you have to buy a minimum of five books; at another, $100 is the minimum order; at yet another, retailers will get a 42 percent discount and free shipping if they place their order in June.

For this reason, Weins says a bookseller must have computer ability along with a strong interest in books; physical mobility is not a requisite. "It takes all your time, but doesn't put you at physical risk because you're not lifting heavy things and you're not exposed to the elements. This makes it an ideal retirement career," says Janine.

"I read all the time. I read more than I did before, and I sample all the books that come in," she adds. "In a month, I'll review 50 books. I work seven days a week because I'd rather be here than anywhere else."

SPECIALTY FOOD BUSINESS— LARGE SCALE

Uncle Dave's Kitchen

Dave Lyon
Bondville, Vermont

Ease of Startup	Difficult
Range of Initial Investment	$10,000
Time Commitment	Full-time
Can You Run the Business From Home?	Yes
Success Potential	Difficult

Description of Business: A small food manufacturing company that sells one or products to stores and wholesalers. Most fall into two categories: elegant or homemade.

Ease of Startup: Difficult. You must go to your state department of agriculture to check out packaging and manufacturing requirements.

Range of Initial Investment: $10,000 is the absolute minimum.

Time Commitment: Full-time

Can You Run the Business From Home? Yes

Success Potential: Difficult. There's a lot of competition out there; this makes it hard to get the attention of a distributor or retailer.

How to Market the Business: Through publicity, tastings, trade shows, brochures.

The Pros: It's fun, and it's satisfying to get good feedback.

The Cons: It's a lot of hard work. Unless your product is different from what's already out there, your chances aren't good.

Special Considerations: For people who love to cook, turning a favorite recipe into big business can quickly dampen the enthusiasm.

For More Information: *From Kitchen to Market* by Stephen Hall (Dover, NH: Upstart Publishing, 1992); National Association for the Specialty Food Trade, 8 W. 40th St., New York, NY 10018

Story of the Business

To a casual observer, Dave Lyon seems to have had the perfect life. He worked in manufacturing for a few decades before moving to Vermont to become a ski bum at the age of 50. He soon tired of that and went off to serve as president of Grolier International Publishing for a few years before he came back to Vermont again to "relax."

In the meantime, his wife was planning to start a specialty food business when their son—who was working for the Dukakis presidential campaign—fell into early retirement and came up to Vermont in 1989. "They wanted to make a new ketchup with no preservatives, made with honey and maple syrup instead of corn syrup," says Lyon. Dave Lyon decided to become involved in the company as Uncle Dave, figuring this would set the company apart from other specialty food businesses by backing the product up with a real person.

In the beginning, Uncle Dave's did a lot of grassroots marketing going to craft shows—one a week at the start—to exhibit the products. People would buy the ketchup and take it back to Minnesota—or wherever—with them. Shortly, Uncle Dave's would get a call from a small store in Minnesota placing an order.

After the ketchup hit the market, Lyon noticed a great need for quality pasta sauces. They developed spicy peanut pasta sauce, a Tex-Mex sauce and sundried tomato sauce. Like the ketchup, the pasta sauces have no preservatives and are all natural. Other products in the line now include mustard, honey and a Bloody Mary mix. The hardest part was getting the first distributor to agree to carry the ketchup.

"Sometimes we went to a supermarket and asked them to carry us. They'd contact a distributor because it's easier for them to order from the distributor than from us," explains Lyon. "Other times, we'd go straight to a distributor, show them our products and what we could do, backing this up with a real Uncle Dave. I volunteered to do demonstrations and to promote the product in other ways. This set us apart from the 2,000 other products they see every year."

The key is to have lots of distributors and to market a product that is different from all the others. "For instance, when we came out with pasta sauces, we came out with sauces nobody else had," explains Lyon. "Then we backed into marinaras, which other people did have. But once we had shelf space with the distributors, we could come out with other items because most distributors automatically take the new items their current producers bring out."

Lyon refers to the marketing strategy for Uncle Dave's as guerrilla marketing. His son works full-time to get publicity for the company. "Once we made the biggest Bloody Mary in the United States—350 gallons—using our mix," reports Lyon. Media mentions include favorable writeups in the *Boston Globe, New York Times* and *Wall Street Journal*. But all this doesn't come cheaply.

Though Uncle Dave's was launched with $10,000, that barely covered getting out the front door. The Lyons borrowed money from friends and investors by selling a minority interest in the company. They also got a loan from a bank via the Small Business Administration, which guaranteed 90 percent of the loan. "We asked for $250,000. By the time the paperwork was done, we needed another quarter million," he recalls. They got the loan after being in business for only two years. "Our enthusiasm helped, along with the fact that we had raised a quarter million on our own before that."

Today, Uncle Dave's grosses over a million a year, up from $100,000 the first year. Lyon acknowledges that not all aspiring specialty food producers want to become as large as Uncle Dave's. "If you just want to do the circuit with a small mail-order business and through craft shows and stores in Vermont, it's very easy," he remarks. "I don't know if you'll make any money, but in Vermont, it's a big cottage industry. When we started, there were only about 50 specialty food companies here. Today there are over 300."

Ideally you have to have a great cook on board. You'll need another person to work on marketing and someone to deal with distributors. Uncle Dave's has all three, but as Lyon puts it, his intention to relax in Vermont has gotten to the point where, he says, "I work 90 hours a day."

Don't say you haven't been warned.

SPECIALTY FOOD BUSINESS— SMALL SCALE

Spruce Mountain Blueberries

Molly Sholes

West Rockport, Maine

Ease of Startup	Moderate
Range of Initial Investment	$5,000
Time Commitment	Part- or full-time
Can You Run the Business From Home?	Yes
Success Potential	Difficult

Description of Business: A business that produces specialty food products either fresh or prepared, sometimes even growing the ingredients.

Ease of Startup: Moderate. If you grow your own produce, it may take a few years to develop the crop.

Range of Initial Investment: $5,000, if you already have the land.

Time Commitment: Part- or full-time

Can You Run the Business From Home? Yes

Success Potential: Difficult. The field is crowded. You need time to build the business.

How to Market the Business: Advertising, trade shows, wholesalers, word of mouth, referrals.

The Pros: If you like to grow things and cook in bulk, this is a perfect business.

The Cons: There's not a lot of money in it. It's hard work to both grow and prepare your products.

Special Considerations: Retirees who like to juggle many different tasks and be tied to the homefront will be happy in the business.

For More Information: *From Kitchen to Market* by Stephen Hall (Dover, NH: Upstart Publishing, 1992).

Story of the Business

What Molly Sholes is doing today on her blueberry farm is the culmination of her experiences during her working life. She spent 19 years as a foreign service wife in India and Pakistan, working with natives to learn about their cuisine. She spent summers at a farm in Maine with a well, gas lights and 35 acres of wild blueberries. In 1986 she moved to the farm full-time and started her business. "I love the subcontinent, and I love blueberries, so I put the two together to form my business," she says.

Sholes has a value-added, integrated blueberry farm, which means she grows the blueberries and sells them to wholesalers to sell fresh-packed or to freeze. She also processes blueberries into six products from her home kitchen. She sells blueberry chutney, chutney with almonds and raisins, blueberry conserve, jam, whole berry syrup and vinegar. She works at the business year-round, but considers it a part-time occupation because in the winter she works as little as eight hours a week at the business.

"The combination of growing your own product and selling it in a packaged form is a wonderful retirement business because you can work both outside and inside," she reports. "Except for harvest season, which is July and August, I can pretty much work when I want."

During the harvest, Sholes has a workforce of 10 people who rake the berries from the fields and then pick them over for foreign matter before packing them. In 1993 she grew 52,000 pounds of blueberries: 68 percent went to a commercial freezing company, 28 percent went to a fresh-pack wholesaler and four percent went into her freezer to make chutney the rest of the year. She also sells fresh blueberries to neighbors as a courtesy. The money she made is disproportionate, however: of her $40,000 gross, she brought in $19,000 from selling the blueberries wholesale and $21,000 from selling her chutney.

She sells chutney direct to wholesalers—she prefers not to have a distributor or reps—and by mail order to her own list of 550 names. The wholesaler sells direct to retail outlets, gift shops and specialty food stores concentrated in the northeast. She hooked up with the wholesaler by exhibiting at trade shows and visiting specialty food stores. When she was beginning her business she did informal test marketing by bringing jars to people she knew at local businesses to see what they thought of her product.

"There's so much competition in every phase of this business that it pays to consult the Small Business Development Corporation or an equivalent service that's available," she says. Like other small states with cottage businesses, the state of Maine has drawn up a booklet for prospective specialty food producers, advising them to develop a marketing strategy and an enterprise budget. "None of which did I do," admits Sholes. Instead, she started out very small, putting a couple thousand dollars into the business each year; and she's stayed small. "If I lost money, it wasn't a disaster because I have enough money to live on from my retirement income," she adds. "I'm not trying to make a living; I'm trying to utilize the land in the best way I can."

STORYTELLER

Tom Weakley
Arlington, Vermont

Ease of Startup	Easy
Range of Initial Investment	$100
Time Commitment	Part- or full-time
Can You Run the Business From Home?	No
Success Potential	Moderate

Description of Business: An individual who entertains groups of adults and/or children by telling stories.

Ease of Startup: Easy. If you're a good storyteller, it's still a good idea to take workshops and seminars to keep up your skills.

Range of Initial Investment: $100 to print a brochure.

Time Commitment: Part- or full-time

Can You Run the Business From Home? No

Success Potential: Moderate. Storytelling is competitive; demand is limited in most areas.

How to Market the Business: Advertising, word of mouth, referrals.

The Pros: Great for the ego.

The Cons: You might have to perform for free in the beginning; even when you're established, bookings can be few and far between.

Special Considerations: For people who love to entertain, becoming a storyteller can be a good sideline.

For More Information: *Storytelling Magazine*, POB 309, Jonesborough, TN 37659.

Story of the Business

Tom Weakley had an inauspicious start as a storyteller. He and his wife moved to Vermont in the late '50s, shortly after their wedding. They started a retail shop in the southwest corner of Vermont, where they made and sold their own antique candles. Tom started teaching Sunday school in 1981, but both he and the kids knew he was not a great teacher. He turned to a teacher's manual for help. "It said don't read the stories or have the kids read the stories. Instead it suggested that the teacher read the stories ahead of time and then tell them to the kids," he recalls. "I did that, and the whole atmosphere in the classroom changed."

When he started, Weakley didn't know he was in the middle of a resurgence of storytelling. He enjoyed it so much he started taking workshops in storytelling. He still participates in workshops several times a year.

The first couple of years, Weakley viewed storytelling as a hobby. He performed for free in churches, schools and libraries. "I vividly remember the first time I performed because it was such a sweaty moment in my life," he recalls. Tom went on performing about once every other month for the first two years before he began to charge for his services. "I only started charging because my storytelling friends charged," he reveals. He began by charging $25 for a 45-minute session—about the length of a typical school class. After a year, he doubled his fee to $50.

"Being a businessman, I looked at it in an entrepreneurial way. I figured I ought to be twice as good in a year, so I doubled my price," he remarks. Tom went up by $25 increments for the next couple of years; then he stayed at $100 for two years. People requested new stories. He realized he was putting in a lot of extra research and rehearsal time, so he raised his price to $125. "The calls began slowing up," he reveals. He went up to $150, and they slowed even more. "The people who had hired me at $100 had enjoyed me," he says, "but their budgets didn't allow for $150." He stayed at $150 for a long time, waiting for their budgets to catch up, but it never happened.

Instead, he raised his price to $200 and changed his niche. He now does less business with churches and small nonprofits. He has turned to the after-dinner banquet circuit; he's frequently hired by businesses and corporations for annual or quarterly meetings.

Weakley's specialty is being a personal storyteller; he tells tales about growing up and stories about his life. He's also known as a humorist. In addition to placing ads in local business newspapers, Tom gets a lot of his work through word of mouth. "Someone will be in charge of planning an annual conference and hears about me from somebody who saw me at another function," he says.

He's busiest from October through December, when a lot of the corporations hold their annual meetings. He'd like to average 50 dates a year. The dates tend to bunch up with dry spells in between.

Weakley has made two tapes; he sells them at his performances for $10 each. He's also sold them in local bookstores. One of them, *Harry and the Texaco Boys*, won a notable recording award for 1993 from the American Library Association; this has helped to boost sales.

Weakley recommends aspiring storytellers design a brochure to hand out, make tapes to sell and publish their stories. "Once your tape is out there and on the counter at storytelling conferences, you have established yourself as a serious contender," he says.

TAX PREPARER

Wayne Nottle
Whitehall, Pennsylvania

Ease of Startup	Moderate
Range of Initial Investment	$500+
Time Commitment	Part-time
Can You Run the Business From Home?	Yes
Success Potential	Easy

Description of Business: An individual who prepares individual, small business and corporate tax returns.

Ease of Startup: Moderate. It's a good idea to take some classes and become certified as a tax preparer, though it's not necessary.

Range of Initial Investment: $500 for school plus $1,300 or more for a computer program that's updated annually if you're going to prepare returns by computer. Plan to spend $2,000 and up for a computer system.

Time Commitment: Part-time, three months out of the year.

Can You Run the Business From Home? Yes

Success Potential: Easy. Tax preparers are in demand, especially if they price their services reasonably: People hate to do their own taxes.

How to Market the Business: Advertising, word of mouth, referrals.

The Pros: You can make good money in a predictable period of time each year.

The Cons: Those few months can be packed. Updating the computer program each year is expensive.

Special Considerations: For those rare people who always got a secret thrill from doing their own taxes, this is a good business.

For More Information: Local H&R Block office.

Story of the Business

Wayne Nottle spent almost 34 years teaching music to kids. For the last 10 years of his teaching career, he spent the time from the end of January through to April 15th working two jobs: music teacher by day, tax preparer by night.

When he retired in June of 1992, he knew the following tax season would be a little easier to take, especially given his predilection for attending Phillies spring training camp for a couple of weeks in the middle of March, right in the middle of tax season.

Nottle runs his business out of a bedroom in his home. His first clients were his colleagues, schoolteachers who didn't want to do their own taxes. "I started with a special price for teachers, and the business grew from there," he explains.

When he first decided to start a tax business, Nottle went to the H&R Block tax school, two nights a week for four months. He learned how to prepare personal tax returns as well as to cope with the myriad forms used by different segments of society.

He started with 15 clients in 1982; he now has a caseload of 225. "It's a good retirement business; it was also a good part-time business," he adds. "I worked until midnight every night, and on Saturday and Sunday during the season as well." He also made house calls to pick up information and to deliver finished returns.

Though he started out preparing returns with a pencil, he says filling out the information on computer is the best thing he's ever done for the business. "I get a new program every year, which takes the new changes in the tax laws into account," he indicates. "If I put something in that won't go, it'll let me know. I can also transfer information from the last year up to the current year, including depreciation." The program costs $1,300 each year. Nottle says it's worth it, because it cuts down the time he spends on each return.

He still prepares returns for a lot of the teachers he worked with. He also places an ad a few days a week in the local daily newspaper during tax season. He charges between $40 and $110 to prepare a return, depending upon how complex the individual's financial picture is. "If they sold a house or sold some stock, I increase the price accordingly," he remarks. "I don't charge per form, though, like a lot of places do."

He's content to keep his current caseload and has no plans to expand into other financial fields. He suggests that a person who's interested in tax preparation as a retirement business should first possess a fundamental understanding of taxes. He recommends the Block school. "It's good basic training. They do offer jobs to some of the students who complete the course," he says.

TIE MAKER

Beau Ties by Jean

Jean Houseman
Saco Island, Maine

Ease of Startup	Easy
Range of Initial Investment	$100+
Time Commitment	Part - or full-time
Can You Run the Business From Home?	Yes
Success Potential	Easy

Description of Business: A cottage industry that produces ties, bow ties and cummerbunds by hand to sell at fairs, stores and privately.

Ease of Startup: Easy. You need fabric and skill.

Range of Initial Investment: $100 or more.

Time Commitment: Part- or full-time

Can You Run the Business From Home? Yes

Success Potential: Easy. Quality handmade products always have an audience.

How to Market the Business: Personal visits to retail shops, advertising and direct mail and booths at special crafts fairs.

The Pros: It's lucrative and satisfying.

The Cons: If you hire workers to help, the quality may not be up to your standards.

Special Considerations: Your work has to be original and of excellent quality to succeed. If you have the patience, you'll do well.

For More Information: Bow Tie Manufacturers Association, 75 Livingston Street, Brooklyn, NY 11201.

Story of the Business

Jean Houseman wouldn't be in the tie business today if her husband wasn't working for architects. In 1989 Bill Houseman decided he was going to change his style of dress and wear bow ties instead of long ties. Jean went shopping with him to check them out. They both thought they looked pretty dull, so she bought a pattern and started to make them herself.

The architects Bill works with like his bow ties because long ties get in the way when they work," says Jean. "A couple of the architects offered to sponsor me if I started making the ties as a business. I thought if they think they're that good, I ought to try it."

She didn't accept their offer, but instead started a mail-order business by herself. She began by placing small display ads in *The Atlantic*, *The New Yorker* and a few other magazines. The orders started pouring in. Every month or so, Jean went to New York to buy fabric for the ties, particularly the Liberty of London shop in Manhattan. Once the staff at the store saw what she could do, they asked her to make ties for them as well. She began to work almost exclusively for Liberty of London, along with a few other shops and some occasional custom work.

When she sold the ties through the mail, she charged $20 to $25 per tie depending upon the fabric. Working for Liberty of London, she earns $8 to $12 a tie; the store provides the fabric. For other local shops, she supplies the fabric herself and has the pleasure of shopping in Manhattan, where she travels on business at least twice a year.

A couple years into the business, she hired a few women to help with the work in their own homes, but they weren't good enough. "They were more interested in speed than perfection," she indicates. "Besides, I didn't want to be an employer and have all the problems, so I do it all myself."

She produces about 800 to 1,000 ties each year. Each tie would probably take an hour if she made them one at a time. Jean finds it much more efficient to perform the same work on a number of ties at once, first cutting the lining, then cutting the fabric. "The work goes more quickly," she remarks.

From April through December, along with her regular orders, she spends a lot of time doing custom wedding work for Liberty of London. "Couples buy the fabric there and send it to me to make their ties and cummerbunds for their weddings. That has been a full-time venture," she reports.

Houseman still has a few regulars she works for through the mail, including a few celebrities whom she declines to name. She says her biggest challenge is making the ties well and getting the special orders out on time. "The most rewarding part of the business is that I often receive thank you notes from the brides and grooms," she says.

Bill and Jean recently moved from a house into a condominium and her home chores were cut down. The time she spends on her business has expanded to fill the empty space. "My days are absolutely filled," she explains. Jean works at home in a separate workroom.

She likes working for herself. As she put it: "I can be an entrepreneur, or I can be a housewife or sneak out and go shopping." Her two Siamese cats keep her company while she works. For others who are thinking about getting into the accessories business, Jean advises, "Be sure it's something you really want to do, and something you're good at if you expect to sell your product. Originality is important, and quality counts for a lot. The stores are full of crafts that if you've seen one, you've seen them all."

TOUR GUIDE

Images from the Past

Tordis Isselhardt
Bennington, Vermont

Ease of Startup	Easy
Range of Initial Investment	$500
Time Commitment	Part- or full-time
Can You Run the Business From Home?	No
Success Potential	Easy

Description of Business: A business in which a person offers group and individual tours of an area to visitors.

Ease of Startup: Easy. Design and map out a variety of thematic tours. Then contact the chamber of commerce and other businesses that deal with tourists.

Range of Initial Investment: $500 for brochure and business card.

Time Commitment: Part- or full-time

Can You Run the Business From Home? No

Success Potential: Easy. Your chances are good; they can improve even more if you put an unusual twist on your tours.

How to Market the Business: Advertising, word of mouth, referrals.

The Pros: You'll meet people and be able to make money from your knowledge of a particular area.

The Cons: Business can be seasonal and sporadic. You might need time to build your reputation as an expert if you're not known already.

Special Considerations: People who love to share their knowledge and enjoy people will do well with this business.

Story of the Business

Tordis Isselhardt has long been known as an expert on Bennington history, from the famous Bennington Battle Monument to the architecture of several of the town's more spectacular historic homes.

In 1988 the Bennington Chamber of Commerce arranged with the three major historical sites in town—the Monument, the Bennington Museum and the Park McCullough House— to offer a group ticket to visitors, charging one price for admission to all three. The director of the Chamber had heard that Chambers in other towns had offered a local guide to groups and bus tours that purchased group tickets. He contacted Tordis to serve as the guide because she had written a brochure for two self-guided tours that the Chamber had published. He then designed and distributed a flier to give to bus tours to alert them to the service. For one price, each person gained admission to three sites, a tour guide and lunch.

A step-on guide is a local expert who gets on a tour bus and provides running commentary to general or specific history of the town. The Chamber ran the program for a year before deciding it didn't want to be in the tour business. They then handed it over to Tordis, who assumed the responsibility of dealing with the bus tour companies and arranging itineraries and schedules. The Chamber continues to refer tour groups to her. She also works with lodging facilities in town which recommend her when tours arrive and ask what there is to see.

Generally, Isselhardt starts off with an introductory 20-minute slide presentation in which she gives a brief historical talk about the town. Then the group gets on the bus to visit two or three of the main attractions; sometimes they drive a special route if the group has requested it. "I do basic tours, but also design special tours for people who request them," she explains. The tours last a few hours or all day.

"I have a solid understanding of what went on here. I can put it in a regional and national context, presenting it to people in a way that is meaningful to them," she adds. "Tours come from all over the country and Canada. I enjoy dealing with different groups because they're all bringing their own experiences and appreciation to what I'm showing them."

For tours that last all day, she includes lunch, having lined up three restaurants to work with her on a variety of menus. To arrive at her price—which averages $20 per person for everything—she figures out what the sites and restaurant will charge her. The Museum charges $4, the Park McCullough House costs $3 and the Monument charges $1. She can get lunch for $7, giving a total of $15; she makes about $5 per person. If 30 people are on the tour, she'll make $150 for a seven-hour day, not including the time it took her to plan the itinerary and make reservations with the various sites.

Her busiest season is the fall, when she does up to four tours a week for five weeks. The bus tour business slows down in a weak economy because commitments by tourists and tour groups have to be made in advance and secured with a deposit. "A tour operator is unwilling to put down deposits on lodging until a certain number of people have signed up," she indicates.

"As a result, people on the tours want more for their money. They're asking more questions," she says. "They don't just want an outing. It has to be a show and a learning experience."

TRAVEL MATCHMAKER

Partners for Travel

Clarice McGarvey
Miami, Florida

Ease of Startup	Moderate
Range of Initial Investment	$15,000+
Time Commitment	Full-time
Can You Run the Business From Home?	Yes
Success Potential	Easy

Description of Business: A company that matches travel partners and offers group tours.

Ease of Startup: Moderate. You need a computer to develop a database; you also need contacts in the travel field for tours.

Range of Initial Investment: $15,000 - $25,000 for promotion and marketing.

Time Commitment: Full-time

Can You Run the Business From Home? Yes

Success Potential: Easy, if you can provide a unique service.

How to Market the Business: Publicity, event sponsorships, speaking regularly to focus groups.

The Pros: Operating a matchmaking service is an extremely portable business; you can do it anywhere. It can be very lucrative.

The Cons: Sometimes people will not be clear about their needs, and you have to figure out what they really mean.

Special Considerations: To run a service that is akin to a dating service, the owner must be a people person and have a lot of energy.

For More Information: American Society of Travel Agents, 1101 King St., Alexandria, VA 22314.

Story of the Business

Partners for Travel is a membership organization designed to help single people find traveling companions. "After all," says Clarice McGarvey, who began the company in 1992, "travel hasn't changed much since the days of Noah's Ark. Everything is based on two people. If you're only one person, most of the time you pay for the other bed that isn't being slept in."

McGarvey got the idea for the business after her father-in-law died. Her mother-in-law was hesitant to travel alone and didn't want to pay the single supplement. "She began to pressure me to travel with her, but I didn't have the time or money to do travel as often as she wanted," she recalls. "So I started to look for a traveling partner for her. A younger person might have looked in the want ads, but that wasn't her thing. I thought I could do it better."

Clarice set up a database and began publicizing her service. People call in looking for a travel partner for a trip they are planning. Clarice sends them an application and a questionnaire that asks for details about their travel plans and what they're looking for in a travel partner. "Once we get their information, we go through the files for people who would be a good fit," she explains. It doesn't always work out.

"People don't always know what they really want," she says. "So at first, we'll send them lists of people who fit the description of what they said they wanted. Then I talk with them on the phone and find out what they're really looking for." While the member is receiving information about other people, Clarice is sending information about them to other members as well. She sends profiles—up to 10 at a time—rather than a list of names. The profiles tell what each person is interested in, if they smoke and if they like to go to bed early or late. For those who give permission, she encloses their name and address with their profile; for those who want to remain anonymous, all contact goes through the office.

People usually get a sense of their compatibility after the first letter. But they're still very cautious; some want to meet with a person several times before they travel. Members are evenly split between men and women. Two-thirds of the women ask for male traveling partners; 90 percent of the men request women.

Partners for Travel has 450 members from 25 to 79 years old; the core group is between 45 and 65. For an annual fee of $120, members receive a monthly newsletter and as many matches as they want. Clarice explains that she's not aware of most matches that are made, since the members don't finalize their trips through her office. "I only find out if someone writes me a letter," she says. "I have a number of women who have taken several trips together, and a few women who've met men through the service. I got a letter from a woman who told me not to send a certain man any more profiles because she wanted him to see only her."

Many members travel several times a year. Some have just retired and want to start traveling right away. Recent trips that materialized through Partners for Travel include two women who are renting a house in Italy for a month and a couple of university professors who will travel cross-country. McGarvey also has several members with motor homes. There are others who prefer cruises or backpacking.

McGarvey recently expanded the business to include group travel and tours. Members get first priority; then she opens the trips to the public. The trips range from weekend trips to weeklong tours.

She cites portability as an advantage to the business. "Last summer, after Hurricane Andrew hit, I operated out of my station wagon," she recalls. "I drove around until I could find a place to plug in my computer, and my 800 number followed me. I operated out of hotels and friends' houses."

A matchmaking service of any kind is particularly great for retired people who are single. "This is a fabulous way to meet people. When I first opened, all the men who called in wanted to meet me," she recalls. "I could have gone on a hundred dates."

USED BOOKSTORE
Lilac Hedge Bookshop

Bob Ericson
Norwich, Vermont

Ease of Startup	Moderate
Range of Initial Investment	$5,000
Time Commitment	Full-time
Can You Run the Business From Home?	Yes
Success Potential	Difficult

Description of Business: A store that sells used books, occasionally offering other merchandise.

Ease of Startup: Moderate. Some people already have enough books to get started.

Range of Initial Investment: $5,000 for shelves, a storefront, and books.

Time Commitment: Full-time

Can You Run the Business From Home? Yes

Success Potential: Difficult. Used bookstores are not as popular among the public as you might think.

How to Market the Business: Advertising, word of mouth, referrals.

The Pros: You'll meet a lot of interesting people. You can indulge your love of books.

The Cons: It's hard to make much money, especially when you exchange books.

Special Considerations: Book lovers who like to stay put and who don't need a lot of retirement income will do well running a used bookstore.

For More Information: *How to Open a Used Bookstore*, by Dale Gilbert (Dover, NH: Upstart Publishing, 1991).

Story of the Business

Book lovers are a breed just a bit different from other folk, but used book lovers are a species unto themselves, and you can spot them a mile away. Those with a particularly acute sense of smell can sniff them out, because their musty scent gives them away every time.

Bob Ericson opened the Lilac Hedge Bookshop in Norwich in 1983 with his late wife, Katherine. Years earlier, when they were living in Putney, Vermont, they opened the first Lilac Hedge, named for the row of lilacs that ringed the shop. When they heard about the impending construction of a new federal prison just down the road, they began to look elsewhere in Vermont.

They wanted to be surrounded by cosmopolitan people even though they were in the country, so they settled in Norwich, across the Connecticut River from Dartmouth College. "College towns are good places for book shops," he remarks. "We don't get a lot of students coming here, but just about everybody who got out of Dartmouth wants to come back to the area. A lot of them are readers."

The Ericsons originally got into the used book business because of their kids. "I'm a compulsive reader," says Bob. "When we sat down at breakfast, I read the labels on the cereal boxes. We always had a lot of books. We had so many that our kids said, 'Why not start a bookstore?'"

So they did. Many people start out in the used book business buying books they like. However, according to Bob, there's one lesson you learn quickly if you don't want to starve. You find out that a lot of books you like don't sell at all.

"Normally, we sell a brand-new book for no higher than 50 percent of the published price, and probably only a quarter of that," he indicates. A book that sells for $20 new, he sells for four or five. "I hope people do keep buying new books because otherwise there wouldn't be any old books for me," he points out. "At used bookstores you find the good ones, since they've already been through a sorting-out process."

Bob does searches for customers, as do most old and new booksellers, but he likens the process to throwing bottles with messages into the ocean. He considers himself lucky if this one in four searches is successful. This isn't very hard to understand when he describes the desired books.

"I get asked to do searches on some very old, fairly esoteric philosophy books," he says. The most unusual search was for an ancient book on horses by a Byzantine writer. Another was for a copy of Alex Wilson's *American Ornithology*; he found a second edition of nine volumes, which he sold for $6,000—the most he's ever sold a book for.

Bob sells some of the paintings hanging in the bookstore and in the adjacent living room. He'll point out some other items for sale, like an oil lamp from the *USS Constitution*, an antique bed warmer and some wood carvings.

He doesn't live off the proceeds from the shop, which is located in a couple of rooms in the front of his house. He relies on pensions and other retirement income.

VIDEO BIOGRAPHER

Lifescope Videos

Stanley Marcus
Berkeley, California

Ease of Startup	Difficult
Range of Initial Investment	$4,000+
Time Commitment	Part- or full-time
Can You Run the Business From Home?	Yes
Success Potential	Difficult

Description of Business: A company that produces broadcast-quality interviews with parents and grandparents for the purpose of family history.

Ease of Startup: Difficult. You need to make a sample video to show your expertise and style.

Range of Initial Investment: $4,000 for the first tape, with at least $1,000 more for promotion.

Time Commitment: Part- or full-time

Can You Run the Business From Home? Yes

Success Potential: Difficult. This is a luxury product that's hard to sell in a recession.

How to Market the Business: Through publicity, advertising, distributing fliers, direct mail, exhibiting at local fairs and appropriate conventions.

The Pros: You're helping perpetuate a family's history.

The Cons: This is an idea that's ahead of its time.

Special Considerations: For people who are proficient in video production and interviewing skills, the field of video biography is wide open.

For More Information: International Society of Videographers, Box 296, Washington Street, Sparkill, NY 10976.

Story of the Business

One afternoon a number of years ago, Stanley Marcus, a journalist who once contributed a weekly column to *TV Guide,* was driving around the Bay Area with an elderly friend. "As we drove, he began to talk about what life meant to him," recalls Stanley. "As I listened, I thought, 'This should be on tape.'"

Thus Lifescope Videos was born. "I thought there were many families that would like to have their parents and grandparents on tape talking about the most important things in their lives," he reflects. The tapes are sold to families. The aim is to capture the essence of the person, their values and what has shaped their lives, not just what happened when.

"It's oral history, but for me, it's much more about the person than events," says Stanley, who interviews the person for 90 minutes before editing down to 60. The final tape is very polished, well-edited and includes still photos.

To prepare for the interview on tape, Stanley first talks with the person on the phone. "I find out about the basic structure of their life history: where they were born, what their parents did, how many siblings, when they got married and so on," he explains. "Then I draw up a long list of questions for the interview, though I never get to all the questions."

Marcus began Lifescope Videos in January of 1992. Before he started promoting it, he put together a sample 26-

minute presentation tape to show prospective clients the content and quality. For this tape, he includes excerpts from the interviews of the parents of four of his friends. "I appear on this tape on camera talking about the concept of the interview and the reactions from family members about having their elders interviewed in such a manner," he explains.

He put the tape together over the course of 2-1/2 years. He then began to promote his service by sending out press releases, placing advertisements in local papers and by distributing fliers in affluent zip codes.

"This concept is really quite novel, and it carries a price tag that people associate with a luxury product," he says. The price is $1,350 and includes three copies of the tape. To achieve broadcast quality video, Marcus employs $150,000 worth of equipment, and many hours go into the editing. "In a family with several siblings," he points out, "this is not much of a reach, considering that what they're purchasing is priceless. Most people think this idea is fantastic, but there is that key transition from thinking it's a good idea to getting them to spend the money."

After he does the interview, Stanley works side by side with a technical film editor from a professional video company who implements his decisions. In all, he spends about 20 hours working on one tape.

"I'd suggest that people tread very warily when starting a video biography service," he warns. The ideal candidate would have interviewing skills—possibly a journalist or social worker—and be enmeshed in a particular community.

"People often say to me, 'I wish I knew you three or four years ago because I had an aunt who was fascinating, and she died a few years ago.' I say, 'Let's focus on the living.'"

"I think this is an idea that's ahead of its time," says Marcus. "Over the next few years, this concept will take hold. It will become normal for people to think of making a video record of their elders."

WATER FILTER DISTRIBUTOR

Lois Elkis
Cherry Hill, New Jersey

Ease of Startup	Easy
Range of Initial Investment	$125
Time Commitment	Full- or part-time
Can You Run the Business From Home?	Yes
Success Potential	Easy

Description of Business: An individual who sells water filters and air filters to consumers and businesses.

Ease of Startup: Easy. Contract with a water filter company to sell their products. Then start canvassing everyone you know while also contacting new people and businesses.

Range of Initial Investment: $125.

Time Commitment: Full- or part-time

Can You Run the Business From Home? Yes

Success Potential: Easy. Clean drinking water is a big concern in many parts of the country. This business capitalizes on this.

How to Market the Business: Advertising, publicity, word of mouth, referrals.

The Pros: This is a product that's is extremely timely; frequently, it's an easy sell.

The Cons: There are 450 different water filter companies out there; there is lots of competition with the bottled water market.

Special Considerations: Aggressive people who are concerned about their health, their friends' health and the environment will succeed.

For More Information: National Safety Associates, POB 18603, Memphis, TN 38181-0603; Lois Elkis, 1246 E. Kay Drive, Cherry Hill, NJ 08034.

Story of the Business

Lois Elkis became involved in selling water filters when a friend who was working as a distributor visited her and put a filter on her faucet. After a few days, she was hooked.

"I wasn't aware of all of the minerals and chemicals in my water," she explains. "After I put the filter on, I started enjoying drinking water more."

Shortly after that, she signed on with the company—National Safety Associates—and began selling water filters and air filters through the company. The company makes several different kinds of air and water filters that sell for different prices. Sales distributors increase their profits as their volume increases.

Elkis sells the filters in two ways; she sells to friends and to companies in the area. She can also build a network of people who sell the filters—just as she was recruited—and make a percentage of their sales.

Lois concentrates on selling the filters to local corporations. She has a person working under her who solicits the hotel and motel industry; Lois sells filters to people she knows and those she meets for the first time.

She sees her competition as the bottled water industry; though to Elkis, there is no comparison due to the cost of bottled water. "We're successful because bottled water costs from 75 cents to $1.50 a gallon. Our water filters cost from three to five cents a gallon," she remarks. Customers can install the filter themselves. It doesn't have to be changed for three years; the company sends the customer a reminder just before a new filter is needed. If the customer returns the used filter, the company sends another filter for less money than the first one cost.

The water filter sells for $179. At the lowest level of profit, a distributor makes $59 from selling one filter. A distributor's initial investment is a $30 application fee and $120 for a water filter. National Safety Associates will also arrange for a convenience charge account so distributors can order up to $500 of filters at one time.

The company doesn't advertise, which allows for a substantial markup. Free training sessions are held throughout the country for distributors, who are not assigned a specific territory. As you become a supervisor of other distributors, your job is to help them, keep in touch with them and encourage them.

Elkis likes selling water filters because the market is large; it can be anywhere she travels. "It's a happy product, and there's no pressure," she says. "Customers can try it for a week. If they don't like it, I'll take it back."

Her biggest challenge is educating customers about the need for a filter. In recent years, the media has helped the public become more aware.

"I feel good about doing this because I believe in the product," she says. "I've personally benefited from it."

WINERY

Chateau Chevre

Jerry Hazen
Yountville, California

Ease of Startup	Difficult
Range of Initial Investment	$500,000
Time Commitment	Part- and full-time
Can You Run the Business From Home?	Yes
Success Potential	Difficult

Description of Business: A vineyard that sells grapes wholesale and makes its own wine on the premises.

Ease of Startup: Difficult. It's expensive, requires permits and takes four to five years to develop the grapes; it takes another one or two to make the wine.

Range of Initial Investment: At least $500,000 for the land and expenses.

Time Commitment: Part-time while you develop the vineyard; full-time when you start making wine.

Can You Run the Business From Home? Yes

Success Potential: Difficult. Competition, poor weather and economy as well as the reduced drinking habits of Americans has made this business difficult in recent years.

How to Market the Business: Through publicity, advertising to tourists, attending wine tastings.

The Pros: If you like wine, you'll feel like a baron once you're up and running.

The Cons: It's expensive, takes a lot of hard work, and there are no guarantees.

Special Considerations: Land in California's Napa Valley is pricey. Small vineyards in out-of-the-way places like Idaho, Washington state and Vermont have a better chance.

For More Information: American Wine Society, 3006 Latta Road, Rochester, NY 14612.

Story of the Business

In 1972 Jerry Hazen was an airline pilot, 50 years old, and starting to think about what he would do when he retired in eight more years. He bought 12 acres in the Napa Valley that was little more than pastureland, with the idea of planting grapes on it.

In 1973 he started to put in the vineyard because he knew it would take at least four years for the first crop of quality grapes to come forth. Though his initial plan was to just sell the grapes, he made a batch of homemade wine from the first crop in 1977. He entered it in some wine tastings where it won blue ribbons. The judges suggested he make wine as well as sell grapes. By the time he was able to sell the first crop of grapes in 1978, Hazen had caught the wine bug.

He spent 18 months applying for the permits necessary to make wine in the Napa Valley. This involved separate inspections by the state and county governments. They checked to see that the property had adequate water, since winemaking uses a lot of water. They considered whether the land is near any earthquake lines, and they wanted to know how he would dispose of waste materials. By the end of 1979, after he'd been through all this, he discovered he could have received a verbal permit to sell the wine in 1978. He had already sold all of that year's crop, so he officially began in 1979.

He named his winery Chateau Chevre, because the 1,300-square-foot building that was converted into the winery once served as a barn for goats; Chateau Chevre is French for goat house.

Hazen produces both red and white wines. He ages them in French oak barrels, which are supposed to be the best. Some wineries are using oak from the Northwest, and he says it's hard to tell the difference.

He ages his table red wine in the barrels for 22 months; his Merlot takes about three years. Hazen also makes Chardonnay, which takes about a year to age. He doesn't grow Chardonnay grapes; instead he buys the grapes from a friend down the road.

Hazen bottles the wine by hand, using semiautomatic corking machines. He and a team of friends can bottle 350-400 cases in a day. Chateau Chevre's annual output is about 1,000 cases a year, down from 5,000 in 1987, when he had a partner who thought bigger was better. Hazen didn't agree; they parted ways. Today he feels that 1,000 cases annually is manageable.

Fall is the busiest season at the winery because the grapes are picked and crushed. "You have to pick the grapes when the sugar's at a certain level. If you pick them a little late in the season, you lose some of the texture of the wine," explains Jerry. He says that the optimal sugar content produces a wine with an alcohol content of 13 to 13-1/2 percent.

"The grapes are what set me apart from everyone else," he remarks. "Merlot is a very popular grape. You can't do much to influence the quality of your grapes, however. You should get good grapes to start with and take care of them. Then do a bit of adjusting in the laboratory, and let nature take care of the rest."

Early reaction to Hazen's wine was positive, so he didn't have to do much in the way of marketing. "They came to me," he recalls, referring to wine brokers and distributors. Chateau Chevre also received favorable ratings in the publications *The Wine Spectator, Wine Advocate* and *Connoisseur's Guide to Wine.* People would read about the wine; they either called the winery directly or asked their local liquor store to order it. Hazen's brokers also visit liquor stores and restaurants to sell the wine.

He lists the winery in local guide maps and trade papers. There are a fair number of tourists who visit the winery by appointment and buy directly from Hazen.

Business has dropped in the last few years. Hazen, setting his price by the supply and demand, has dropped a couple of dollars off the price of each bottle. He doesn't feel that the fact that people are drinking less is responsible; he believes lack of easy money is the problem. "I still sell the wine, but more slowly," he reports. A bottle of Merlot goes for $14, and Chardonnay costs $12. Hazen grosses about $70,000 each year, with grape sales accounting for about 40 percent of that.

YACHT REPAIR YARD

Wayfarer Marina

Harvey Picker
Camden, Maine

Ease of Startup	Difficult
Range of Initial Investment	$100,000
Time Commitment	Part- or full-time
Can You Run the Business From Home?	No
Success Potential	Moderate

Description of Business: A business that services and repairs yachts; it can also store them off-season.

Ease of Startup: Difficult. It's necessary to buy a piece of land and publicize your services.

Range of Initial Investment: $100,000 and up for land and equipment.

Time Commitment: Part- or full-time

Can You Run the Business From Home? No

Success Potential: Moderate. Repair and restoration services offered on a large scale provide steadier work than building small craft.

How to Market the Business: Advertising, word of mouth, referrals.

The Pros: Customers are friendly, business can be steady and you get to work at a job you probably have dreamt about your whole life.

The Cons: It's dangerous work; this can be an expensive business to start.

Special Considerations: People who have salt water in their blood and who are willing to make a profit off the land when they sell are ideal prospects for the business.

For More Information: American Boat Builders and Repairers Association, POB 1236, Stamford, CT 06904.

Story of the Business

Harvey Picker, who worked as a professor and dean at Columbia among other things, knew he wanted to pick a retirement business where his customers would hold him in as high esteem as his students did.

"When I first came here, the head of the boatyard told me when he called a busy executive, there were two people who would be put through immediately," Picker recalls. "One is his wife. The other is the man who says, 'I'm calling about his yacht.'"

Since Picker had spent much of his working life with intellectuals "whose problems are never-ending," as he puts it, he looked forward to having the chance to work with people who work with their hands. "It's a different group of society," he says. "They don't take their work home with them, and they know right away whether or not they've solved the problem."

Picker had spent his summers sailing with his wife to Maine from Long Island Sound, and he was always aware of Wayfarer. Back in the early '80s he found out that the yard was for sale. The owners were two brothers, the heads of IBM. Harvey already knew them, so he approached one of the brothers about buying it after the other had died.

"I might be a bad mechanic, but I don't have to buy a whole boatyard to get a job," Harvey jokes. He visited the boatyard out of curiosity. "I was very impressed with the employees because they had the artisan attitude of the 18th and 19th centuries and were dedicated to doing the job right." Picker bought the marina a few years later.

"I originally didn't plan to move to Camden, but I found the town so intellectually stimulating that we moved here in 1984," he says. "It's given me a chance to enlarge my retirement."

Wayfarer is a complete yacht repair yard. It takes a more highly skilled worker to work in a repair yard than in a building yard. "They have to figure out the wiring or reconstruct a boat that's been in a collision sometimes based only on a photograph," he says.

The length of the jobs varies from a few hours to several months. "Some come with scratched paint or a refrigerator that's not working. A yacht that needs its engine room rebuilt can take three months," indicates Harvey.

Traditionally, most yards are very busy in the spring, when the workers are painting the boats and repairing the engines, and the fall, when there's a great rush to haul the boats in for storage. Winter and summer are downtime. Most repair yards keep people on in the busy season, but Harvey retains all 125 employees year-round. He has rebuilt the yard completely to enable workers to work on yachts in the wintertime.

The business has its hazards. "It's a dangerous business," he reports. "People are working up high. You can't organize the workers to make the workplace completely safe like you can in a factory."

Picker describes different variations on the theme of yacht repair yard as retirement business. "This is a very manageable size of a business for my retirement. Anyone can do this with $20,000 to $100,000 for a small yard that's not full-service and on a piece of land that's near, but not on, the water," he says. "You can haul the boat to the shop, let the person work on his own boat and provide a mechanic in case he needs it." A bigger yard would require an upfront investment of anywhere from one to fifteen million dollars. The gross from a repair yard—depending on its size—can range from $100,000 a year up to $20 million.

PART THREE

Planning Your Business

Developing a Business Plan

Once you have chosen a business, careful planning gets you started out on the right foot. A business plan helps lay out goals, provides stability and direction, and makes sure you focus your efforts where you will receive the most benefits. Only someone with a strong will to fail fails to plan.

Instructions

(1) If your proposed retirement business is complicated or requires a large investment, a full-blown business plan with three-year financial projections and a large marketing section is recommended. The outline of a business plan (see p. 377) provides a starting point, but if you have not written a business plan for a small business before, you would be well advised to get in touch with the nearest SCORE chapter or SBDC. They both provide free one-on-one help with business and marketing plans, as well as seminars and workshops addressing small business topics.

(2) If your retirement business is less ambitious, the Business Plan Sketch (see p. 376-383) will meet your needs. Although you can never know too much about your own small business and its markets, you don't want to get bogged down in endless planning efforts. Since the risks and the dangers are limited, your plan doesn't need to be as comprehensive as that for a more elaborate venture.

(3) Experience will correct most planning errors—but in either case, the planning process will alert you to most of the pitfalls that await new entries in the small business arena. Your written business plan will give you a working model of your business, a model that is cheaper to tinker with before you start your business. A plan poses and

answers a more or less comprehensive list of questions based on extensive small business experience that you may lack. Answer the questions as best you can. If you need more information, help is available from many sources, including trade associations, Small Business Administration programs such as the SBDCs and SCORE, and books and periodicals.

Retirement businesses aren't different from other kinds of business in most important respects. You have to match up a limited range of product or service with a tightly defined target market. You have to find out what the people in your chosen market want and expect from you. You have to have a way to reach that market — that is, to make them aware of your goods or services, as well as an answer to the "what's in it for me?" that motivates them to actually purchase something from you. This is a complex and interesting puzzle. To make it even more challenging, you have to try to solve this puzzle in a fluid and competitive environment. People and markets change with remarkable abruptness. If you are working a profitable vein, other people will wish to jump your claim. New products and services and marketing approaches and competitors spring up all too often.

What can you do about all this? Write a business plan.

What is a business plan? A business plan is a short written document used to communicate the details of your business to interested parties, ranging from bankers to investors to employees. More importantly, the process of writing the business plan helps you take a thorough and objective look at your business. The end result, a written plan, is used to identify goals and set budgets, measure progress and keep the business on a steady course.

Business plans contain three sections. The first and most important section describes the business, the markets the business will serve and how the business will be managed to make the venture a success. This is a difficult task. It calls for some research, some experience and a great deal of thinking.

Outline of Business Plan

Section One: The Business

A. Description of Business
B. Product/Service Description
C. Market Description
D. Competition
E. Location
F. Management
G. Personnel
H. Application & Expected Effect of Loan
I. Summary

Section Two: Financial Data

A. Sources & Applications of Funding
B. Capital Equipment List
C . Balance Sheet
D. Break-even Analysis
E. Income Projections
F. Cash Flow Projections
G. Deviation Analysis
H. Historical Financial Reports

Section Three: Supporting Documents

(from *The Business Planning Guide* by David H. Bangs, Jr., Dover, NH: Upstart Publishing Co., Inc., 1992.)

The second section, expressing your business ideas in financial terms, is often looked at as a daunting task. However, this is actually the simplest part of all. There are plenty of accountants, including bookkeeping services such as General Business Services or Comprehensive Accounting, to help you translate your ideas into financial terms. Even better, there are free resources including but not limited to Small Business Development Centers and SCORE programs

Sources of Free Help

1. **Libraries and librarians** are underutilized by small business owners. Librarians are trained researchers who are delighted to exercise their skills. For example, there are over 35,000 trade associations, one of which will have more than enough information for your retirement business. See "For More Information" in each of the 100 businesses for a start. There are books such as *The Small Business Sourcebook* which direct you to other resources. For many businesses, there are how-to books which are very business-specific.

2. **Small Business Administration.** The SBA is found in the white pages under the U.S. Government heading. Its main mission is helping small businesses through educational programs. They publish a wide range of material, most of which is free or low-cost. They provide some financial grants and loan guarantees, but their greatest contribution is through their SCORE and SBDC programs. See below.

3. **The Service Corps of Retired Executives (SCORE)** provides excellent one-on-one business counseling in addition to workshops and seminars addressing specific small business problems and techniques. Their business planning workshops are superb. Staffed by volunteer retired executives and business owners and loosely governed by the SBA, SCORE is a must-visit for any prospective retirement business owner.

4. **Small Business Development Centers (SBDCs)** are found in over 40 states. Staffed by professional small business experts, SBDCs provide the most extensive range of business counseling of any of the SBA programs. They offer workshops, seminars, publications and long-term one-on-one business counseling. The SBDCs are as close to a one-stop business center as you are likely to find and are another must-visit.

5. **Economic Development Corporations (EDCs)** are an example of the kind of resource some states provide, usually in areas where the economy is particularly sluggish. If you have one in your area it's worth a phone call to see

just what they offer. It varies. Some states have programs which you can access through the Secretary of State. For example, in Maine there is a fine program called FAME, Finance Authority of Maine, which works closely with small businesses throughout the state.

6. **Bankers** are good to get on your side. If you are going to need outside financing they are invaluable, but even if you are providing all the money yourself you would benefit from their assistance. While they won't be expert in your business, they are expert in the financial end of small businesses and have seen about all the financial errors (and their solutions) you might commit. As with any expert, shop around until you find a banker you like and can communicate with. Like librarians, they seldom are fully utilized as a source of small business help.

7. **Voc techs, colleges, universities, business faculty and students.** If you have a college with business courses nearby, check them out. Many professors moonlight as consultants (although this can be expensive) or will steer you to students needing experience or to pertinent and targeted information if you want to keep your costs down.

8. **Chambers of Commerce** differ in their small business aptitudes and interests, but if you are planning a retail or business-to-business venture, check them out. Some Chambers have active small business programs, which range from workshops to networking cocktail parties.

9. **Competitors and noncompetitors** in the same field can be a wonderful source of information. Look for businesses closely resembling yours in another market area (another city or state). A good technique is to ask for an appointment (small business owners are often pressed for time) and then send a list of the questions you want to ask. This makes getting an appointment easier, as it sets an agenda. You will almost invariably find that the conversation gets much deeper than you expect. Small business operators like to talk about their businesses and rarely get a chance. My favorite question to ask is: "If you knew then what you know now, what would you have done differently?" It tends to open the floodgates.

(see pp. 374-375) where you can obtain confidential and professional one-on-one counseling. Unless you are well trained
in financial management accounting, don't try to do this part
alone.

The third and final section consists of whatever supporting material you might need. This includes copies of leases
or franchise agreements and other legal papers. Just what
goes into this catch-all depends on your retirement business.
Once again, the more ambitious the business, the greater the
detail you will wish to provide.

The Retirement Business Plan

Your business plan stands on three legs: Concept, Customers
and Cash. While there are refinements that apply to each of
these, your plan will be more than adequate if you develop a
clear sense of what your business is (the Concept). Next find
out who your markets are and why they buy whatever they
buy from you (the Customer). And whether you have enough
financial resources to afford to serve those markets (Cash).

Business Plan Sketch

To sketch out your retirement business plan, take out your
three-ring binder again. Your answers to the 17 questions
immediately below will, if you jot down your brief but considered responses to them, provide enough of a business
plan to go forward with. You may want to go into greater
depth on some of them or seek assistance with the financial
questions.

Concept
1. **What business are you in?** There should be three elements in your answer: the industry or generic name of
   the business, the product or service and the market.
   Consider the cat kennel on p. 84. What business is Toni
   Miele really in? Try putting yourself in her shoes. For
   example, "cat kennel, boarding cats for a day or a month,
   pet owners within driving distance of my kennel" would
   give a brief but adequate description of her business. One

way to approach this question is to pretend you are stuck over O'Hare waiting to land, and your seatmate asks what it is you do for living. If you just said "board cats," he or she would think that inadequate.

2. **What are your products or services?** It is almost impossible to know too much about your products or services. Many businesses will offer more than one; the challenge is coming up with the most important or defining product or service. Think about the cat kennel again. What are Toni Miele's products and services? For example: "boarding cats, but we also sell top quality cat food and cat accessories...we make sure the cats are well looked after and that they get enough exercise and attention..." You can spin this out further for your business. In fact, the further you spin it out the more apt you are to be able to come up with an award-winning answer to the next question.

3. **What benefits do your products (services) provide your customers and prospects?** Answer this one right and you become rich and famous. Customers never buy products or services. They buy benefits. (The classic benefit/product distinction is Charles Revson's oft-quoted "My factories make cosmetics. We sell hope." For example: "security because owners know their cats are well taken care of, safe and content... convenience because they don't have to worry about getting a neighbor or friend to check up on the cats . . ." and so on.

Customers

4. **Who are the people in your target markets?** Since you are undertaking a small business, the market should be small also. The more highly targeted your market, the better off you will be. You cannot know too much about your customers, actual or potential. If you select a market small enough to understand and tight enough to fit your advertising muscle, you stand a better chance of making your retirement business a pleasure instead of a dull ache.

This is so central to your success that an extra form is provided (see p. 383) entitled **Who Are Your Customers?**

People who know their customers succeed. Those who don't sooner or later run into trouble.

5. **What benefits do your customers and prospects seek from you?** This is not possible to answer from the depths of the armchair. You have to go out and ask. You will find some good secondary research at the library, in trade publications and in books. But there is no substitute for asking real live individuals. A client for the cat kennel might say, "Loving care for our cats when we can't be there. We can leave the family pet for months and know she'll be fine and healthy and not lack for attention . . ." Benefits are the emotional goodies people want to receive. Think of why women buy lipstick. Or why balding men go to great lengths to have hair implants.

6. **Promotion: How (and what) do they know about your company?** Even the smallest company has to advertise, if only by putting up a sign or telling the neighbors you are in business. The better you know your market, the easier it becomes to advertise and choose the right form of advertising for your business. Ads (Yellow Pages, newspaper, fliers, etc.) are one way to promote a business. Another involves getting stories about your unique business in the local press. The message should be as focused as possible: "Loving care for lonely cats" or some such is far warmer and benefit-laden than "Cat kennel, cheap and convenient," even if cost and location are important factors.

7. **Competition: Who are your leading competitors?** Every business has competitors. If yours doesn't, then either you are a pioneer) or other people have decided for good reasons there is no future for such a business. They may be wrong—but probably not. Make a list of your nearest competitors, then set up "competitor files" for the three or four closest. Put all the information you can into that file, and within a few weeks you'll know a lot more about them than they know about you. Clip copies of their ads, notices of "help wanted" or legal notices. Everything. Visit with them. Observe. Ask questions. And keep notes.

8. **What do they do better than you?** You want to learn from your competitors. If they do something better than you do, why not emulate them? Likewise, if they make mistakes, you can avoid those mistakes. Look at it this way: Baseball managers and theatrical impresarios keep an eye out for what other folks in their trades are up to. It isn't spying. It's common sense. It doesn't mean you have to imitate everything they do. Just be aware of what they are up to and you'll avoid unpleasant competitive surprises.

9. **What is your location ?** Why did you choose it? Some businesses live or die on their location. Restaurants and other hospitality businesses are location-sensitive. So are most retail businesses, while many services performed on the client's turf are not. For example, people don't mind taking their cats to the cat kennel. It is easy to find—a destination that is not a problem. "We run the cat kennel in our house, which is conveniently located for our customers . . ." Where do your customers want you to be? How important is it to them? Notice that you can't answer this if you don't know what your customers think is important. The orchid growers on p. 272 went out of business in the past because of its location. "We hung ourselves by coming to such a remote area," a lament worth heeding from John McKinnon, one of the owners.

10. **When are you open—and why did you pick those hours?** What accords best with your customers' needs? "The Cat Kennel is open all the time. Holidays and vacation times are our busiest . . ." If you aren't open when your customers want you to be, they will go somewhere else.

11. **Management: Who is in charge?** Even the smallest business (one person part-time) has to be managed. That means all the traditional management functions[1] have to be covered (by you or someone in your employ). To do that, some scheduling is needed. This can be quite simple, especially for a hobby business, but you want to make sure products are properly inventoried and stored, promotional efforts made rationally and the books kept up to date. And so on. The large-scale specialty food

business, *Uncle Dave's Kitchen* on p. 329, provides an especially clear example of how important management can become as a business grows. Dave Lyon's experience applies to all retirement businesses—so read it over even if you have no interest in a specialty food business! Experience is the best teacher for what has to be done. Barring years of experience, trade publications are full of stories about what has to be done and when it is best to do it. Or ask other people in the same business what they have to find time to do. Bob and Lorraine Caristi, owners of the Westport General Store (p. 149) opted to have no employees, figuring that longer hours for themselves more than offset any values employees would provide.

12. **What are your personnel needs?** This can be as simple as "just me." To answer it sensibly you have to know what has to be done and who will do it. You may find it more profitable to hire someone part-time to do bookkeeping than to do it yourself. Or to hire an extra salesperson to boost sales. Or whatever your business needs. The only inviolable rule is: Never hire before the need is pressing.

13. **Who are your outside advisors?** Running a small business, even a part-time retirement business, can be immensely lonely. Outside advisors range from your professional advisors (lawyer, accountant, SBDC or SCORE counselor) to business acquaintances or friends who can be objective about your business decisions and tell you when you are about to put your fingers in the fire. The Lone Ranger or John Wayne approach simply doesn't work. You don't have to do what your advisors suggest, but for your own sake you should at least (a) have outside advisors and (b) listen closely to their advice.

Cash

14. **What are your projected sales for the next year?** Unless you are buying a going business that you are thoroughly familiar with, this is apt to be a very tough question to even approach, let alone answer. But answer it you must, since so much rides on your estimate. Some costs will vary directly with sales, others will be fixed costs estab-

lished by your answer. See the form on p. 387, Sales
Projections, and work through it before answering this
question. Aim a ballpark figure that is based on realistic
assumptions. At best, you are making an educated guess.
"$50,000 last year, which we expect to increase to $60,000
next year . . ." But make sure you can substantiate that
figure; it must be credible or you heighten the risks of
making disastrous errors of judgment. To make it credible,
you have to know a great deal about your product or service, how to price it, how to market it—and even more
importantly, how to make those customers buy.

15. **How much capital do you need to meet your sales goals?**
Bankers will tell you that lack of capital (cash invested in
the business) is the biggest managerial mistake made by
small business owners.

    The amount needed varies from nothing (see the
Clown business on p. 95) to over $10 million (for the
country club on p. 113). Approximate initial investment
figures are provided for each business—but that initial
investment will probably have to be augmented. You can
estimate how much capital you need by consulting trade
figures (available through trade associations in most
cases) and looking for the "Sales-to-Worth" ratio. If you
estimate that next year's sales will be $60,000, and your
trade association says the best-managed businesses have
a sales-to-worth ratio of 10/1, then you need to have
$6,000 invested in the business. Much less than this will
make you spin your wheels; much more would probably
represent capital that is resting rather than working.
(Nobody ever went broke by being overcapitalized,
though.) This is another example of the need to closely
project sales. See also Q. 17.

16. **How much debt can you safely carry?** Another handy
trade figure is the debt-to-worth ratio much beloved of
bankers, who want to know how much of your own
money is at risk before they'll commit a dime of their
depositors' hard-saved cash. A rule of thumb some
bankers use is 0.5 to 1, or 50¢ of debt for every $1 of net
worth. If you borrow too much you'll spend all your time

making interest payments instead of profits, nobody's idea of a good time. See also the next question.

17. **What does your *cash flow pro forma* tell you?** A "pro forma" is a financial projection formatted to make analysis of the numbers easier for bankers and other interested parties. It also facilitates comparisons with other similar businesses. The best way to decide how much capital you need, or how much debt you can afford to carry, or even how much a business is worth[2] is to push a cash flow *pro forma* until it turns definitely positive. This is the kind of financial analysis that most people need to get help with. While there is nothing conceptually difficult about cash flow projections (money flows in and flows out of your business, with most ins and outs being easily

---

A Note on Financial Statements and Management

Don't try to become a financial manager or accountant yourself. You have a business to run, or will shortly. Use your professional advisors from the SBDC, SCORE or other sources.

Here are 10 good questions to ask your financial advisors:

1) How do we establish an effective *cash flow budget?*
2) What is our break-even point? Why is it important?
3) How can we reach and/or maintain a positive cash flow?
4) How do we compare with similar businesses?
5) How much money—and when—do we need to borrow?
6) How can I know on a daily or weekly basis if we are making money?
7) Can we afford to do this?
8) Should I try to build revenues, cut costs or both?
9) Do you know a good tax accountant? (There are over 40,000 pages of our simplified tax code . . .)
10) Do you think *this* retirement business makes sense for me, based on the amount of money I can invest and the amount I'd like to earn?

The answers you get will help you make more profitable retirement business decisions.

determined in both timing and amount), the detailing becomes complicated in the extreme, and the format is also very important. The SBDCs and SCORE counselors are wonderfully skilled at helping people over this hurdle. So are most bankers and accountants.

The reason the cash flow *pro forma* is so especially important is simple enough. You can run out of cash while making a profit, especially in fast growth or startup situations. Your cash flow *pro forma* is also a carefully worked out cash budget—and businesses which operate without budgets are called bankrupt sooner rather than later.

Furthermore, your cash flow *pro formas* are a fine working model of your business and the assumptions you make about how the business will perform. Keep in mind that the first objective of your retirement business is to stay in business long enough to make a profit. The cash flow will tell you how much and when to borrow money (if needed), when to hire more people or lay people off or take a vacation. It will help you make "what-if" tests of pricing changes, new or different products or markets, establish proper inventory levels, and do most of the financial management things that separate winning businesses from the living dead.

If you only have one financial tool, make it be your cash flow *pro forma*.

Who Are Your Customers?

You should try to describe your markets in enough detail so you can pick out the best segments of those markets in the following form. Some markets will be better for your business than others. By focusing on your best markets you can use your resources more effectively (including promotion and advertising monies), fit products and services to the people in those markets and avoid wasted efforts. Be as specific as you can. You can always improve on or change your answers. You can also get help from the usual sources: SBDCs, SCORE, trade association publications and so on.

Who Are Your Customers?

1. Describe your *best* customers

_____
age

_____
sex

_____
income level

_____
occupation

If industrial or business:

_____
type of business (SIC)*

_____
size

2. Where do they come from? (check one)

☐ local   ☐ regional   ☐ national
☐ international   ☐ tourist

3. What do they buy?

☐ product(s)   ☐ services   ☐ benefits

4. How often do they buy? (check one)

☐ daily   ☐ weekly   ☐ monthly
☐ every now and then ☐ other

5. How much do they buy?

_____
Units

_____
Dollars

6. How do they buy? (check one)

☐ credit (you invoice them) ☐ cash   ☐ contract

_____

* *Standard Industrial Classification code used to find information in many databases and government publications.*

7. How did they learn about your business? (check all that apply)

☐ advertising: newspaper, radio/TV   ☐ word of mouth

☐ location   ☐ direct sales   ☐ other (specify)

8. What do they think of your business/products/services? (Customer perceptions)

_____

_____

_____

9. What do they want you to provide? (benefits they are looking for that you can or should provide)

_____

_____

_____

10. How big is your market?

_____

geographically

_____

population

_____

potential customers

11. What is your share of that market? (market share)

_____

_____

_____

12. How do you want your markets to perceive your business? What do you want your business to be known for?

_____

_____

_____

_____

_____

Sales Forecasting

Before starting this process, remember that forecasts are at best estimates based on incomplete information. Don't try to make them 100 percent accurate; you'll just frustrate yourself. You want to establish a sales range which you have good business reasons to trust to be about 90% accurate if you are lucky as well as astute.

The best method for small business owners to forecast sales for the next 12 months takes three steps. First, "chunk" your business up by product lines, markets or other natural segments. For most businesses, this will mean no more than five "chunks." As an example, Upstart Publishing used to use newsletters, books and "other"[3] as their three products for forecasting purposes. They could have used banks, bookstores and random businesses (chunking by market). The cat boarding business would have short-term lodgers, long-term lodgers, emergency or special lodging, plus some product sales. The trick is to make these divisions natural and pertinent to your business.

Second, develop scenarios for each chunk. Start with the Worst Case scenario: what happens if everything goes wrong? "Everything" in this case means realistically looking at the downside. You won't have $0 for sales (realistically). Going businesses often take last year's performance to be the lowest acceptable forecast amount, barring special environmental factors such as local economic downturns or major technological change. Turn next to the Best Case: What if everything works just fine? Finally, between these two extremes, what do you think will most likely happen? Figure each of these scenarios *by chunks*, then add them. The Worst Case and Best Case scenarios become a contingency plan (so keep them for reference).

Third, take the Most Likely scenario and break it out by months. All businesses have seasonal patterns—you don't just divide by 12 and get meaningful monthly figures. For example, the cat boarding business has peak seasons around the holidays and again when people go off on summer vacation. Their forecasts will reflect this seasonality and dramatically influence their cash flow.

Your forecasting abilities will improve over time, faster if you take and keep notes about the scenarios than otherwise. It can be very educational as well as somewhat abashing to look back at your assumptions a year or two later.

Sales Projections

Product/Service (or Market)	WORST CASE	MOST LIKELY	BEST CASE
1.			
2.			
3.			
4.			
5.			

Summary

Once you have answered the 17 questions, you aren't exactly finished. Business plans are always works in progress, at least if they are to yield the benefits you are seeking from your retirement business. *Use* your plan. The cliché is: "Plan your work and work your plan." This has a lot of truth in it, since using the plan will keep your efforts concentrated on doing what has to be done rather than chasing off after enticing but expensive distractions.

You will need more financial information than is shown in the business plan sketch. At the very least you will need a Balance Sheet and an Income (or Profit & Loss) statement. If you are not familiar with these basic tools, have your accountant explain them to you. Monthly statements make running the business easier, alerting you to both opportunities and problems early enough to take informed action before the opportunities flee or the problems grow out of control. This is one area where your personal computer will pay for itself fast.

A word of warning: Make sure to keep your personal and business finances separate. Your retirement business will have some very lucrative tax shelters (ask your accountant how to take advantage of the tax minimization small businesses afford), but commingling personal and business records will almost guarantee an audit. And that is something to avoid at almost any cost.

Finally, good luck. Your retirement business will keep you active and interested—and provide extra income, new challenges and a chance to make a lot of new friends.

Notes

[1] *Planning, organizing, directing, controlling* and *innovating* are the most commonly cited management functions.

[2] Asset value plus the discounted value of future cash flows give a ballpark value for most small businesses. There are many complications, including hidden liabilities and potential legal liabilities and taxation issues, so *always* seek professional help when buying a business.

[3] "Other" was a small and stable amount from over the transom work, sometimes copy writing, or design, or even consulting work. It never exceeded 5% of revenue, so it wasn't broken out further.

Resources for Small Business

Upstart Publishing Company, Inc. These publications on proven management techniques for small businesses are available from Upstart Publishing Company, Inc., 12 Portland St., Dover, NH 03820. For a free current catalog, call (800) 235-8866 outside New Hampshire, or 749-5071 in state.

The Business Planning Guide, 6th edition, 1992, David H. Bangs, Jr. and Upstart Publishing Company, Inc. A manual that helps you write a business plan and financing proposal tailored to your business, your goals and your resources. Includes worksheets and checklists. (Softcover, 208 pp., $19.95)

The Market Planning Guide, 1990, David H. Bangs, Jr. and Upstart Publishing Company, Inc. A manual to help small-business owners put together a goal-oriented, resource-based marketing plan with action steps, benchmarks and time lines. Includes worksheets and checklists to make implementation and review easier. (Softcover, 160 pp., $19.95)

The Cash Flow Control Guide, 1990, David H. Bangs, Jr. and Upstart Publishing Company, Inc. A manual to help small-business owners solve their number one financial problem. Includes worksheets and checklists. (Softcover, 88 pp., $14.95)

The Personnel Planning Guide, 1988, David H. Bangs, Jr. and Upstart Publishing Company, Inc. A 176-page manual outlining practical, proven personnel management techniques, including hiring, managing, evaluating and compensating personnel. Includes worksheets and checklists. (Softcover, 176 pp., $19.95)

The Start Up Guide: A One-Year Plan for Entrepreneurs, 2nd edition, 1994, David H. Bangs, Jr. and Upstart Publishing Company, Inc. This book utilizes the same step-by-step, no-jargon method as *The Business Planning Guide* to help even those with no business training through the process of beginning a successful business. (Softcover, 176 pp., $19.95)

Managing By the Numbers: Financial Essentials for the Growing Business, 1992, David H. Bangs, Jr. and Upstart Publishing Company, Inc. Straightforward techniques for getting the maximum return with a minimum of detail in your business's financial management. (Softcover, 160 pp., $19.95.)

Building Wealth, 1992, David H. Bangs, Jr. and the editors of *Common Sense*, Upstart Publishing Co., Inc. A collection of tested techniques designed to help you plan your personal finances and how to plan your business finances to benefit you, your family and employees. (Softcover, 168 pp., $19.95)

Buy the Right Business—At the Right Price, 1990, Brian Knight and the Associates of Country Business, Inc., Upstart Publishing Company, Inc. Many people who would like to be in business for themselves think strictly of starting a business. In some cases, buying a going concern may be preferable—and just as affordable. (Softcover, 152 pp., $18.95)

Borrowing for Your Business, 1991, George M. Dawson, Upstart Publishing Company, Inc. This is a book for borrowers and about lenders. Includes detailed guidelines on how to select a bank and a banker, how to answer the lender's seven most important questions, how your banker looks at a loan and how to get a loan renewed. (Hardcover, 160 pp., $19.95)

Can This Partnership Be Saved?, 1992, Dr. Peter Wylie and Dr. Mardy Grothe, Upstart Publishing Co., Inc. The authors offer solutions and hope for problems between key people in business. (Softcover, 272 pp., $19.95)

The Complete Guide to Selling Your Business, 1992, Paul Sperry and Beatrice Mitchell, Upstart Publishing Company, Inc. A step-by-step guide through the entire process from how to determine when the time is right to sell to negotiating the final terms. (Hardcover, 160 pp., $21.95)

The Complete Selling System, 1991, Pete Frye, Upstart Publishing Company, Inc. This book can help any manager or salesperson, even those with no experience, find the solutions to some of the most common dilemmas in managing sales. (Hardcover, 192 pp., $21.95)

Creating Customers, 1992, David H. Bangs, Jr. and the editors of *Common Sense*, Upstart Publishing Company, Inc. A book for business owners and managers who want a step-by-step approach to selling and promoting. Techniques include inexpensive market research, pricing your goods and services and writing a usable marketing plan. (Softcover, 176 pp., $19.95)

Export Profits, 1992, Jack S. Wolf, Upstart Publishing Company, Inc. This book shows how to find the right foreign markets for your product, cut through the red tape, minimize currency risks and how to find the experts who can help. (Softcover, 304 pp., $19.95)

Financial Troubleshooting, 1992, David H. Bangs, Jr. and the editors of *Common Sense*, Upstart Publishing Company, Inc. This book helps the owner/manger use basic diagnostic methods to monitor the health of the business and solve problems before damage occurs. (Softcover, 192 pp., $19.95)

Financial Essentials for Small Business Success, 1994, Joseph Tabet and Jeffrey Slater, Upstart Publishing Company, Inc. Designed to show readers where to get the information they need and how planning and recordkeeping will enhance the health of any small business. (Softcover, 272 pp., $19.95)

From Kitchen to Market, 1992, Stephen Hall, Upstart Publishing Company, Inc. A practical approach to turning culinary skills into a profitable business. (Softcover, 208 pp., $24.95)

The Home-Based Entrepreneur, 1993, Linda Pinson and Jerry Jinnett, Upstart Publishing Company, Inc. A step-by-step guide to all the issues surrounding starting a home-based business. Issues such as zoning, labor laws and licensing are discussed and forms are provided to get you on your way. (Softcover, 192 pp. $19.95)

Keeping the Books, 1993, Linda Pinson and Jerry Jinnett, Upstart Publishing Company, Inc. Basic business recordkeeping, both explained and illustrated. Designed to give you a clear understanding of small business accounting by taking you step-by-step through general records, development of financial statements, tax reporting, scheduling and financial statement analysis. (Softcover, 208 pp., $19.95)

Marketing Your Invention, 1992, Thomas Mosley, Upstart Publishing Company, Inc. This book dispels the myths and clearly communicates what inventors need to know to successfully bring their inventions to market. (Softcover, 232 pp., $19.95)

The Small Business Computer Book, 1993, Robert Moskowitz, Upstart Publishing Company, Inc. This book does not recommend particular systems, but rather provides readers with a way to think about these choices and make the right decisions for their businesses. (Softcover, 190 pp., $19.95)

Steps to Small Business Start-Up, 1993, Linda Pinson and Jerry Jinnett, Upstart Publishing Company, Inc. A step-by-step guide for starting and succeeding with a small or home-based business. Takes you through the mechanics of business start-up and gives an overview of information on such topics as copyrights, trademarks, legal structures, recordkeeping and marketing. (Softcover, 256 pp., $19.95)

Target Marketing for the Small Business, 1993, Linda Pinson and Jerry Jinnett, Upstart Publishing Company, Inc. A comprehensive guide to marketing your business. This book not only shows you how to reach your customers, it also gives you a wealth of information on how to research that market through the use of library resources, questionnaires, demographics, etc. (Softcover, 176 pp., $19.95)

On Your Own: A Woman's Guide to Starting Your Own Business, 2nd edition, 1993, Laurie Zuckerman, Upstart Publishing Company, Inc. *On Your Own* is for women who want hands-on, practical information about starting and running their own business. It deals honestly with issues like finding time for your business when you're also the primary care provider, societal biases against women and credit discrimination. (Softcover, 320 pp., $19.95)

Problem Employees, 1991, Dr. Peter Wylie and Dr. Mardy Grothe, Upstart Publishing Company, Inc. Provides managers and supervisors with a simple, practical and straightforward approach to help all employees, especially problem employees, significantly improve their work performance. (Softcover, 272 pp., $22.95)

The Restaurant Planning Guide, 1992, Peter Rainsford and David H. Bangs, Jr., Upstart Publishing Company, Inc. This book takes the practical techniques of *The Business Planning Guide* and combines it with the expertise of Peter Rainsford, a professor at the Cornell

School of Hotel Administration and restaurateur. Topics include: establishing menu prices, staffing and scheduling, controlling costs and niche marketing. (Softcover, 176 pp., $19.95)

Successful Retailing, 2nd edition, 1993, Paula Wardell, Upstart Publishing Company, Inc. Provides hands-on help for those who want to start or expand their retail business. Sections include: strategic planning, marketing and market research and inventory control. (Softcover, 176 pp., $19.95)

The Woman Entrepreneur, 1992, Linda Pinson and Jerry Jinnett, Upstart Publishing Company, Inc. Thirty-three successful women business owners share their practical ideas for success and their sources for inspiration. (Softcover, 244 pp., $14.00)